AF799980

The Economic and Political Dangers of Globalization

Dipak Basu · Victoria Miroshnik

The Economic and Political Dangers of Globalization

A Non-Western Perspective on Global Capitalism

palgrave
macmillan

Dipak Basu
Nagasaki University
Nagasaki, Japan

Victoria Miroshnik
Reitaku University
Chiba, Japan

ISBN 978-3-030-79894-9 ISBN 978-3-030-79895-6 (eBook)
https://doi.org/10.1007/978-3-030-79895-6

© The Editor(s) (if applicable) and The Author(s), under exclusive license to Springer Nature Switzerland AG 2021
This work is subject to copyright. All rights are solely and exclusively licensed by the Publisher, whether the whole or part of the material is concerned, specifically the rights of translation, reprinting, reuse of illustrations, recitation, broadcasting, reproduction on microfilms or in any other physical way, and transmission or information storage and retrieval, electronic adaptation, computer software, or by similar or dissimilar methodology now known or hereafter developed.
The use of general descriptive names, registered names, trademarks, service marks, etc. in this publication does not imply, even in the absence of a specific statement, that such names are exempt from the relevant protective laws and regulations and therefore free for general use.
The publisher, the authors and the editors are safe to assume that the advice and information in this book are believed to be true and accurate at the date of publication. Neither the publisher nor the authors or the editors give a warranty, expressed or implied, with respect to the material contained herein or for any errors or omissions that may have been made. The publisher remains neutral with regard to jurisdictional claims in published maps and institutional affiliations.

This Palgrave Macmillan imprint is published by the registered company Springer Nature Switzerland AG
The registered company address is: Gewerbestrasse 11, 6330 Cham, Switzerland

This book is dedicated to the Memory of our Uncle
Anil Dutta
Who was the source of our inspiration

Introduction

This book should open the eyes of the people who are the victims of massive propaganda since 1992 that a market economy can invite a glorious world by removing the 'evil' socialism from the world. 'Destruction' of the Soviet Union in 1991 December created this idea. New institutions were created to push this idea all over the world, in which the World Bank and the IMF played a major role by creating the 'Structural Adjustment' in the late 1980s. 'Structural Adjustment' was imposed on the highly indebted developing countries to remove all traces of 'socialist' policies from the public policy structure of these countries so that they can pay back their debts. Developing countries had no choice, as the financial supports would come as an exchange from the IMF and the World Bank. Refusal to accept the 'structural adjustment' means that country would be cut off from the world financial system. However, the question is how the developing countries became the highly indebted countries in the first place.

In 1974, there was a sudden increase in the price of crude oil by the Arab oil producing countries, who then formed the Organization for Petroleum Exporting Countries (OPEC). The massive amount of money of the oil producers went back to the Western banks, who had the problem to recycle these monies effectively. Initially, that money created the debt crisis for Argentina and Mexico who could not pay back their debt in time. Then, the developing countries took this money as debt when the interest rate was low. President Reagan then tried to stimulate the American economy by over-spending and had to raise the interest rate. Most of the debt of the developing countries was with the Western banks, so they had to cope with two dangers: increased price of crude oil and high interest rate on their foreign debt. Most of these countries were in near bankruptcy and had to go to the IMF, who suggested them to accept 'Structural Adjustment.'

That structural adjustment was another name of the 'Washington Consensus' the combined policy of the US Treasury, IMF, and the World Bank, which was promoted after 1992 as the only savior of the world. World Trade Organization, which was the enhanced GATT (General Agreement on Trade and Tariffs) with provision for the implementation of the 'Washington Consensus' was created in 1995. Developing countries were told unless they become members of the WTO, they would be cut off from the world trade, although both China and Russia were not members of the WTO at that time, but that has not stopped them from trade.

Even before 2001, China was allowed to dominate the world trade. China with a very low exchange rate had created the 'Asian Financial Crisis' in 1998, when one after another South East Asian and East Asian countries started collapsing with very low export earnings as China had taken over their markets already. However, IMF and the World Bank refused to blame China and put the blame on 'Crony Capitalism,' where the politicians in South East and East Asian countries gave the trade and industrial contracts to their friends and relatives. 'Crony Capitalism' had nothing to do with the 'East Asian Financial Crisis'; in fact, India is following that 'Crony Capitalism' today, and IMF and the World Bank are praising India.

After the Tiananmen Square massacres in 1989, where 8000 students were killed because they demanded democracy, foreign investors flooded into China hoping that the government would allow them to do anything they like with the force of the state power in the 'Special Economic Zones.' In 2001, China was allowed to join the WTO, and the destruction of the US started. American industrialists moved their factories to China, taking advantage of the dictatorial political system with low wages and absence of any trade union rights. There is a historical similarity. Henry Ford and other American capitalists also financed the NAZI party in Germany in the 1930s. In the same way today, American capitalists and their institutions are supporting China today.

This book analyzed these events in a systematic way. We have quoted from various essays and blogs scattered around the cyberspace and libraries to assimilate these into a book so that the public can understand the dangers they are facing. That is the purpose of this book.

Contents

List of Figures

List of Tables

CHAPTER 1

The First Globalization

Globalizations took place under every empires, whether Greek, Persian, Maurya, Roman, Turkish, but the real globalization was under the British Empire, which by geographical expansion was the biggest of all other empires and created industrialization of Britain. British historians normally are shy about answering some basic questions: Where the investments came from, and where was the market for the products of Industrial Revolution in Britain. In the analysis of the first globalization, we concentrate on India and Africa through the slave trade, although the British Empire expanded throughout the world.

For centuries, India had been an exporter of fine textiles, to such an extent that Great Britain had to impose tariff protection to save its domestic manufacturers from Indian competition. After the Industrial Revolution, India was importing one-fourth of all British exports of cotton piece goods and had to supply raw cotton to Britain.

A blow to Great Britain's eighteenth-century dreams of empire, however, came from the revolt of the 13 American colonies. These colonies were at the heart of the old, or what is often referred to as the first, British Empire, which consisted primarily of Ireland, the North American colonies, and the plantation colonies of the West Indies. The assimilation of the French Canadians, control of the Indians and settlement of the trans-Allegheny region, and the opening of new trade channels created a host of problems for the British government. To cope

© The Author(s), under exclusive license to Springer Nature Switzerland AG 2021
D. Basu and V. Miroshnik, *The Economic and Political Dangers of Globalization*, https://doi.org/10.1007/978-3-030-79895-6_1

with these problems, new imperial policies were adopted by the mother country: Raising (for the first time) revenue from the new colonies in India; tightening mercantile restrictions against Indian exports; imposing firm measures against New England's substantial trade with the West Indies.

Conquest of India

Starting with the assumption of control over the province of Bengal (after the Battle of Plassey in 1757) and especially after the virtual removal of French influence from the Indian Ocean, the British waged more or less continuous warfare against the Indian people and took over more and more of the interior.

The national debt of the UK was at a staggering £140,000,000 in 1760 (Cook, 1995). The Battle of Plassey left a handful of Company executives as masters over the vast territories of Bengal. Imperial glory was the ambition of this group of traders turned governors. British government was responsible for granting and renewing their charter as that would provide the massive wealth of Bengal in particular and India in general to finance industrial development in Britain.

Clive, as the first military governor of Bengal, appointed Mir Jafar to be the Nawab (Tax Collector and administrator) of Bengal and took annual gifts from his appointee of at least £234,000 (James, 1995). Then, the agents of the East India Company began the process of economic exploitation of Bengal. "As public officials, they had the rights to accept bribes, steal tax revenues, and involved in illicit trading of goods, and used these administrative rights as a means to steer the wealth of India into their hands" (James, 1995; Webster, 2007).

These lawless officials, who were called "Nabobs," brought back vast fortunes to England by straining the economy of Bengal, causing famines and serious economic distress for the people but paved the way for the Industrial Revolution in Britain. In the Treaty of Allahabad, Clive bribed the Mogul Emperor to legally give the East India Company the right of taxation of Bengal, Behar, and Orissa with the justification that these revenues would finance the civil administration of the areas in the "Agreement on 12 August 1765" (Keith, 2003). Under this system, the English took over the military affairs of Bengal in addition to their new duty of tax collection.

With the income of up to £3,000,000 annually, this new power gave the East India Company officials with a very secure form of income and served the insatiable greed of British Nabobs (Marshall, 1996; Marshall et al., 1998; Marx, 1957). The reforms of Lord Bentinck introduced of new cash crops Indigo and Opium and the increased income of the East India Company (Smith, 1960).

Since 1765, the "East India Company" in Bengal did not need any silver to buy any textile from Bengal. In 1767, Clive can only limit the "Loot," but he cannot eliminate it (Reinhard, 2015). "There is a silent agreement for more enrichment in Bengal on a low level because the directors deny rise of salaries for the company's staff members. Therefore it's easier for the company tolerating the enrichment" (Keene, 1887). Since 1767, the Company is obliged to pay 400,000 pounds to London every year because England is spending yearly 480,000 pounds for the "American" colonies.

After the installation of the "dual system" in Bengal since 1767, the East India Company was provoking more speculation expecting high returns (Reinhard, 2015). The capital of the Company was increased again by 1 million pounds. The importations of spices, fabrics, and stimulants were about 10–15%. The exportations of European goods to Asia are marginal. In 1760, Great Britain has got a total capital of 130 million pounds, and until 1770, there is a people's income of estimated 140 million pounds. The total profits of England from India are 17,828.071 pounds; thus, from 140 million pounds, these 17.8 million are almost 13%. The goal in India was only the personal enrichment (Reinhard, 2015), which went on financing Industrial Revolution in Britain.

Prior to the 1780s, most of the fine quality cotton muslin in circulation in Britain had been manufactured in India. American historian Brooke Adams has recorded that "the plunder from the Nawab of Bengal's treasury was so excessive that it fuelled Britain's Industrial Revolution from 1760 and changed the worlds lifestyle forever as money alone is capable of being transmuted in any form of activity" (Brooke Adams, 1895).

Before 1760, the technology of spinning cotton in England was as simple as it was in Bengal and England's iron industry was in decline. Before the inflows of Indian treasure and credit, no force sufficient for the purpose of turning scientific inventions into commercial projects was there in England. After 1757, a complex system of credit and the joint-stock investment were developed based on immense wealth coming from Bengal.

The British sent away an estimated 1 billion pounds to Britain after 1757, and Industrial Revolution took place in 1760. Robert Clive collected 2.5 million pounds for the East India Company and 2,34,000 pounds for himself. To put these figures in perspective, an annual income of 800 pounds was considered sufficient for luxurious living by British nobleman of those days (Keene, 1887). Thus, the plunder of Bengal after the Battle of Plassey rapidly auto-mechanized the British textile industry.

Indian exports to Britain went up from £1.5 million pounds in 1750–1751 to £5.8 million pounds in 1797–1798. "The Company used its political power to dictate terms to the weavers of Bengal who were forced to sell their products at a cheaper and dictated price, even at a loss. Many of them were compelled to work for the Company for low wages and forbidden to work for Indian merchants" (Adams, 1895). The East India Company eliminated its rival traders, both Indian and foreign, Dutch and French by force.

The servants of the East India Company monopolized the sale of raw cotton and made the Bengal weaver pay exorbitant prices for it. Thus, the weaver lost both ways. At the same time, Indian textiles had to pay heavy duties to enter the British market as the British wanted to protect the product of its very new machine tools. Once England established industrial capital, it needed markets to sell the products and it was there in Bengal, which was forced to absorb these products to sustain the British Industrial Revolution.

This drain of wealth destroyed Indian industries, and undue tax collections created a series of famines. R. C. Dutt (1904) writes, "The people of Bengal had been used to tyranny, but had never lived under an oppression so far reaching in its effects, extending to every village market and every manufacturers loom. They … had never suffered from a system which touched their trades, their occupations, their lives so closely. The springs of their industry were stopped; the sources of their wealth dried up. This domineering British control pushed India hundreds of years behind in economic development."

In 1769, the British industrialists forced the East India Company by law to export every year over £380,000 worth of British manufacturing goods, mainly textiles. In 1793, they forced the East India Company to provide them the use of 3,000 tons of its shipping every year to carry their products to India. "Exports of British cotton goods to the East, mostly to India, increased from £156 in 1794 to nearly £110,000 in 1813, that is, by nearly 700 times" (Dutt, 1904). That had destroyed Bengal's textile industries.

The drain of wealth from Bengal began in 1757, when the Company's sent home nearly £6 million between 1758 and 1765. This amount of drain did not include the trading profits of the Company. In 1765, the Company acquired the right to collect taxes of Bengal. The East India Company began to purchase Indian goods out of the revenue of Bengal and to export them. These purchases were known as 'Investments.' Thus, through 'Investments,' Bengal's tax-revenue was sent to England. For example, "from 1765 to 1770, the Company sent out nearly £4 million worth of goods or about 33 per cent of the net revenue of Bengal" (Dutt, 1904). The drain took the form of an excess of India's exports over its imports, that surplus was not for India but for the East India Company. The wealth drained out of India played an important part in financing Britain's industrial development, especially during the late eighteenth century and the beginning of the nineteenth century. Britain was at that time investing in industry and agriculture about 7% of its national income, most of that came from Bengal alone (Adams, 1895; Keene, 1887) (Table 1.1).

In 1756, before Bengal was occupied, the national debt of Britain was about 75 million pounds, mainly to Holland with annual interest obligation of about 3 million pounds. The national debt of the UK was went up to £140 million in 1760, but in 1815 that debt was reduced to 86 million pounds but within a few years Britain has wiped out its debt and became an exporter of capital to the US and Argentina. The East India Company had to export silver worth of 0.6 million pounds annually from 1740 to 1760 to buy tea from China and textiles from Bengal.

Table 1.1 Estimated state income, 1667–1853 (million £)

	1667	*1707–1709*	*1764*	*1800*	*1818*	*1853*
British India	–	–	3	8	13	21
Revenues of Indian states	26	38	–	14–21	–	13

Source Cook (1995)

After the occupation of Bengal in 1757, it became reverse; from 1810 to 1820, annual imports of silver from India to Britain became about 3 million pounds per year as Britain took silver out of Bengal. "It was not long before greedy Company agents lost all restraint and began the process of economically plundering Bengal with their schemes. As public officials, they readily assumed the rights of accepting bribes, pocketing tax revenues, and smuggling goods, which had all been the understood prerogatives of their native predecessors, and used these administrative inefficiencies as a means to steer the wealth of India into their hands" (Reinhard, 2015).

In the eighteenth century, Great Britain was a net debtor, but in the nineteenth century the UK was lending in many other countries. These facts have consequences for the methods by which investment was financed, as a surplus in the current account means that national saving financed domestic investment as well as investment abroad, while a deficit means that investment was financed not only by domestic saving but also through capital inflows (Marshall et al., 1998).

In 1770, Dutch investments in the English East India Company alone stood at around £10 million. In 1791, one-sixth of Bank of England stock was held by the Dutch. In 1773, the British government borrowed £1 million sterling from Holland to finance sugar plantations in the British West Indies paying 8% interest, compared with 2–3% in Holland. As regards the public debt, Dutch investment in British public debt in 1737 stood at £10 million (27.7% of the total gross debt), in 1762, at £30 million (25% of the total gross debt), and in 1774 at £46.6 million (25% of the total gross debt). The gross foreign debt was £100 million in 1770 (Deane & Cole, 1967). However, between 1790 and 1815, the UK passed from being a debtor to being a creditor nation. The balance of foreign net debt in 1800 varies from £18 million to wealth supplied the funds that bought national debt back from the Dutch and others £167 million depending on the transfer series. Davis (1979) wrote, 'It is altogether more probable that Indian leaving Britain nearly free from overseas indebtedness.'

From 1740 to the end of the eighteenth century, the national saving rate increased by 50% and the investment ratio by 80%. This means that, for the century as a whole, national saving was not sufficient to finance investment; there was a need for inflows of foreign capital. During most of the eighteenth century, almost one-third of the investment was financed by inflows of foreign capital from India, particularly Bengal. The data also reveal that the decrease in government saving which occurred during the Napoleonic Wars was not completely offset by an increase in private domestic saving, since the national saving ratio decreased. However, this decrease in the saving rate did not constrain the investment ratio since the UK got money from Bengal. The decrease in national saving at the end of the eighteenth century was counterbalanced by an increase in the current account deficit, financed by flows of capital from Bengal (Adams, 1895; Dutt, 1904; Marshall et al., 1998).

In the eighteenth century, along with improvements in technology, came the necessity of investing in fixed assets, and saving was no longer sufficient to finance both working and fixed capital. The fact that working capital was one and a half times greater than fixed capital implies that the financing of working capital was crucial to the operation of the enterprise. Usually working capital was provided by a merchant banker and did not come from the entrepreneur's own saving. The link existing between merchant bankers and non-domestic financiers allowed the channeling of the foreign flows of capital to investment in working capital. In 1761–1770, the ratio of capital inflow to nominal output was 2.2% and the investment ratio was 6.0%, while national saving was only 3.8%. Two completely different interpretations of these figures are possible: On the one hand, all capital flows could have been directed toward investment, including a portion of domestic saving (the other portion going toward financing the budget deficit). Most British historians subscribe to that view. On the other hand, foreign capital from India could very well have financed the budget deficit, with domestic saving being directed into investment. The period 1740–1790 constitutes the first stage of British industrialization. The investment ratio could not attain 11% until 1820 (Adams, 1895; Dutt, 1904; Marshall et al., 1998). The data show that Britain repaid its debt during the war years. Davis argued for a substantial increase in remittances (amounting up to £15 millon per annum on average) from the Indian Empire during the last decade of the eighteenth century (Davis, 1979; Philips, 1961).

After gaining the right to collect revenue in Bengal in 1765, the Company largely ceased importing gold and silver, which it had hitherto used to pay for goods shipped back to Britain. In addition, as under Mughal Empire rule, land revenue collected in the Bengal Presidency helped finance the Company's wars in other parts of India. Consequently, in the period 1760–1800, Bengal's money supply was greatly diminished because of the exploitation of the East India Company, adding to the economic downturn. During the period, 1780–1860, India changed from being an exporter of processed goods for which it received payment in bullion, to being an exporter of raw materials and a buyer of manufactured goods. More specifically, in the 1750s, mostly fine cotton and silk were exported from India to markets in Europe, Asia, and Africa; by the second quarter of the nineteenth century, raw materials, which chiefly consisted of raw cotton, opium, and indigo, accounted for most of India's exports (Adams, 1895; Dutt, 1904).

Initial Exploits

Early in the second half of the eighteenth century, two events presaged a change in this process. In 1761, the Peshwa's army lost at Panipat. And in 1765, the Company received the taxation rights of Bengal from the Mughal Emperor. The proportion of the military in total expenditure was universally high in the second half of the century. The Company could not finance wars from its income. The proportion of interest-bearing-debt-to-revenue ratio rose from 120% in 1793 to over 300 in 1809, declining to 200% in 1833. 90% of the war finance was raised in India. In British India, in the decade of the third Anglo-Maratha wars, debt service as a percentage of revenue fell from nearer 20% to 12%. Bengal revenues increased from a figure nearer £2 million in the last days of the Nawab 1757 to over £5 million 25 years after Company takeover 1793 (Mukherjee, 1939).

The access to increasing sums of money allowed the Company to expand its standing army between Plessey and the Sikh war. From the very beginning in 1757, when Sirajuddowla was defeated, the British plundered Bengal and this plunder directly contributed to the Industrial Revolution in England. The plunder from Bangla (Bengal) was invested in the new British industries. To discourage Indian exports, Indian goods were taxed heavily, tax of 67.5% was levied of Indian calicos, and a tax of 37.5% was levied on muslins on entry into Britain. Over 300% import tax was placed Indian sugar. Possession of Indian imported goods in England such as cotton items was fined heavily to further hurt the Indian industry. While massive industrialization began in Britain, Bengal (and the rest of India) was deindustrialized. Indian exports were slowly being stifled, with that its economy and goods combined and caused the final ruin of Bengal (Adams, 1895; Dutt, 1904; Marshall et al., 1998).

Bengal was hurt tremendously since it was an exporting province. They took raw materials from Bengal and sold industrial products from Britain back to the Bengal. The muslin still caused a threat for sale of British fabric and so the weavers were forced to stop producing muslin or passing on their skill to their children. To enforce these thumbs of the weavers were cut off. Muslin was the softest fabric ever produced in human history. 20 meter length of muslin fabric could be folded into a matchbox… today it survives in museums only. Muslin production began 3000 years ago or maybe has its roots in the Indus Civilization which is 5000 years old and survived various foreign invaders in Bengal. However, it did not survive the vengeful British colonial period (Adams, 1895; Reinhard, 2015).

By 1756, the English East India Company's servants send home nearly 6 million pounds; this amount is more than four times the total land revenue collection of the Nawab of Bengal. By 1765–1770, the English East India Company sends out nearly 4 million pounds worth of goods or about 33% of the net revenue of Bengal, in the form of the Company's 'Investments.' From 1766 to 1767, nearly 5.7 million pounds are drained from Bengal to England. In the early nineteenth century, the drain of wealth from India to Britain in the form of the English East India Company's 'Investments' constitutes nearly 9% of India's national income. The first Governor-General of British India, Warren Hastings, acknowledged "violent" tax collecting after 1771: Revenues earned by the Company were higher in 1771 than in 1768. Globally, the profit of the company increased from fifteen million rupees in 1765 to thirty million in 1777 (Dutt, 1904; Marshall et al., 1998).

There had been a great demand for muslin from Bengal and silk from Bengal and Benaras. British merchants bought these Indian products in large quantities. However, at the beginning of the eighteenth century, Britain and other European countries passed laws prohibiting the entry of cotton and silk textiles from India although there was a demand for it. After the advent of the Industrial Revolution, India was forced to produce cotton, indigo, and other products which British industries required. Indian markets were flooded with cheap, machine-made textiles manufactured in England. Indian hand-made textiles could not compete with the cheap machine-made textiles. India was transformed into a supplier of raw materials and a market for British manufactured goods (Adams, 1895; Dutt, 1904).

While British goods were exempted from duties while entering Indian markets, Indian goods entering England were burdened with heavy customs duties. Thus, the self-sufficient economy of India collapsed under the impact of British colonial policies. With the decline of the cotton industry, the towns that had flourished as centers of trade or industry also declined (Dutt, 1904).

In 1769–1770, there is a big famine in Bengal because of droughts and crop failures provoking millions of dead, because the East India Company is just ignoring the shortage of food there, not taking any measure, or forced the farmers to plant wrong products in times of a famine. Estimations indicate 10 million persons killed by this famine (Adams, 1895).

In 1778, the Company has 67,000 soldiers. The income of 3.8 million pounds a year was confronted with payments of 5 million pounds a year (included the tax for London for the "American" colonies which are normal since 1767). In 1786, the looser of the battle of Yorktown of the war of independence, Mr. Charles Marquis Cornwallis, is becoming the new Governor-General of Bengal, until 1793. Britain was performing Industrial Revolution now with the weaving machine, since the 1790s. English technicians invent the weaving machine with the possibility of weaving large fabrics competing the Indian production by hand. Thus, the sales of Bengal textiles in England went down. In 1760, Great Britain has got a total capital of 130 million pounds, and until 1770, there is a people's income of estimated 140 million pounds. There is a yearly accumulation of capital of 9.4 million pounds. 500,000–600,000 pounds of transferred private profits are just 0.36% of the people's income. The total profits of England from India are 17,828.071 pounds, and thus, out of 140 million pounds, these 17.8 million are almost 13% (Adams, 1895; Dutt, 1904; Reinhard, 2015).

East India Company

Prior to the start of the Industrial Revolution in the late eighteenth century, Mughal India was the most important manufacturing center in world trade, producing about 25% of the world's industrial output, with the Mughal Bengal province prominent in the textile manufacturing industry. Real wages in eighteenth-century southern India were also comparable to those in southern England at the time. In early modern Europe, there was significant demand for textiles from Mughal

India, including cotton textiles and silk products. European fashion, for example, became increasingly dependent on Mughal Indian textiles and silks. In the late seventeenth and early eighteenth centuries, Mughal India accounted for 95% of British imports from Asia (Guha, 1995; Tripathi, 1957).

During the second half of the seventeenth century, the newly established factories of the East India Company (EIC) in India started to produce finished cotton goods in quantity for the UK market. The imported Calico and chintz garments competed with and acted as a substitute for indigenous wool and the linen produce, resulting in local weavers, spinners, dyers, shepherds, and farmers petitioning their MPs and in turn the UK Government for a ban on the importation, and later the sale of woven cotton goods, which they eventually achieved via the 1700 and 1721 Calico Acts. Indian cotton textiles, particularly those from Bengal, continued to maintain a competitive advantage up until the nineteenth century. In order to compete with India, Britain invested in labor-saving technical progress, while implementing protectionist policies such as bans and tariffs to restrict Indian imports.

At the same time, the EIC's rule in India contributed to its de-industrialization, opening up a new market for British goods, while the capital amassed from Bengal after its 1757 conquest was invested in British industries such as textile manufacturing and greatly increased British wealth, contributing to Britain's Industrial Revolution. Britain eventually surpassed India as the world's leading cotton textile manufacturer in the nineteenth century.

Bengal and Britain's Industrial Revolution

American historian Brooke Adams (1895) has recorded that the plunder from the Bengal's Nawabs Treasury was so excessive that it fueled Industrial Revolution of Britain from 1760 and changed the world's lifestyle forever.

After the battle of Plassey in 1757, the pattern of the Company's commercial relations with India underwent a qualitative change. Now the Company could use its political control over Bengal to acquire monopolistic control over Indian trade and production and push its Indian trade. Moreover, it utilized the revenues of Bengal to finance its export of Indian goods (Dutt, 1904).

The inventions between 1764 and 1785 were the spinning jenny by Hargreaves, the water frame by Arkwight, the mule by Crompton, and the power-loom by Cartwright. John Kays had invented the flying shuttle and coal began to replace wood in smelting, while in 1768 Watt matured the steam engine. However, it needs a lot of money to convert these inventions into commercial success that produced the Industrial Revolution. That money came from Bengal since 1757.

As R. C. Dutt (1904) the effort of the Parliamentary Select Committee of 1812 was "to discover how they (Indian manufacturers) could be replaced by British manufacturers, and how British industries could be promoted at the expense of Indian industries." The British manufacturers looked upon the East India Company, its monopoly of eastern trade, and its methods of exploitation of India through control of India's revenues and export trade, to be the chief obstacles in the fulfillment of their dreams. Between 1793 and 1813, they launched a powerful campaign against the Company and its commercial privileges and finally succeeded in 1813 in abolishing its monopoly of Indian trade. With this event, agricultural India was to be made an economic colony of industrial England. The Government of India now followed a policy of free trade or unrestricted entry of British goods.

The British exported to Britain part of India's wealth and resources for which India got no adequate economic or material return. Englishmen, working and trading in India, nearly always planned to go back to Britain, and the Indian government was controlled by a foreign company of merchants and the Government of Britain. The British, consequently, spent a large part of the taxes and income they derived from the Indian people not in India but in Britain, their home country. By the end of the eighteenth century, the drain constituted nearly 9% of national income. The actual drain was even more, as a large part of the salaries and other incomes of English officials and the trading fortunes of English merchants also found their way into England (Keene, 1887).

Drain theory was the core of critique of colonialism that Britain was draining and bleeding India. R. C. Dutt (1904) made this theme the subject of his Economic History of India. Drain, he declared, was the basic cause of India's poverty. Naoroji (1901) observed in 1880:

> It is not the pitiless operations of economic laws, but it is thoughtless and pitiless action of the British policy; it is pitiless eating of India's substance in India and further pitiless drain to England, in short it is pitiless perversion

of Economic Laws by the sad bleeding to which India is subjected, that is destroying India.

John Sullivan, President of the Board of Revenue, Madras, added—"*Our system acts very much like a sponge, drawing up all the good things from the banks of the Ganges, and squeezing them down on the banks of the Thames*" (Mukherjee, 1939). The 'Drain of Wealth was nothing but a unilateral transfer of fund. For the first six years from 1766 to 1771, the total receipt was 13,066,764 pounds, or about 13 million pounds a year. If we add total charges with it (salaries, expenses, service charge to the Nawab for military expenses, etc.), the amount would go up to about 22 million pounds per year. These are extracted only from Bengal area, as the remittances sent from Bombay and Madras areas were about 7% of the gains from Bengal. As we can see, land revenues used to be the main components of the total receipts. Land revenues went up to an extraordinary level in the years 1766, 1882, 1805, and 1826 causing famines in which millions perished (Richards, 2011).

From 1757 to 1919, India also had to meet administrative expenses in London, first of the East India Company, and then of the India Office, as well as other minor but irritatingly extraneous charges. The cost of British staff was raised by long home leave in the UK, early retirement, and lavish amenities in the form of subsidized housing, utilities, rest houses, etc. Under the rule of the East India Company, official transfers to the UK rose gradually until they reached about £3.5 million in 1856, the year before the mutiny. The real blow to Indian handicrafts fell after 1813, when they lost not only their foreign markets but, what was of much greater importance, their market in India itself. The Industrial Revolution in Britain completely transformed Britain's economy and its economic relations with India.

Britain had come to capture and monopolize many foreign markets by means of war and colonialism. These export markets enabled its export industries to expand production rapidly, utilizing the latest techniques in production and organization. Africa, the West Indies, Latin America, Canada, Australia, China and above all India provided unlimited opportunities for export. This was particularly true of the cotton textile industry which served as the main vehicle of the Industrial Revolution in Britain. Britain had already evolved the colonial pattern of trade that helped the Industrial Revolution which, in turn, strengthened this pattern: The colonies and underdeveloped countries exported agricultural and mineral raw materials to Britain while the latter sold them to its manufactures (Hobsbawn, 1968; Marx, 1957).

There was sufficient capital accumulated in the country for investment in new machinery and the factory system. Moreover, this capital was concentrated, in the hands of merchants and industrialists who were keen to invest it in trade and industry. Here again the immense wealth drawn from Africa, Asia, the West Indies, and Latin America, including that drawn from India by the East India Company and its servants after the battle of Plassey played an important role in financing industrial expansion.

Any government wedded to Indian interests alone would have protected Indian industry through high tariff walls and used the time thus gained to import the new techniques of the West. Britain had done this in relation to its own industries in the eighteenth century; France, Germany, and the US were also doing so at the time; Japan and the Soviet Union were to do it many decades later; and free India has done that before it has joined the WTO and a new colonial exploitation stated in the name of free trade.

However, not only were Indian industries not protected by the foreign rulers but foreign goods were given free entry. Foreign imports rose rapidly. Imports of British cotton goods alone increased from £1,100,000 in 1813 to £6,300,000 in 1856. While the doors of India were thus thrown wide open to foreign goods, Indian products which could still compete with British products were subjected to heavy import duties on entry into Britain. The British would not take in Indian goods on fair and equal terms even at this stage when their industries had achieved technological superiority over Indian handicrafts. Duties in Britain on several categories of Indian goods continued to be high till their export to Britain virtually ceased. For example, in 1824, a duty of 67½% was levied on Indian calicos and a duty of 37½% on Indian muslins. Indian sugar had to pay on entry into Britain a duty that was over three times its cost price. In some cases, duties in England went up as high as 400%. As a result of such prohibitive import duties and development of machine industries, Indian exports to foreign countries fell rapidly (Adams, 1895; Mukherjee, 1939).

The unfairness of British commercial policy has been summed up by the British historian, H. H. Wilson (1848), in the following words:

> It was stated in evidence, that the cotton and silk goods of India up to this period could be sold for a profit in the British market, at a price from 50 to 60 per cent lower than those fabricated in England. It consequently became necessary to protect the latter by duties of 70 to 80 per cent on their value, or by positive prohibition. Had this not been the case, had not such prohibitory duties and decrees existed, the mills of Paisley and of Manchester would have been stopped in their outset and could scarcely have been again set in motion, even by the power of steam.

They were created by the sacrifice of the Indian manufacture. Had India been independent, she would have retaliated, would have imposed preventive duties upon British goods, and would thus have preserved her own productive industry from annihilation. This act of self-defense was not permitted her. Recently, the WTO has imposed a similar regime.

British goods were forced upon her without paying any duty; and the foreign manufacturer employed the arm of political injustice to keep down and ultimately strangle a competitor with whom he could not have contended on equal terms. Instead of exporting manufactures, India was now forced to export raw materials like raw cotton and raw silk which British industries needed urgently, or plantation products like indigo and tea, of food grains which were in short supply in Britain.

In 1856, India exported £4,300,000 worth of raw cotton, only £810,000 worth of cotton manufactures, £2,900,000 worth of food grains, £1,730,000 worth of indigo, and £770,000 worth of raw silk. The British also promoted the sale of Indian opium in China even though the Chinese put a ban on it because of its poisonous and other harmful effects. But the trade yielded large profits to British merchants and fat revenues to the Company-controlled administration of India. Interestingly enough, the import of opium into Britain was strictly banned. By the end of the nineteenth century, Indian exports consisted primarily of raw cotton, jute and silk, oilseeds, wheat, hides and skins, indigo, and tea. Thus, the commercial policy of the East India Company after 1813 was guided by the needs of British industry. Its main aim was to transform India into a consumer of British manufactures and a supplier of raw materials (Adams, 1987; Dutt, 1904; Wilson, 1848).

Revenue from Taxation, Opium and Indigo

The main burden of providing money for the trade and profits of the East India Company, the cost of administration, and the wars for British expansion in India had to be paid by the Indian people. The Indian state used to take a part of the agricultural produce as land revenue. It had to do that directly or indirectly through intermediaries, such as zamindars, who collected the land revenue from the cultivator.

E S. Brezis (1995) wrote, it will be shown that in the eighteenth century Great Britain was running a current account deficit and was a net importer of capital, whereas in the next century the UK was running *a* current account surplus and was a net exporter of capital. How that could happen? The data show that, while domestic saving financed two-thirds of the investment during the second half of the eighteenth century, the current account deficit financed the remaining one-third. Therefore, foreign capital cannot be disregarded in the determination of British investment.

Another major, though erratic, export item was indigo dye, which was extracted from natural indigo, and which came to be grown in Bengal and northern Bihar. In late seventeenth- and early eighteenth-century Europe, blue clothing was favored as a fashion, and blue uniforms were common in the military; consequently, the demand for the dye was high. In 1788, the East India Company offered advances to ten British planters to grow indigo; however, since the new (landed) property rights defined in the Permanent Settlement, didn't allow them, as Europeans, to buy agricultural land, they had to in turn offer cash advances to local peasants, and sometimes coerce them, to grow the crop (Guha, 1995).

The peasant discontent in Bengal eventually led to the Indigo rebellion in 1859–1860 and to the end of indigo production. However, indigo production continued well into the twentieth century. Recent acts of Modi government to satisfy the demands of the WTO is very similar to that contract farming introduced by the British to promote the cultivation of cash crops like Indigo and Opium (Tripathi, 1957).

From the 1850s, the strategy of using governments to source and secure capital was extended to India and the rest of the empire. In India, the British had no interest in developing a sector of the economy that they were doing so much to develop at home. Beyond what was necessary to achieve a favorable balance of payments, there was no serious attempt to develop manufacturing. British economic policy in India was designed to draw tribute while minimizing social and political change. In order to sustain tribute, the administration worked to maintain a trade surplus of exports over imports. Exports were principally opium, cotton, and grains together with jute, hides, indigo, and tea (Government of India, 1880). The aversion to industrial manufacturing ensured that India's main exports were raw agricultural materials rather than manufactures. In 1878–1879, only 6.5% of total exports were manufactured goods.

When the Famine Commission sought to promote alternative employment, it did so with industries that would ensure that India remained firmly in an agricultural state. These industries were associated with India's primary exports: Sugar refining; leather tanning; the manufacture of cotton; wool and silk; tobacco; the manufacture of paper, pottery, glass, soap, oils, and candles. In the decade 1869–1879, when state-constructed railways began, India's export surplus averaged roughly £16m per year.

This export earning was repatriated as the Home Charges—roughly half as returns on capital investment and the rest as administrative costs (Government of India, 1880). Cain and Hopkins wrote that the 'India's role' 'was to be that of a tributary province' (Cain & Hopkins, 1993). The British Raj functioned to source and stabilized the transmission of tribute from India to Britain. In the process, the Indian public debt rose from £30m in 1837 to £220m by 1900 (Charlesworth, 1982). Loan financed public works, mainly canal irrigation and the railways, represented a significant part of what the Raj did in India as revenue figures indicate. In 1878–1879, total gross revenue stood at just over £65m. Land revenue accounted for the greatest single contribution at £22.5m, opium accounted for £9m, and salt at just under £7m. Receipts from 'productive public works' accounted for as much as salt at nearly £7m and more than the combined total of customs and excise at £2m and £2.5m, respectively. Canals and railways were not built to modernize India's economy. Development was merely rhetoric to legitimize actions taken purely in the interests of capital.

Capital's shift to India in the 1850s came in the wake of financial failures in the US and growing competition for the City on continental Europe (Jenks, 1971). More renowned for his efforts at reform and 'improvement,' Governor-General Dalhousie (1848–1856) did much in this period to make India safe for British capital. First, he set about expanding the revenue base to enable India to meet its external financial obligations. Beginning with Punjab in 1849 and finally Awadh in 1856, Dalhousie's administration witnessed one of the largest and most determined periods of territorial annexation since the early decades of British expansion. With these various territorial acquisitions Dalhousie calculated, he had added roughly £4m to the revenue of India. Behind Dalhousie's rhetoric of reform and modernization lay the determined drive for revenue and markets for British capital (Adams, 1895; Dutt, 1904; Marshall, 1996).

Africa, the West Indies, Latin America, Canada, Australia, China, and above all India provided unlimited opportunities for export. This was particularly true of the cotton textile industry which served as the main vehicle of the Industrial Revolution in Britain.

Britain had already evolved the colonial pattern of trade that helped the Industrial Revolution which, in turn, strengthened this pattern: The colonies and underdeveloped countries exported agricultural and mineral raw materials to Britain while the latter sold them its manufactures.

Man-Made Famines in British India

The British brought an "unsympathetic and ruthless economic agenda to India" and that "the creation of famine" was brought about by British "sequestration and export of food for enhanced commercial gain." Three important factors caused devastating famines in India under British rule. First, India's indigenous textile industries were destroyed by London's high tariffs and the import of cheap British manufactured products, impoverishing millions of town dwellers, who were forced into the countryside to compete for dwindling land. Second, India's traditional granary reserve system, designed to offset the impact of bad harvests, was dismantled. Third, India's peasants were pressured into growing crops for export, making them dependent on fluctuating world market prices for their means of subsistence. As a result, tens of *millions* of people died of starvation. These famines were not caused by shortages of food. They took place at the very same time that annual grain exports from India were increasing.

One-third of the population of the then province of Bengal, which includes today's Bangladesh, West Bengal, Orissa, Bihar, and South Assam, were wiped out in the famine of 1770, immediately after Bengal was occupied by the British Easy India Company, due to their inhuman tax system. According to Davis (2001), during the famine of 1876, "the newly constructed railroads, lauded as institutional safeguards against famine, were instead used by merchants to ship grain inventories from outlying drought stricken districts to central depots for hoarding...In Madras city, overwhelmed by 100,000 drought refugees, famished peasants dropped dead in front of the troops guarding pyramids of imported rice."

The British refused to provide adequate relief for famine victims on the grounds that this would encourage indolence. Sir Richard Temple, who was selected to organize famine relief efforts in 1877, set the food allotment for starving Indians at 16 ounces of rice per day—less than the diet for inmates at the Buchenwald concentration camp for the Jews in Hitler's Germany. British disinclination to respond with urgency and vigor to food deficits resulted in a succession of about two dozen appalling famines during the British occupation of India. These swept away tens of millions of people. "The frequency of famine showed a disconcerting increase in the nineteenth century," under the British rule (Bhatia, 1963).

Very few would be aware of the horrendous calamities inflicted on Indians by the British. The annual death rate in 1877 in British labor camps during the Deccan famine was about 94%. Extraordinarily low population growth between 1870 and 1930 (due to famine, malnourishment-exacerbated disease and cholera, plague and influenza epidemics) was due to this exploitative policy. In 1943 Bengal Famine in British-ruled India, about 5 million people were perished, but it was never mentioned in the British history books, because it was caused by a deliberate British "scorched earth policy" to deprive the Azad Hind Army and the Japanese to receive any support from the local people (Bhatia, 1963, Mukherjee, 2010).

The annual death rate in India before 1920 was about 4.8% but this declined to 3.5% by 1947 and is presently about 0.9% (http://countrystudies.us/india/32.htm). Using a baseline "expected" annual death rate value of 1.0% and assuming an "actual" pre-1920 value of 4.8%, one can estimate that the avoidable (excess) mortality was about 0.6 billion during 1757–1837, 0.5 billion during 1837–1901, and 0.4 billion during 1901–1947. Thus, the British rule of India was associated with an excess (i.e., avoidable) mortality totaling 1.5 billion—surely one of the greatest crimes in all of human history (Davis, 2000).

An extraordinary feature of the appalling record of British imperialism with respect to genocide and mass, worldwide killing of huge numbers of people (by war disease and famine) is its absence from public perception. There is no mention of famine in India or Bengal in the British textbooks of history. New historians in India are now putting the blame on the victims. Meghnad Desai et al. (1983) in his article in Cambridge History of India puts the blame on the Indian speculators; Amartya Sen (1981) suggested that people in that area had eaten too much to create the famine.

The progress made in India under British Rule like the coming of railways, postal system, telegraphic communications, etc., was all undertaken by the British Administration to facilitate their rule. The aim of British policy was to integrate the Indian economy with that of the British in way such that India supplied Great Britain with cheap raw material for being manufactured into valued-added (costly) finished products. It is not true that if India remained independent it could not have developed railways or telegraphic system; Japan or Thailand was never colonized but they have today much better infrastructure than that in India.

India during the British rule was to provide a ready captive market for British goods made from Indian raw materials. The resultant enrichment and industrial development were to take place in Britain and not in India. Thus, at the dawn of independence, India inherited an economy that had the worst features of both the feudal and the industrial ages without the advantages of either. As Rabindranath Tagore wrote in 1941, in his letter from the deathbed to British member of parliament Mrs.Rothbone, that "...in the Soviet Union illiteracy was eradicated with two decades but in India even after two centuries of British rule only 15 percent of the Indians were literate" (Tagore, 1997).

Occupation of Africa

Here, we describe the colonization of the African continent by European powers during the period of 1881 and 1914. In 1870, only the Portuguese, Dutch, and British colonized Africa in the coastal areas, whereas by 1914 almost 90% of the continent, except Ethiopia (Abyssinia), a part Somalia, and Liberia, was unoccupied. The Berlin Conference of 1884 divided up Africa among the European powers. In the beginning, slave trade was the main motive to occupy Africa. Later, Africa became the source of raw materials for the industry in Europe and Americas (Bourne, 1903; Gjersø, 2015; Robinson & Gallagher, 1962).

During the Long Depression (1873–1896), Africa offered Britain, Germany, France, Holland, and other countries an open market where the surplus capital can be invested in various plantation industry and mining where abundant raw materials could made a greater profit possible.

However, in Africa, the amount of capital investment by Europeans was comparatively small. Some of the best-known companies were Cecil Rhodes's De Beers Mining Company and Léopold II of Belgium's rubber company in the Congo Free State. John A. Hobson argued in his book imperialism that this "shrinking of continental markets was a key factor of the global new imperialism period" (Langer, 1935; Sanderson, 1974; Von Strandmann, 1969).

Weltpolitik (world policy) was the foreign policy of Germany encouraged by Kaiser Wilhelm II in 1890, whose ambition was to transform Germany into a global colonial power through the acquisition of overseas colonies, just like the British. Soon, Germany became the third-largest colonial power in Africa with Southwest Africa, Togoland, the Cameroons, and Tanganyika. Due to the brutality of King Leopold II of Belgium, up to 8 million of the estimated 16 million native people of Congo inhabitants died between 1885 and 1908 and unknown number of people lost their limbs for producing enough rubber. A similar situation occurred in the neighboring French Congo (Hochschild, 2006; Robinson et al., 1961).

Theophilus Shepstone annexed the South African Republic (or Transvaal) in 1877 for the British Empire, after it had been independent for twenty years. In 1879, after the Anglo-Zulu War, Britain fought against the Dutch settlers in leading to the First Boer War (1880–1881). The Second Boer War, fought between 1899 and 1902, was about control of the gold and diamond industries (Darwin, 1997; Shillington, 2005).

Slave Trade and Its Contribution to the British Finance

European settler in the Americas emerged from adventurers, pirates, soldiers, farmers, and tradesmen, and a few from the aristocracy. Settlers traveling to the newly discovered continents included the Dutch of New Netherland, the Swedes and Finns of New Sweden, the English Quakers of the Province of Pennsylvania, the English Puritans of New England, the English settlers of Jamestown, Virginia, Germans who settled the mid-Atlantic colonies, and the Ulster Scots people of the Appalachian Mountains. These groups all became part of the US when it gained its independence in 1776.

Colonists came from European kingdoms that had military and naval capabilities. The Spanish and Portuguese' centuries-old experience of conquest and colonization during the Reconquista coupled with new oceanic ship navigation skills. England, France, and the Netherlands had also started colonies in the West Indies and North America.

The British economy had begun to grow rapidly at the end of the seventeenth century and, by the mid-eighteenth century, particularly since Bengal, India was occupied by the East India Company. Small factories in Britain, financed by the returning 'Nawabs,' as the former employees of the company used to be called, of the East India Company, were producing much more than the nation could consume. Britain found a market for their goods in the British colonies of North America, increasing her exports to that region by 360% between 1740 and 1770. British merchants offered credit to their customers; this allowed Americans to buy a large amount of British goods. From Nova Scotia to Georgia, all British subjects bought similar products, creating and anglicizing a sort of common identity and culture. Earning from the slave trade also made serious contribution.

About 600,000 slaves were imported into what is now the US. The great majority went to sugarcane-growing colonies in the Caribbean and to Brazil, where life expectancy was short and the numbers had to be continually replenished. Life expectancy was much greater in the North American colonies because of better food, less disease, lighter workloads, and better medical care, so the numbers grew rapidly by excesses of births over deaths, reaching 4 million by the 1860 Census (Williams, 1944).

Bengal (India) was effectively occupied by the East India Company in 1757. Thus, 1750's decade gives suddenly a substantial profit, which went on increasing in 1760. Balance of trade and net exports showed substantial improvements. The slave trade contributed substantial amount in these periods.

Portugal and Britain were the two most 'successful' in transporting and enslaving the people of Africa, with 70% of all Africans transported to the Americas due to these two countries. Britain was the most important between 1640 and 1807, when the abolition of slave trade took place. Estimates showed that Britain transported 3.1 million Africans (of whom 2.7 million arrived) to various British colonies (Williams, 1944, 1994).

From 1660, the British Government passed various laws to facilitate British companies on the West Coast of Africa and to supply slaves to the North American colonies. The East India Company was engaged in the collection of slaves from West Africa and to send them to East Africa, South Africa, India, and Asia.

Britain was the most important European country in the Slave Trade. Of the 80,000 Africans transported from Africa to the Americas each year, 42,000 were by British companies. By the end of the eighteenth century, four million pounds came into Britain from its West Indian plantations and slave trade. In Britain, those who had made much of their fortune from the slave trade built fine palaces, established banks such as the Bank of England, and invested in new industries. The grandfather of Winston Churchill, John Churchill built the Blenheim Palace near Oxford with the money he earned from the slave trade. Another important beneficiary was William Gladstone, the Prime Minister of Britain (Williams, 1944).

British slave ship owners made 20–50% profit on each ship. Large sums of money were made by ship owners, who stayed in England, from buying and selling Africans slaves. Plantation owners in the American colonies used slave labor to grow their crops mainly cotton and sugar. Slaves were unpaid workers. They invested their profits in new factories and inventions. The ports like Bristol and Liverpool became major ports as a result. Banks and finance houses grew fabulously rich from the fees and interest they earned from merchants who borrowed money for their voyages. The Transatlantic Slave Trade created many jobs for people in Britain. Many people worked in factories selling their products to West Africa. Birmingham used to sell 100,000 guns a year to the slave traders.

With the expansion of agriculture, African black slaves became an even more important factor for the British Colonialists. They promoted American economic growth in agriculture. Slaves were considered as real estate. In the mid-1700s, in the South, the cotton industry was developing fast and demand for slaves was growing. However, in 1808, the importation of slaves into America was banned. After the Civil War, President Abraham Lincoln in 1865 abolished slavery everywhere. In 1833, the British government abolished slavery in Great Britain and its colonies.

Profits from slave trade benefitted universities in Britain like Oxford, established a score of banks, including Barclays, and financed the experiments of James Watt, inventor of the steam engine. Liverpool merchant bankers, made gigantic profits in the slave trades, invested in the early cotton manufacturers of its Lancashire. West Indian planters built stately homes—some, ridiculously extravagant dwellings. Others were investing in building canals.

The British Empire at that time was composed of Ireland, the North American colonies, and the plantation colonies of the West Indies. Capitalism was developed as a result. The Spanish, Portuguese, English,

French, and Dutch colonization in America was capitalist. Its objectives were organizing production and to place products on the world. The colonization has capitalist objectives, to make profits. However, no financial institutions attempted to provide funds for entrepreneurs, and banks financed foreign trade. Dynamic sectors of the economy, cotton manufacturing, iron production, coal mining, and ceramics, were initially starved of capital until the vast tax revenues started flowing into Britain from Bengal (Marx, 1957).

Between 1692 and 1815, debt rose from 5% of GDP to more than 200%. Peaking at over 200% after the end of the Napoleonic Wars, debt eventually fell to 100% of GDP by the middle of the nineteenth century. The question is how. After 1760, investment as a percentage of GDP probably increased from around 8% to over 12%, because of the huge finance coming from Bengal, India. The rate of return on capital in Britain also grew from 10% in 1770 to over 23% by 1860 (Mukherjee, 1939).

In 1815, after the end of the Napoleonic Wars, Britain's debt amounted to £792 million; in 1914, to £843 million, some 6% higher. At the same time, the debt/GDP ratio declined to 1/10th of its former level, from 226 to 25%. Government expenditure took the form of military expenses. The state owned neither the means of production nor infrastructure. Elsewhere, government played an important role in promoting industrial developments as in Germany and Japan or in encouraging and subsidizing private sector industrialization, as in the US, but in Britain industrial development was mainly supported by individual efforts financed by the revenues from Bengal, India (Reinhard, 2015).

The creation of a large national debt enabled Britain to finance its navy and colonial armies. As a result, Britain could meet the increasing costs of the global wars. A financial–military nexus emerged. Merchants, city financiers, and parts of the aristocratic landed elite supported this nexus and benefited from it, and the British economy prospered. The Indian Empire and the trade it generated expanded markets, enabled specialization, and provided surplus capital and raw materials.

In his 1944 book (it was republished in 1994) 'Capitalism and Slavery,' Eric Williams argued that profits from colonies 'fertilized' many branches of the metropolitan economy and set the scene for England's 'Industrial Revolution.'

At crucial moments during the onset of industrialization in Britain, colonial markets, colonial supplies, and colonial profits made a significant contribution. Early capitalist manufacturers needed wider markets to reach the levels of output that would allow for the widespread adoption of new industrial methods.

The ability of British merchants to penetrate European markets declined steadily in the eighteenth century, but the growth of transatlantic trade and the trade with India more than compensated for this. The early industrial manufacturers had quite modest capital requirements for the purchase of machinery, but needed extended credit to reach overseas markets. An early cotton mill might cost no more than £1,000, but the manufacturer might need to invest 10 times this sum in wages and raw materials before they received any money back from sales. It often took a year or more for the manufacturer to receive payment from overseas. In the meantime, they needed to pay their workers and suppliers. This is where the merchants' credit came in. The buoyancy of the colonial trade, including profits on the trade in slaves and slave produce, revenues from Bengal put merchants and bankers in a position where they were willing and able to supply that credit.

Colonial purchases of British goods were a major stimulus to the economy. Around 1770, 96.3% of British exports of nails and 70.5% of the export of wrought iron went to colonial markets. Around the same time, British exports of iron manufactures took 15–19% of domestic iron production (Adams, 1895; Mukherjee, 1939).

Textile exports accounted for between a third and a half of total production, with colonial markets again taking a huge share. In the periods 1784–1786 and 1805–1807, the growth of exports accounted for no less than 87% of the growth of British output. During the French Wars (1793–1802, 1804–1815), British exporters often found that, excluded from Europe, they had to rely on colonial and American markets. The merchant and finance houses that facilitated the import of sugar and cotton also helped to extend badly needed credit to the textile and metal manufacturers.

Around 1770, total investments in the domestic British economy stood at £4 million (or about £500 million in today's money). This investment included the building of roads and canals, of wharves and harbors, of all new equipment needed by farmers and manufacturers, and of all the new ships sold to merchants in a period of one year.

Around the same time, slave-based planting and commercial profits came to £3.8 million (or about £450 million in contemporary terms). Of course, profits were not all reinvested, but they did furnish a convenient pool of resources available for this purpose. British West Indian planting profits can be estimated at £2.5 million in 1770, while trading profits on the West India trade were around £1.3 million, at a time when annual slave trading profits were at least £1 million. Even if not all reinvested, the slave-generated profits were large enough to have covered a quarter to a third of Britain's overall investment needs. The rest came from Bengal (Williams, 1944).

The broad case for a colonial stimulus to the British economy is very strong. Pomeranz and Topik (1999) estimated that the acreage required to grow the cotton, sugar, and timber imported by Britain from the New World in 1830 would have been somewhere between 25 and 30 million acres—or more than Britain's total arable and pasture land combined. They observed: Raising enough sheep to replace the yarn made with Britain's New World cotton imports would have required staggering quantities of land, almost nine million acres in 1815 and over 23 million acres by 1830.

One might add that cotton yarn was much more suitable for early industrial processes than wool, and that the price paid for each pound of raw cotton dropped by one half between 1790 and 1820 as an expanding slave population, the new cotton gin and steam transport opened the inland states to cotton cultivation. As late as 1860, six million slaves toiled in the fields of the American South, Cuba and Brazil, producing vast quantities of cotton, sugar, and coffee. Britain got off to a good start at the time of the Industrial Revolution, and Britons today still enjoy a consequent afterglow of prosperity (Adams, 1895; Richards, 2011; Williams, 1944).

Slavery and the Wealth of Nations

In 1858–59, the American economist and sociologist Henry Charles Carey (1858), known for his defense of protectionism, described the slave-owning planter prior to emancipation as mere superintendent of slaves for British merchants, to whom he was usually in debt. In 1839–1841, Herman Merivale (1839) even affirmed the evident solidarity between colonial slavery and the industrialization of England: What raised Liverpool and Manchester from provincial towns to great cities? What maintains now their ever active industry and their rapid accumulation of wealth?

Marx (1969) considered the turning of Africa into a warren for the commercial hunting of black-skins as one of the processes of primitive accumulation, which signalized the rosy dawn of the era of capitalist production. In the same spirit, in 1894, John Atkinson Hobson, a heterodox liberal economist later known for publishing "Imperialism, A Study," in 1902, evaluated the part played by the slave trade in the advent of modern capitalism the following way: "The black population of Africa was, of course, the great reservoir for the new tropical economy of the European colonial system. The profits of the European companies embarking in early colonial trade were very large, for slave economy is not in itself and in all circumstances bad. It is for this reason that colonial economy must be regarded as one of the necessary conditions of modern capitalism" (Hobson, 1902).

Karl Polanyi (1966) has postulated that the establishment of large slave plantations by the Portuguese, the Dutch, the English, and the French, from the middle of the seventeen century on, constituted an epochal event as specific as the invention of the steam engine by James Watt some 130 years later. Eric Williams (1994) systemized this theory with regard to England in Capitalism and Slavery. In his opinion, the slave trade represented one of the principal channels of capital accumulation required by the British Industrial Revolution.

Slave Traders Versus Industrialists?

Max Weber (1923) was to suggest a quite different interpretation, giving impetus to a distinct analysis of the historiography of relations between colonial expansion, the slave trade, and the rise of capitalism, mostly developed after the Second World War by emphasizing the antinomy between slave-trade profits and modern capitalism. In the period from the sixteenth to the eighteenth centuries, wrote Weber, slavery signified as little for the economic organization of Europe as it did much for the accumulation of wealth in Europe. This analysis bears certain similarities with Joseph Schumpeter views on late nineteenth-century imperialism, which he considered above all as an anachronistic survival of the Ancien Regime.

Industrial Revolution and Triangular Trade

India, a net exporter of textile (cotton) to Europe in the eighteenth century, was importing two-thirds of its textile consumption by the late nineteenth century, chiefly from Britain. After the abolition of the East

India Company's trade monopoly in 1813, the Indian market was flooded with textile products manufactured more cheaply by the developed countries. This opening hastened the decline of the local textile industry. That dynamic growth of British industry was made possible by a large and sustained inflow of resources extracted from India and, indeed, colonized societies everywhere.

The 'Triangular Trade' financed the Industrial Revolution in Britain (Blackburn, 2010; Williams, 1994), showed that Britain sold textiles to Africa, and used the proceeds to capture slaves who were sold at great profit in the West Indies. With that money, Britain brought sugar for Britain. He estimated the profits from that triangular trade to amount to £14,000 in 1739 increasing to £303,000 by 1759.

That wealth, he argued, made the Industrial Revolution possible. Economic historians have treated the Williams' thesis with derision (Crouzet, 1972). They have, however, failed to see the real argument that underlies Williams' thesis, for the flow of wealth into England was not limited to that arising from what Williams calls the Triangular Trade. There was a huge flow of resources into Britain from the colonial enterprise all over the world. If then we look at the figures of the flow of wealth from India alone, the argument no longer appears to be derisory.

We made a very conservative estimate of the annual net flow of resources from India to England, at the time of the Industrial Revolution, of about £2 million per year (Alavi, 1980). That figure compares with estimates made by Marshall of some £3 million before 1757 and an average of £5 million between 1757 and 1784 (Marshall, 1996). Other estimates are equally large. We can compare these estimates of the annual flow of resources from India to Britain, during the critical period of the Industrial Revolution, to estimates of annual industrial capital formation in Britain at the time.

Crouzet (1972), for example, estimates gross capital formation in the British economy at a grand total of £9.4 million in 1770 and £16 million in 1790–1793. Of that grand total, investment in machinery was £ 0.8 million in1770 and £2 million in 1790–1793 and additional investments in stocks were £ 1.5 million and £ 2million, respectively. If we compare these figures of the amount of resources that went into industrial capital formation in Britain, even the estimate of the flow of resources from India to Britain of £ 2 million annually is no longer derisory—and other, better informed, estimates are twice that figure.

The flow of resources from India underpinned capital formation in British industry to a very large degree. To that we must add the tribute extracted by Britain from the rest of the colonial world. It can be said that indeed the bulk of capital formation in British industry during the Industrial Revolution was paid for by the colonial tribute. The surplus arising in the colonies was accumulated not at home but in the metropolis.

It is noteworthy that it was not until the late nineteenth century that the relationship between India and Britain conformed to the classic colonial pattern of export of raw materials from the colony and imports of manufactured products. Indeed, the initial trading activities of the East India Company, concentrating on export of Indian manufactured textiles, were virtually the reverse of the familiar colonial pattern. The classic pattern of the colonial economy, as we know it today, namely that of colonized India as an exporter of raw materials and importer of manufactured goods from England did not take shape until the second half of the nineteenth century.

The American Civil War and the Manchester cotton famine that followed it played a large part in that change. There was a new urgency in developing canal irrigation for cotton cultivation. Cropping patterns in agriculture were changed to suit the needs of the colonial economy. British capital began to be invested in India mainly in plantations and extractive industries, railways, and harbors.

In the rural areas of India, the old pattern of Indian feudalism was replaced by a new system. A class of landed magnates became subordinate to the colonial regime. They were also principal allies in India. Beginning with the 'Permanent Settlement' imposed by Lord Cornwallis in 1793 in Bengal, the structure of the rural economy had changed beyond recognition. The main impact of that and successive changes was the elimination of the petty sovereignties of chieftains and Zamindars or landlords. Indeed, one might say that land Lords were turned into land owners. The localized structure of power which is characteristic of feudalism was dissolved. The power of landowners was subsumed under the colonial state into which they were integrated.

It was that 'alliance' between the colonial state and the Indian landlord class that made possible the sustained colonial rule and exploitation of India, which in turn underpinned the development in the metropolis itself. A colonial mode of production was established in India with great implications.

Naoroji (1901) gave estimate for just one year's transfer to Britain, in 1866, which suggests a total amount of 9,360,000 pounds for salaries of the British officers and their families only. The profit of the East India Company was not included. If we take into account the value of the purchases of government stores of British manufacturers per year, annual charge can exceed 1,000,000,000 pounds.

Naoroji gave the estimates of these charges (salaries and costs of the army, navy, judges, and police) in India before 1866 (Table 1.2).

The total amount of these charges from 1787–1788 to 1828–1829 was 596,528,000 pounds. If the total acquirement by England before 1788 was 300,000,000 pounds, interest charges before 1866 was 800,000,000 pounds, and the rough estimate of wealth derived by England from 1829 to 1866 was 488,331,000 pounds, we can calculate the total charges on India for England up to 1866 as 1,647,983,000 pounds. Naoroji (1901) also provides the estimates of the total value of imports in pounds, including treasures, from India as follows in Table 1.3

These give a figure of 32,000,000 as average for these four years. The years after the 1858 Mutiny show extraordinary increase in imports from India which amounts to 'Loot' after the fantastic treasures of old Delhi, Agra, and Lucknow were available to the East India Company's soldiers (Table 1.4).

Table 1.2 Home charges from India, 1787–1866

1787–1788	5,275,000
1797–1798	8,254,000
1807–1808	15,000,000
1817–1818	17,763,000
1827–1828	23,932,000
1829–1830	13,536,000
1839–1840	14,103,000
1849–1850	17,170,000
1856–1857	26,316,000
1857–1858	35,678,000
1858–1859	43,590,000
1859–1860	44,622,000
1860–1861	40,408,000
1865–1866	40,615,000

Source Naoroji (1901)

Table 1.3 Value of imports from India, 1868–1871

1868	31,629,315
1869	35,309,973
1870	30,357,055
1871	28,826,264

Source Naoroji (1901)

Table 1.4 Imports from India, China, and Singapore (Malay)

1854	22,098,653
1855	23,505,311
1858	24,450,274
1859	27,021, 805
1860	27,759,150
1861	35,203,641
1862	51,150,767
1863	68,150,997
1864	73,213,187
1865	54,719,071

Source Naoroji (1901)

We can go backward to the middle of the eighteenth century to estimate the contribution of Bengal in the Industrial Revolution of Britain. In 1765, the East India Company formally assumed territorial control over Bengal—now part of India and Bangladesh—and began to gradually establish a colonial empire that spanned the Indian subcontinent. By 1833, it had relinquished all monopoly rights to trade in the East and become a purely colonial power. In 1858, after the Sepoy Mutiny, the colonial empire became the British Raj. This colonial administration was the cornerstone of the British overseas empire.

Phyllis Deane and W. A. Cole (1967) identify a turning point in British economic growth in 1745, but find that real acceleration occurred after 1780 (Deane & Cole, 1967: p. 80). Crafts later amended this to argue that growth did not really begin a marked upward movement until after 1820 (Crafts, 1985), arguing additionally that even the gradual structural shifts leading up the change were not in evidence until the beginning of the eighteenth century (Crafts, 1985). The same researchers have pointed out that although industrialization occurred in Britain prior to 1830, it was confined to a few localities that accounted for a small proportion of the total economy—reinforcing the point that the national economy did not experience a strong acceleration until after 1830 (Mokyr, 1985/2018).

Private trade also became increasingly important as a source of capital for the Company itself. In its overseas ports, the Company frequently fell short of the necessary funds to supply return voyages and turned to its own employees for infusions of capital. The country trade of the factors served as an additional source of overseas capital that was used to fund the purchase of return goods in Asia. There is also evidence that the private trade attracted employees, encouraging individuals to work for the company and lowering the wage necessary to induce appropriate behavior. The English East India Company in the private trading period is therefore an early example of a decentralized firm.

Wallerstein (1974, 2011) has long held that the world system, essential to the growth of modern capitalism, was not fully integrated until at least 1760, when a colonial apparatus was able to funnel raw materials from Asia and the Americas to the industrial capitalists in Northern Europe (Wallerstein, 2011). Even the invention and adoption of the steamship might have been delayed had not long-distance trade already become an important part of European commerce.

The role of the East India Company was to introduce Indian textiles to the mass market. The export cotton industry in India had been in existence since at least the thirteenth century. Trade between Europe and Asia—by other paths and through other hands—had also existed for centuries, so it was not that cotton was unknown in England. Surplus production in Asia and the rise of living standards in England must have contributed to the boom in textile consumption, but there is little reason to believe that India would have begun to ship cotton to England.

Prakash (2005, 1976) found that together the English and Dutch companies supported 8.69 to 11.11% of the workforce through their trade in Bengal in the early eighteenth century, and that overall, the companies increased the output and incomes of the region, as well as employment rates. The exchange of European silver for manufactured goods (i.e., cotton textiles) was particularly beneficial for the Bengal economy (Prakash, 1976).

Prakash also finds that the cultivation of arable lands increased in Bengal during the 1700s, tax revenues grew, and trade expanded (Prakash, 2005). Frank Perlin (1983) argued that the expansion of overseas trade from 1500 to 1800 stimulated an existing trend toward the development of merchant capitalism in the Indian subcontinent, which included the expansion of peasant settlements, a rising urban population, the development of new financial institutions and taxation techniques, monetization, and a rise in manufacturing (Perlin, 1983).

There is widespread agreement that British Imperial authorities either began or hastened a process of de-industrialization in India. Both structural forces and British colonial rule depressed the cotton trade: Technological innovations in textile production made British goods more competitive, political instability and drought conditions in India raised grain prices, and the British government imposed free trade agreements that acted to the detriment of Indian industry (Chingingsmith & Williamson, 2008).

The result in India was a significant decrease in secondary industry employment rates and a reduction of available capital. In Bengal, the English Company used its newly acquired political power to exclude other European Companies from the region's trade while eroding the autonomy of Indian merchants, thus destroying the foundations for a competitive market (Prakash, 2005).

Further, once the Company was able to collect bullion through tax revenues in its colonial territory, the influx of foreign bullion ceased. Instead, Company operations and related English trade began to drain bullion out of the country, with considerable negative economic consequences. The autonomy of the merchant class in Coromandel was diminished as the Company used its political power to establish direct control over weavers, and, according to Christopher Bayly (1998), urbanization rates began to decrease across the board under Company rule.

Beginning in the 1690s, the Company had turned to the British government for assistance in patrolling eastern waters for pirates (Stern, 2011) and the late eighteenth-century conquest of Indian territory relied upon British government forces. Without the increased military powers of the British state, such interventions would not have been possible. By the early eighteenth century, public outlay outstripped public income by over £2 million, and the shortfall was made up through public debt. The English East India Company played a significant role in this process, along with the Bank of England and the South Seas Company.

At the most basic level, the English East India Company was a major source of short- and long-term capital for the government. In the late seventeenth century, the English East India Company had long found it necessary to make repeated loans to the Crown in order to secure 65 support for its monopoly privileges, but after 1688 the scale of the loans increased. From 1675 to 1679, Charles II received what would have been considered an extremely large sum of £200,000 through a series of loans from the Old East India Company. In 1698, the New East India Companies loaned the government £2 million, and the United East India Company, which combined the New and Old Companies, had loaned the government an additional £1.2 million within a decade (Dickson, 1967). Thus, the English East India Company directly contributed to the military successes of the British government by financing a significant portion of them.

The East India Company was able to supply these large funds to the government because of the concurrent development of the London stock market and the creation of new financial instruments. Because the East India Company was a joint-stock company whose shares were traded in a public market, they were able to transfer the cost of the public debt they funded on to third parties through the creation and sale of India Bonds. As has recently been demonstrated by Pilar Marco and Camila van Malle-Sabouret (2007), these were sophisticated financial instruments that incorporated an early version of call and put options. These India Bonds were popular because they were extremely liquid, but still returned interest (Marco & van Malle-Sabouret, 2007). Thus, the English East India Company's sale of India Bonds greatly increased the liquidity of public debt.

The East India Company's role was therefore not only to loan money, but also to facilitate the transfer of funds between private investors and government. The main question still is what the source of funds of these private financiers was.

The sheer number of links between the company and the new political economists is somewhat remarkable. David Ricardo was a member of the Company's court of proprietors. Ricardo's close friend, James Mill wrote his major life's work on the history of the British in India and went on to serve as Assistant Examiner of the India Correspondence, a very respectable position within the East India Company. His even more influential son also worked for the Company. Thomas Malthus served as the chair of history and political economy at Haileybury, the East India Company's college for the education of young men. And, although eventually passed over, even Adam Smith at one time put considerable effort into seeking a position within the Company.

Soon after the Company acquired political control of Bengal, in the aftermath of the 1757 Battle of Plassey, the region began to experience severe silver shortages, which disrupted both the local economy and the English export trade, mainly because Clive and his people robbed everyone of everything. By taking political control of Bengal, the Company had finally found a way to end the debate over exporting bullion, by using Bengal tax revenues as a source of silver. In the seventeenth century, the region was popularly understood in Europe as a thriving center of trade and manufacture. After Mill, it came to be viewed as a static, if not backward, traditional economy—a stereotype that has persisted to at least the twentieth century (Barber, 1975).

The Battle of Plassey was fought over the fate of Bengal. British took away whatever they can from the Treasury of the Nawab. That wealth financed the initial development of Industrial Revolution in Britain. In 1765, the Company was declared the Diwan of Bengal, the court-appointed tax-collector for the Mughal Empire (Marshall, 1996); with these vast resources of silver, Industrial Revolution was stimulated further.

India had an extraordinarily powerful manufacturing industry, a complex and thriving commercial economy, and a relatively stable government that encouraged commercialization through its taxation policies (Findley & O'Rourke, 2007).

Before the founding of the East India Company, England was a rural country with a largely agricultural economy. Europe itself was a relative, if rapidly developing, backwater, and England was scrambling to emerge out from under the shadow of the Dutch in their Golden Age. By the time of its dissolution, India was a colony of Britain, which had become the preeminent global political power.

The Industrial Revolution had transformed Britain into "the workshop of the world." The English East India Company played an important role in these events. Its success generated a tremendous amount of wealth, handed the British government the foundation of a global empire, and permanently altered the trade and economies of Britain and Asia.

The private trade of its employees was of great importance as it supplied much needed capital to the new industries when the traditional banking sector in Britain was very reluctant to invest in new industries. A conservative estimate of the size of the private trade, counting only private freights aboard Company ships, put it at eleven percent of the value of Company goods (Mentz, 2005); other estimates put it at equal to or greater than the trade of the Company by the early eighteenth century (Krishna, 1924).

The Company and those operating under its auspices also benefited the private traders. The trade of the captains suffered tremendously after the 1813 and 1833 Parliamentary Acts stripping the Company of monopoly rights (Sutton, 2010). It was the Company that had borne the costs of defending the trading privileges—that were also extended to its employees—all along through loans to the government and vigorous prosecution of interlopers.

Although the Company was a monopoly, it did not operate on monopolistic principles. And although the private trade flourished alongside the Company, this does little to indicate that unregulated trade would have survived without the infrastructure created and maintained by the Company. The Company was not operating in a completely competitive marketplace, but it also never achieved a monopoly of any good. It was somewhere between the two.

Capital flows in the two globalizations are very different in kind, owing to technological and informational changes unlike today; the first globalization was not characterized by the internationalization of production. In 1913, multinational firms accounted for 3–6% of global output. According to Bordo et al. (1999), overseas operations did not contribute significantly to US corporate profits. Foreign direct investment (FDI) made up a mere 10–20% of investment abroad, which consisted mainly of portfolio investment. Today, the relative shares of FDI and portfolio investment are more evenly balanced.

In 1914, FDI was mainly aimed at facilitating access to raw materials rather than internationalizing production. The main FDI destinations were the raw materials-rich US and Russia: 55% of the global FDI stock went to the primary sector, 15% to manufacturing, and 10% to banking. True, the introduction of protectionist measures in Europe from 1879 on had triggered the relocation of production units to countries where customs barriers hampered market penetration. One notable example was the Swiss textile industry, which shifted production to Italy after the adoption of protectionist tariffs there. However, these circumvention practices did not represent a full-fledged internationalization of the production process.

Technological obstacles and imperfect information restricted capital flows to the small set of assets least affected by information asymmetry. Investors concentrated on tangible assets (raw materials, railroads) and transparent assets (sovereign financing), and on bonds rather than stocks. Sovereign financing, railroads, and raw materials industries attracted the bulk of investments: 40% of British portfolio investment went to railroads, 30% to sovereign debt, and 10% to raw materials. At the time, technological and informational constraints limited short-term investment opportunities. The modest status of international financial institutions also restricted the scope for verifying information and enforcing contracts. Today, these constraints have been lifted.

Marx (1957) saw the unrequited transfer of capital from the colony to the metropolis in various forms (what the early Indian historians called the "drain") as a "bleeding process" ruinous to the colony but critical to the process of primitive accumulation and therefore to the transition to and growth of industrial capitalism in the metropolitan countries (Table 1.5).

Attempts are made to argue that Europe was ahead of the rest of the world centuries before the Industrial Revolution, an assertion which when looked at from the vantage point of ancient civilizations such as China and India looks very questionable indeed. After all, Europe was still buying textiles from India, the then world's largest exporter of cloth, till the end of the eighteenth century and had nothing to offer in return except gold and silver "looted" from Latin America.

At the heart of colonialism lay surplus appropriation from the colony to the metropolis or the colonizers. With industrialization and capital becoming the key factor of production, there was always huge transfers

Table 1.5 Share of world GDP (% of world total)

Year	*1500*	*1700*	*1820*	*1870*	*1913*	*1950*	*1973*	*2001*
UK	1.1	2.9	5.2	9.0	8.2	6.5	4.2	3.2
Western Europe[a]	17.8	21.9	23.0	33.0	33.0	26.2	25.6	20.3
US	0.3	0.1	1.8	8.8	18.9	27.3	22.1	21.4
China	24.9	22.3	32.9	17.1	8.8	4.5	4.6	12.3
India	24.4	24.4	16.0	12.1	7.5	4.2	3.1	5.4
Asia (excluding Japan)	61.9	57.7	56.4	36.1	22.3	15.4	16.4	30.9

[a]Western Europe here includes Austria, Belgium, Denmark, Finland, France, Germany, Italy, Netherlands, Norway, Sweden, Switzerland, UK, Portugal, Spain, and a small general category "other" which generally remained way below 1%

Source Extracted from Angus Maddison, The World Economy: Vol. I, A Millennial Perspective, Vol II, Historical Statistics, OECD, 2006 of capital from the colonies to the metropolis. It is significant that, till as late as the early nineteenth century, China and India combined produced more than double the GDP of entire Western Europe, thus bringing into question the notion of Europe's superiority since antiquity. However, from the nineteenth century, the share of India and China begins to shrink (India's share begins to shrink from the eighteenth century and China's since the nineteenth century, as they got colonized in those centuries, respectively) and becomes less than half that of Western Europe by 1913 and only a third of that of Western Europe in 1950 (Maddison, 2006).

It was only by the last quarter of the twentieth century after spending several decades "un-structuring colonialism" that independent China and India began to regain their position in the global economy. The former colonies experienced growth only when the colonial contact was broken.

India was the largest economy of the world for the entire thousand years of the first millennium, accounting for close to 30% of the world's GDP. The decline started soon after and, by 1950, at the end of nearly 200 years of colonial rule, during which apologists of colonialism like Tirthankar Roy (2002) claims "colonial India experienced positive economic growth" when India's share was reduced to a mere 4.2%, less than two-thirds that of Britain.

The growth of per capita income in India in the colonial period, between 1820 and 1913, was either zero or very low, while the independent countries of Europe, the US and Japan grew substantially faster. After decades of colonial rule, after colonialism had had its full impact, the per capita income in India actually declined at an annual rate of –0.22% between 1913 and 1950 (Maddison, 2006).

Britain was able to subjugate and colonize India by about the middle of the eighteenth century. Britain, however, had trading contacts with India for a long period before that, though her trade with India increased rapidly during the first half of the eighteenth century. The "trade" during the first half of eighteenth century consisted primarily (about three-fourths) of imports of textiles and silk from India, which was the largest grower of raw cotton and the largest producer and exporter of cotton textiles in the world till the end of the eighteenth century. While Indian textiles were much in demand in earlier centuries in European markets, as well as, to exchange for spices from East Asia, one major impetus for the spurt in demand for Indian textiles was the facilitation of the "golden age" of the Atlantic slave trade. Indian textiles constituted the single largest item with which the slave-traders were paid for, accounting for about 27% of all goods shipped from England to Africa during the eighteenth century. Since Britain had nothing to sell to India which she needed, therefore, the imports from India were financed by export of treasure or bullion, i.e., silver and gold, obtained from the exploitation of Latin America leading to the virtual extinction of the Amerindian people in many areas (Mukherjee, 1939).

Britain now began to use the "revenues" raised by taxing the people of the conquered territories to pay for her imports from India. A bizarre form of international trade was thus imposed by Britain, the leading European economy at that time, whereby India was made to pay for her own exports!

The East India Company's imports of treasure into India which amounted to Rs 3.1 million in 1757–1788 absolutely ceased thereafter. The entire Indian exports that were paid for by Indian revenues and hence remained unrequited thus constituted the "drain" or the "tribute" paid by India to Britain as the cost of being "colonized" (Chaudhury, 1995).

Chingingsmith and Williamson (2008) mention that while the maximum revenue extracted by the Mughals as high as 40%, this paled in comparison with the effective tax rate in the early years of colonial rule: "*as central Mughal authority waned, the state resorted increasingly to revenue farming (raising) the effective rent share to 50% or more...*".

After initial attempts at revenue farming, Company officials aggressively introduced new taxes in an attempt to reduce their dependence on agrarian production, thus worsening the tax burden on the common man. As Richards (1997) points out, "*Land revenue continued to be the mainstay of the regime until the end of British rule in India, but its share of gross revenues was far less than under the Mughal emperors..Javier Cuenca Esteban estimates these net financial transfers from India to Britain reached a peak of £1,014,000 annually in 1784–1792 before declining to £477,000 in 1808–1815*".

However, even these high figures are significantly lower than the estimates by Richards (1997). Like all other commentators, Maddison (2006) too has mentioned the debilitating effect of the drain of funds from India: "*There can be no denial that there was a substantial outflow which lasted for 190 years. If these funds had been invested in India they could have made a significant contribution to raising income levels. About a quarter of Indian savings were transferred out of the economy, and foreign exchange was lost which could have paid for imports of capital goods.*"

Naoroji (1901) estimated the economic costs and drain of resources from India to be at least at 12 million pounds per annum. Here is an extract from one of his essays, "The Benefits of British Rule, 1871."

> Financially: All attention is engrossed in devising new modes of taxation, without any adequate effort to increase the means of the people to pay; and the consequent vexation and oppressiveness of the taxes imposed, imperial and local. Inequitable financial relations between England and India, i.e., the political debt of 100,000,000 pounds clapped on India's shoulders, and all home charges also…
>
> Materially: The political drain, up to this time, from India to England, of above 500,000,000 pounds at the lowest computation, in principal alone…The further continuation of this drain at the rate, at present, of above, 12,000,000 pounds per annum, with a tendency to increase.

Richards (1997) mentioned that: "*Between 1757 and 1859… ….Officials of the East India Company… tapped the productive people and resources of Bengal and the eastern Gangetic valley to fund the protracted military campaigns necessary to conquer India. Over the same century, these same resources also supplied the wherewithal for a century-long transfer of wealth from India to Great Britain. Burke estimated that in the four years ending in 1780 the investment averaged no less than one million sterling and "commonly Nearer Twelve hundred thousand pounds." This was the value of the goods sent to Europe for which no Satisfaction is made. The transfer continued without interruption and with formal approval from Parliament.*"

In 1793, this devious system of extortion was given official sanction and thus was paved the path to financial ruin: "*By this 1793 Parliamentary directive, the Company was enjoined to take ten million current rupees (1 million sterling) each year for the investment from the territorial revenues of colonial India…. After 1793, the Company zealously maintained its annual investments. Between 1794 and 1810, the average annual cost of the investment was 1.4 million sterling*" (Richards, 1997).

> …In a recent contribution, Javier Cuenca Esteban …puts the "arguably minimum transfers" from India to Britain between 1757 and 1815, Plassey and Waterloo, at 30.2 million sterling. This figure is the estimate of exports from which there was no compensating import for India. (Richards, 1997)

Post 1833, when the Company's commercial operations ceased, the "drain" took the form of "Home Charges" which represented the expenses in Britain borne by the Indian Treasury. These "Home Charges" were a huge burden on the finances and contributed to a sustained and continuous deficit in the budget throughout the nineteenth century. As Richards (1997) notes, "*there were few years in which the Indian budget was not in deficit. For the entire period (1815–1859), deficits reached a cumulative total of 76.9 million sterling or an annual average of 1.7 million sterling.*"

This systematic drain was nothing short of a loot—albeit carried over 200 years and under the cover of colonial trade. It left the economy in ruins and reduce this great country within 190 years from one of the powerhouses of the world economy to a land of destitute who were barely able to sustain itself.

The collective impact of these policies and system of exploitation was severe. Chingingsmith and Williamson (2008) have this to say: "*India was a major player in the world export market for textiles in the early 18th century, but by the middle of the 19th century it had lost all of its export market and much of its domestic market…While India produced about 25 percent of world industrial output in 1750, this figure had fallen to only 2 percent by 1900.*"

Measuring Secular De-industrialization in India

As defined, the evidence of de-industrialization in India during the first global century is pretty clear. Some time ago, Paul Bairoch (1982) offered evidence to measure de-industrialization not only in India, but across the whole non-European periphery.

In 1750, China and India combined to account for almost 57% of world manufacturing output, while India itself accounted for almost a quarter. By 1800, India's world share had already eroded to less than a fifth, by 1860 to less than a tenth, and by 1880 to less than 3%. Note that India's share in world manufacturing output declined precipitously in the half century 1750–1800, before factory-led industrialization took hold in Britain. Furthermore, per capita manufacturing output fell over the period too, so it wasn't just a benign boom in the core at work, but rather a slump in the periphery as well. More evidence supporting the magnitude of de-industrialization is offered by the share of manufacturing exports in total exports: Between the mid-late eighteenth century and 1913, that share fell in Asia from about 42 to 21% (Findley & O'Rourke, 2003).

The Indian world manufacturing output share dropped by 4.8 percentage points between 1750 and 1800, when it rose in China and dropped only one percentage point in the rest of the periphery. India's share was dropped by 6.9 percentage points over the longer period between 1750 and 1830. China lost 3 percentage points, and the rest of the periphery lost 2.6 percentage points.

Bairoch's data suggest unambiguously that during the century before 1830, well before European factories flooded world markets with manufactures, India suffered much more pronounced de-industrialization than did the rest of the periphery. An attempt to measure de-industrialization looks to the early nineteenth century; years which anecdotal evidence has always suggested were ones of most dramatic de-industrialization (Bairoch, 1982).

Since cotton spinning was performed at home using simple technology, it may seem implausible to argue that the demise of cotton spinning in the early nineteenth century destroyed India's platform for modern industrialization. Yet British economic historians assign the same importance to home-based cotton spinning: Seventeenth- and eighteenth-century "proto-industrial" cottage industries are said to have supplied the platform for the factory-based British Industrial Revolution that followed (Mokyr, 1993), and employment of women and children was central to the process then too (de Vries, 2008).

There was a huge decline in yarn used for Indian handloom production, from 419 million pounds in 1850 to 240 in 1870 and to 221 in 1900. This indirect evidence suggests that the decline in hand spinning documented for Gangetic Bihar in the early nineteenth century was widespread, that it was followed by a decline in hand weaving during the mid-century, and that the decline of both hand spinning and weaving was almost complete by 1870. This is confirmed by Bairoch's per capita manufacturing output figures (1982): "somewhere between 1860 and 1928, the index bottoms out and starts to rise for both China and India, while it soars after 1860 for Japan." The percent of industrial workers who were spinners fell from 82 to 15 between 1809–1813 and 1901 in India (Bairoch, 1992).

External Price Shocks and Indian De-industrialization

The most popular de-industrialization hypotheses being considered here is the one associated with what economists now call globalization shocks. Nehru's Discovery of India (1947) argued that India became progressively ruralized in the nineteenth century owing to the destruction of artisan employment in the face of British factory-made goods. Furthermore, he thought that the appalling poverty of the Indian people was of recent origin and that it could be blamed on anti-industrial colonial policy (Nehru, 1947). The economic logic underlying this hypothesis is that rapid productivity advance in European manufacturing lowered the relative price of textiles, metal products, and other manufactures in world markets.

After the French Wars, British factory-made yarn and cloth took away India's local market from her own producers, and India experienced de-industrialization over the half century following 1780 as the terms of trade moved in its favor. This relative price movement is illustrated best by trends in Britain's terms of trade which fell by 40% over the four decades between 1801–1810 and 1841–1850 (Mitchell & Deane, 1962). Thus, the price of British exports (manufactures) fell dramatically compared with that of its imports (primary products).

India's textile producers faced a big negative price shock on that score alone in nineteenth century. Failing to keep up with the factory-based productivity growth achieved abroad, the Indian textile industry took the price hit, became less profitable, and de-industrialization ensued. Having defeated India in export markets, "after 1813 Lancashire invaded India as well" (Moosvi, 2000): The import-competing sectors slumped, the export sectors boomed, and de-industrialization was reinforced.

The most important agricultural commodities for India in the 14 first half of the nineteenth century were opium, raw cotton, raw silk, and sugar, and they were a growing fraction of India's exports by the forced cultivation by the Company. By 1811, they accounted for 57% of India's exports by value compared to 33% for cotton piece goods (Chaudhuri, 1983).

Rest of the Periphery

Did nineteenth century India face a big or a small de-industrializing global price shock compared with other parts of the periphery? If it was "small," then domestic de-industrialization forces must have been more important in India than they were elsewhere in the periphery. Over the half century between 1800–1804 and 1855–1859, India's terms of trade rose "only" 28.6%, or less than 0.5% per annum. No doubt this was a significant secular price shock, but it was far smaller than what happened in other parts of the periphery. For example, the Egyptian terms of trade rose by two and a half times between 1820–1824 and 1855–1859, or 2.7% per annum, *more than five times* that of India; the Ottoman terms of trade increased by two and a half times between 1815–1819 and 1855–1859, or 2.4% per annum, *almost five times* that of India; the Indonesian terms of trade increased 2.7 times between 1825–1829 and 1865–1869, or 2.5% per annum (Korthals Altes, 1994), *more than five times* that of India; and the Latin American terms of trade increased by 1.7 times between 1820–1824 and 1855–1859, or 1.7% per annum, *more than three times* that of India.

Finally, over the fifteen years following Japan's emergence from isolation in 1858, its terms of trade rose 3.5 to 4.9 times (Williamson & Clingingsmith, 2004), or about 10% per annum, *twenty times* that of India! External price shocks facing India were quite modest compared to the rest of the periphery.

* * *

The drain that the Indian economy faced through this continuous process of unrequited exports was enormous in size and critical to Britain. It has been calculated by Irfan Habib that in 1801, at a crucial stage of Britain's Industrial Revolution, drain or unrequited transfers to Britain from India represented about 9% of the GNP of the British territories in India which was equal to about 30% of British domestic savings available for capital formation in Britain. The unrequited transfer from Asia and the West Indies put together was calculated to be 84.06% of British capital formation out of domestic savings in the same year. These figures show how critical transfers from the colony were to the process of capital accumulation for Britain and how debilitating it was for the colony.

Javier Cuenca Esteban (2001) has convincingly shown the net inflows from India to Britain, through 1765–1812, were very large and "arguably the least dispensable," playing a critical role in maintaining British balance of payments which were under major stress in this period. The process of primitive accumulation in capitalism or the initial phase of industrialization is a painful one as the initial capital for investment has to be raised on the backs of the working class or the peasantry. To the extent that Britain and other metropolitan countries were able to draw surplus from the colonial people, to that extent they did not have to draw it from their own working class and peasantry.

This form of direct seizure of surplus therefore continued to sustain the development of capitalism in Britain and the standard of living of its people. However, the subsequent stages evolved other methods of surplus appropriation as well and met metropolitan interests in different ways. In fact, as Britain began to industrialize at the turn of the eighteenth century, she was no longer interested in exporting Indian textiles, she was seeking to expand the markets for her own textile manufactures including in India. Indian raw cotton was short stapled and did not suit British industry. The solution was found in the early nineteenth century in opium. A triangular trade with China was now to lead to the realization of Indian tribute in an enlarged form. Exports of opium from India shot up by more than six times between 1816 and 1830. Indian export of opium to China in 1855 was worth £6.23 million paying for most of the tea and silk worth about £8.5 million that Britain took from China for Japan to earn silver from Japan.

By the second half of the nineteenth century with many other countries apart from Britain industrializing, rapidly the global demand for food and raw materials had expanded enormously and transport of bulky goods had become easier with development of the railways, opening of Suez, etc. India's tribute in this period till First World War began to be realized though a multilateral trading pattern whereby India generated an export surplus with countries in the European continent, Japan, the US, and other countries by exporting large quantities of food and raw materials like raw cotton, indigo, and pig iron. Britain had a huge export surplus with India exporting textiles and other manufactured goods including railway stock to India. Britain, however, had developed a massive balance of payment deficit with the rest of the world largely because of the massive investments it was making globally including in the US and the white colonies. British net foreign investments as a percentage of her net domestic capital formation in fixed assets were as high as 86 between 1880 and 1889 and had peaked at 114 between 1905 and 1914 (Chaudhuri, 1978).

In this situation, Britain used its export surplus with India and India's tribute to adjust her balance of payment deficit with the rest of the world. British claims on India or the tribute was now realized by appropriating India's export surplus with a number of other countries to the extent of the tribute claims. India's tribute alone was estimated to have financed more than two-fifths or 40% of Britain's balance of payment deficit in this period.

It has been calculated that between 1871 and 1916 the surpluses transferred from India, calculated after applying a compound rate of interest of 4%, amounted to a conservative estimate of about £3.2 billion. If one compares this figure with an estimate of about £4 billion as what constituted total British foreign investments abroad in 1913 (including reinvestment of interests and dividends), it becomes clear what a preponderant role India played in British capital transfers abroad which made it the "economic hub of the world between 1870 and 1913." India thus fitted into the so-called third stage of colonialism during which massive transfers of capital occurred from Britain. However, contrary to expectations, she did so not as a receiver of capital from Britain but as a supplier of capital to Britain. A capital which then Britain used to invest all over the world—Asia, Africa, the "white" colonies, and the "west"—to great advantage to itself (Chaudhuri, 1978; Davis, 2001).

"That flow... supported the largest flow of migrants (from Europe) in recent human history as recorded between the 1870s and 1920s... (it) not only led to the peopling of the US and its rise as the most economically advanced country in the world but also helped improve the living conditions of the Europeans left behind" (Davis, 2001). The flow of capital from India to Britain as "tribute" was to continue after the First World War though it took a different form and performed a different role.

Another critical role was played by India in sustaining the process of British industrialization. As Britain industrialized, it was soon faced with the challenge of finding markets for its industrial products. By the early nineteenth century it would no longer do for Britain to allow India to be the chief exporter of textiles globally. British political control over India was now used to manipulate the instruments of state policy that British cotton manufactures rapidly began to displace Indian production not only from the global markets but over time even from the Indian home market. Indian produce was forcibly kept out of British and other global markets, and then, the classical/Ricardian theory of comparative advantage in international trade was used to deny modern Indian industry any protection in the domestic market and a policy of "free trade" was cynically imposed on India right up to the 1920s.

This resulted in India, which was the largest grower of raw cotton and the largest producer and exporter of cotton textiles in the world till the end of the eighteenth century, and which had a share of world manufacturing output estimated to be as high as 19.7% in 1800, rapidly losing that position and her share falling sharply to 8.6 in 1860 and a mere 1.4% in 1913. British exports of cotton goods to India on the other hand increased dramatically, by over a hundred times, in less than 25 years, from 0.8 million yards in 1815 to 100 million yards in 1839. The total cloth imported into India increased by another ten times crossing a 1,000 million yards in 1872 and doubled again to 2,000 million yards by 1887. By 1887, Britain had captured over 66% of the Indian domestic market. The ousting of Indian textiles from its global and domestic market which was critical for British industrialization set in motion a process of de-industrialization in India causing untold misery to millions dependent on this industry (Chaudhuri, 1983). It must be emphasized that the dependence of the British textile industry on the colonial, non-industrialized (in the Indian case de-industrialized) part of the world increased in tandem with the development of modern industry in Europe, the US, and other countries of the "free" world (Bandyopadhyay, 2008) (Table 1.6).

Europe and the US, took a majority, more than 60%, of the British cotton goods in 1820 but as this part of the world itself industrialized, this market virtually disappeared, and by 1900 absorbed only about 7% of British exports. This shift was more than compensated by the increase in British dependence on the markets of the underdeveloped world, which by 1900 were absorbing more than 86% of British textiles. While Latin America, particularly Brazil, was the chief importer of British textiles in

Table 1.6 Exports of British cotton piece goods, 1820–1900 (% of total)

Year	*Europe and US*	*Underdeveloped world*	*Other countries*
1820	60.4	31.8	7.8
1840	29.5	66.7	3.8
1860	19.0	73.3	7.7
1880	9.8	82.0	8.2
1900	7.1	86.3	6.6

Source Hobsbawm (1968, p. 146)

the first half of the nineteenth century, Asia, primarily India, became the chief market in the second half of the nineteenth century.

Given the fact that India was increasingly a critical market for Britain as well as the supplier of huge amounts of capital through tribute, it was not surprising that the liberal imperialist claim that the objective of British rule was to train Indians for self-government never found any takers among the British ruling elite.

On the contrary, Britain had to keep India, its "jewel in the crown" at any cost. As Curzon, the British viceroy at the turn of the nineteenth century was to emphatically state that India was the "pivot" of the British Empire, and if the empire lost any other part of its dominions, it could survive, but if it lost India the sun would set on the empire. Apart from the direct seizure of the Indian surplus through "tribute" being collected by appropriating a large part of India's export surplus, there was another form of surplus appropriation in favor of Britain which began to occur in the "free trade" that grew between Britain and India after Britain industrialized and India was de-industrialized. This was the surplus appropriated through the process of "unequal exchange" between an industrialized country with higher labor productivity and a non-industrialized (or less industrialized) low productivity country (Chaudhury, 1995).

To the extent, the theory of comparative advantage was used to prevent industrialization and consequently prevent the rise in productivity in India; to that extent, the productivity difference between India and Britain, a growing one in the colonial period, ensured that a transfer of surplus to Britain continued to occur through unequal exchange. The two processes were thus complementary.

India was not to be left behind in contributing to Britain's growing need for labor to work the labor-intensive plantations and build roads, railways, and other infrastructure in the Caribbean, Mauritius, Fiji, South Africa, Malaya, Sri Lanka, Burma, etc. With the abolition of slavery in 1834, there was an acute shortage of labor. India again came to the rescue.

Millions of rural poor, their ranks swelling with the destruction of Indian industries, were now transported to various parts of the world as "indentured" labor in virtual slave like conditions. By one estimate, more than two million indentured laborers were exported from India between 1831 and 1920, and other estimates put the total number of Indian emigrants during this period much higher. In any case, by the late 1830s, nearly 65% of population in Mauritius was Indian, 42% in British Guyana, 34% in Trinidad, and 43% in Fiji (Chaudhury, 1995; Davis, 2001).

The Indian economy underwent some industrial growth between 1914 and 1947 leading to considerable import substitution, especially in consumer goods industries. The most dramatic change was that the Indian cotton textile industry essentially regained the domestic market which it had lost to Britain. Britain was forced to concede substantially her imperial industrial interest in the colonial market in favor of imperial financial interest, i.e., using the colony as a source of capital through unrequited remittance or "drain." It was a switch from one imperial interest to another, not a switch from imperial to Indian national interest (Palme Dutt, 1939, 1955).

The British economy was in crisis in the twentieth century. Having lost its industrial supremacy in the world (first in consumer goods and later in capital goods) by the second half of the nineteenth century, she became critically dependent on colonial markets controlled by her to avoid a deep crisis for her industries.

Since the First World War, Britain's need for foreign funds to shore up its own financial status and for the maintenance of the pound sterling became critical. Also, the Great Depression of the 1930s and the Second World War, coming in quick succession, greatly exacerbated the crisis in the British economy. As in the past, Britain once again turned to her colonies, principally India. British financial demands on India increased manifold since First World War.

For example, Home Charges, constituting a substantial part of the tribute, increased from approximately £2 million in 1913–1914 to £32 million in 1924–1925. Military expenditure doubled from £5 million to £10 million and interest charges on external public debt increased from about £6 million to £14.3 million between 1913–1914 and 1934–1935.46. In 1917, India supplied goods worth £100 million without any payment and in 1918 decided to make another gift of £45 million to the British war effort. During the Second World War, defense expenditure increased by over nine times, from about Rs 50 crore in 1939–1940 to Rs 458 crore in 1944. The proportion of the total expenditure of the Indian central government accounted for by the defense services was about 55% in 1920–1921 rising to 75% by the end of Second World War. Far from decolonizing, retaining India had become even more critical for Britain (Palme Dutt, 1939, 1955).

Again, the only possible area where revenue could be increased substantially was customs revenue, which primarily meant import duties. (Land revenue, the principal item in the revenue since the mid-eighteenth century, could not be raised any further as it had already reached the maximum economic and political limit.)

Thus, between 1901–1905 and 1936–1937 while the total revenue raised by Government of India more than doubled, customs revenue alone met about 72% of the increase in total revenue. Customs which had overtaken land revenue as the principal source of revenue by 1921–1925 were thus critical in the maintenance of the rapidly increasing remittances of the Government of India on account of home charges, military expenditure, etc. The import duties on cotton goods went up from 3.5% in the 1890s to 25% for British cotton goods in 1931. Duties on non-British, mainly Japanese goods, were raised to 75% by 1933. This opportunity of protection, provided inadvertently to Indian industry, was seized by it and Indian industry made rapid progress (Chaudhury, 1995).

It was stated that about 60% of the Indian government's budget, i.e., about £60 million out of £100 million, was absorbed by military expenditure, sterling debt charges, and liabilities in respect of salaries and pensions for officials for which the secretary of state was responsible. Of this, defense expenditure alone absorbed 45% of the central revenues. This could not be permitted as India had to generate an export surplus at any cost so that the smooth flow of remittance to Britain could be sustained, as imperial financial interests would not countenance any interruption in that process (Davis, 2001).

A total breakdown of the remittance mechanism was averted by the massive export of gold from India that the government encouraged in this period. The gold exports were crucial in compensating for the drastic drop in India's export surplus on commodity transactions. Between 1931–1932 and 1938–1939, on an average, more than half (about 55%) of the total visible (positive) balance of trade (i.e., balance of transactions in merchandize and treasure) was met through the net exports of treasure, with the exports of gold increasing sharply in years when the commodity balance of trade was particularly low.

For example, in 1932–1933, gold exports constituted about 95% of the total visible positive balance of trade. Clearly, remittance had to be maintained at all costs; if the export surplus in commodities (necessary to convert the rupee revenues into remittance) fell short, it was made up through export of gold. At a time when Britain was facing a balance of payment crisis, it played a major part in strengthening the value of sterling vis-à-vis gold and other currencies. Britain took massive forced loans from India (popularly called the sterling balance) of about Rs 17,000 million (estimated at 17 times the annual revenue of the Government of India and one-fifth of Britain's gross national product in 1947) at a time when over three million Indians died of famine! (Davis, 2001; Richards, 1997).

The sterling balances got accumulated as a result of the "large purchases of goods and services...made by the British Government, in India," against sterling bills or securities placed in reserve in London. The rapid expansion of currency that occurred as a result (the total notes issued increased by nearly four times between 1939 and 1944) combined with the fact that large quantities of goods and services were made available to England for which no goods or services came back to India in return, led to severe shortages and a runaway inflation in India. Britain made a serious bid toward defaulting on repayment of the loans raised at such tremendous cost to India. This of course meant India being bled of anything between 5 and 10% of her GPD annually for close to two centuries! (Davis, 2001).

Development in the Late Nineteenth and Twentieth Centuries

The early development of Indian industry was one of the first instances of long-distance foreign investment in manufacturing. However, the flow of British capital was restricted to certain industries irrespective of rates of return. In eastern India, the export industries drew capital from investors in Britain and expatriates living in India and entrepreneurship from British firms. In contrast, the main industry that developed in western India was cotton textiles, an import substituting activity, which drew capital and entrepreneurship from Indian merchants in the hinterland.

Corporate interest in manufacturing industry dates back to the mid-nineteenth century. Industrial firms were set up in Britain and in India. Firms were floated on the London Stock Exchange as sterling companies or in India as rupee companies. The sterling companies raised their capital in Britain and traded their shares on the London stock market. Some sold block shares to British expatriates in India. The rupee companies raised capital from Indians as well as British expatriates.

While British capital dominated investment in infrastructure, in particular the railways, the picture appears to be quite different when we focus on manufacturing industry. British capital was concentrated in export-oriented sectors, such as tea and jute, and in coal, which catered to the railways. However, the major import substituting industry, cotton textile, was an indigenous initiative. The magnitude of rupee investment in cotton was much larger than the investment in jute and coal and only lower than the investment in tea. The cotton mills, on the other hand, were set up in and around Bombay on the west coast and in the neighboring province of Gujarat.

Modern Scramble for Africa

After the decolonization process during the mid-1960s in most cases, the bulk of a nation's economy relied on cash crops or natural resources. Structural adjustment programs encouraged by the IMF and the World Bank led to the privatization and liberalization of many African economic assets to force Africa to the global capitalist market (Chamberlain, 2014).

In the era of globalization, many African countries became oil-producing countries; Sudan, Cameroon, Nigeria, and Angola are the prime examples. These countries and their ruling classes collaborate with the Western and Chinese oil companies; they ignore the requirements for development of their countries. Thus, for Africa, globalization era became neo-imperialism. Chinese state oil companies have invested in the oil sector of Africa in countries, where there are Western sanctions and who are prepared to take huge loans to build infrastructure in theory. China National Petroleum Corporation purchased 40% of Greater Nile Petroleum Operating Company. Sudan exports 50–60% of its domestically produced oil to China, making up 7% of China's imports. China has also been purchasing equity shares in African oil and mine fields, invested in industry-related infrastructure development and acquired continental oil and mining concessions throughout Africa (Basu & Miroshnik, 2016; Southall & Henning, 2009).

Comments

The current globalization, which began in the 1990s, is not unprecedented: Between 1757's occupation of Bengal-India and 1945, the opening of national economies went hand in hand with a rapid expansion of trade and investment beyond national borders. This period, described as the first globalization, displays similarities with the second globalization, which began in the 1992 with the destruction of the Soviet Union.

Before the first globalization, India was destroyed. Before the second globalization, the Soviet Union was destroyed. In the first globalization, initially Britain gained but ultimately the US won. In the second globalization, initially the US won, but ultimately China won.

Appendices

Table A.1.1: Extraction from Bengal by the East India Company: (in Pounds, Current Price)

	Total receipts	*Total charges*	*Remittances from Madras & Bombay*	*Total receipts and charges from Bengal*
1766	2,121,244	1,210,360	458,029	3,331,604
1767	2,690,930	1,274,093	340,276	3,965,023
1768	2,620,634	1,487,383	370,923	4,108,017
1769	2,587,682	1,573,129	351,543	4,002,861
1771	2,112,245	1,732,093	17,213	3,844,338
Total	13,066,764	9,029,616	1,668,564	22,096,380

For 6 years

Total land revenue		*Tributes and plunder*	
1762	914,748	until 1771	4,920,468
1763	940,165	1782–1790	8,332,685
1764	909,524	1791–1800	14,604,875
1766	2,019,520	1801–1810	35,413,000
1767	3,042,055	1811–1821	17,616,511
1768	2,900,454	1822–1827	3,297,832
1769	2,886,697	Total up to 1827	84,185,371
1770	2,742,411		
1771	2,675,228		
1782	3,610,620		
1783	4,003,871		
1805	10,436,762		
1814	12,232,690		

(continued)

(continued)

Total land revenue		*Tributes and plunder*
1826	14,398,050	
1827	14,565,793	

Sources S. Lambert, House of Commons Sessional papers of the eighteenth century, 1975.

John F. Richards, The Finances of the East India Company in India, c. 1766–1859, Working Papers No. 153/11, LSE, 2011.

Table A.1.2: Estimated Income of the East India Company, 1667–1853 (£Million)

	1667	*1707–1709*	*1764*	*1800*	*1818*	*1853*
British India	–	–	3	8	13	21
Revenues of Indian states	26	38	–	14–21	–	13

Source Statistical Papers relating to India, London: East India Company, 1853.

Table A.1.3: Area, Population, and Estimated Revenue, Area (Sq Miles), British Empire in India, 1853

	Population (millions)	*Revenue (million £)*	*Revenue per capita*	*Revenue/sq mile*
Bengal Presidency	155,000	42.5	0.26	72.4
Bombay Presidency	123,000	12.9	0.37	38.3
Madras Presidency	139,000	22.0	0.24	38.3

Source Statistical Papers relating to India, London: East India Company, 1853.

Table A.1.4: Index Numbers of British Eighteenth-Century Real Output (1700 = 100)

	Agriculture	*Export*	*Home industries*	*Total industry and commerce*	*Rent and services*	*Govt and defence*	*Total real output*
(weights)	(43)	(18)	(12)	(30)	(20)	(7)	(100)
1700	100	100	100	100	100	100	100
1710	104	08	98	104	103	165	108
1720	105	125	108	118	103	91	108
1730	103	142	105	127	102	98	110
1740	104	148	105	131	102	148	115
1750	111	176	107	148	105	172	125
1760	115	222	114	179	113	310	147
1770	117	256	114	1 99	121	146	144
1780	126	246	123	197	129	400	167
1790	135	383	137	285	142	253	190
1800	143	544	152	387	157	607	251

Source Deane and Cole (1967).

Table A.1.5: Extraction from Bengal by the East India Company: (in Pounds, Current Price)

	Total receipts	*Total charges*	*Remittances from Madras & Bombay*	*Total receipts and charges from Bengal*
1766	2,121,244	1,210,360	458,029	3,331,604
1767	2,690,930	1,274,093	340,276	3,965,023
1768	2,620,634	1,487,383	370,923	4,108,017
1769	2,587,682	1,573,129	351,543	4,002,861
1771	2,112,245	1,732,093	17,213	3,844,338
Total	13,066,764	9,029,616	1,668,564	22,096,380

For 6 years

Total land revenue		*Tributes and plunder*	
1762	914,748	until 1771	4,920,468
1763	940,165	1782–1790	8,332,685
1764	909,524	1791–1800	14,604,875
1766	2,019,520	1801–1810	35,413,000
1767	3,042,055	1811–1821	17,616,511
1768	2,900,454	1822–1827	3,297,832
1769	2,886,697	Total up to 1827	84,185,371
1770	2,742,411		
1771	2,675,228		
1782	3,610,620		
1783	4,003,871		
1805	10,436,762		
1814	12,232,690		
1826	14,398,050		
1827	14,565,793		

Sources S. Lambert, House of Commons Sessional papers of the eighteenth century, 1975.

John F. Richards, The Finances of the East India Company in India, c. 1766–1859, Working Papers No. 153/11, LSE, 2011.

Table A.1.6: Estimated State Income, 1667–1853 (£)

	1667	*1707–1709*	*1764*	*1800*	*1818*	*1853*
British India	–	–	3	8	13	21
Revenues of Indian states	26	38	–	14–21	–	13

Table A.1.7: Area, Population, and Estimated Revenue, 1853 Area (Sq Miles)

	Population (millions)	*Revenue (million £)*	*Revenue*	*Revenue per capita*	*Revenue/sq mile*
Bengal Presidency	155,000	42.5	11.22	0.26	72.4
Bombay Presidency	123,000	12.9	4.71	0.37	38.3
Madras Presidency	139,000	22.0	5.32	0.24	38.3

Source Statistical Papers relating to India, London: East India Company, 1853.

Table A.1.8: Index Numbers of British Eighteenth-Century Real Output (1700 = 100)

	Agriculture	*Export*	*Home industries*	*Total industry and commerce*	*Rent and services*	*Govt and defence*	*Total real output*
(weights)	(43)	(18)	(12)	(30)	(20)	(7)	(100)
1700	100	100	100	100	100	100	100
1710	104	108	98	104	103	165	108
1720	105	125	108	118	103	91	108
1730	103	142	105	127	102	98	110
1740	104	148	105	131	102	148	115
1750	111	176	107	148	105	172	125
1760	115	222	114	179	113	310	147
1770	117	256	114	199	121	146	144
1780	126	246	123	197	129	400	167
1790	135	383	137	285	142	253	190
1800	143	544	152	387	157	607	251

Source Deane and Cole (1967: 78).

Table A.1.9: Indian Population, 1751–1871 Year Millions

1600	142
1650	142
1700	164
1751	190
1801	207
1811	215
1821	205
1831	216
1841	212
1851	232
1861	244
1871	256

Sources Mahalanobis and Bhattacharya (1976) and Visaria and Visaria (1983).

Table A.1.10: Real Wages of Indian Unskilled Laborers, 1600–1871 Year 1871 = 100

1600	207.9
1650	179.8
1700	171.9
1751	140.7
1801	120.8
1811	106.7
1821	94.4
1831	101.5
1841	109.1
1851	117.5
1861	108.3
1871	100.0

Source Broadberry and Gupta (2006: 14) and Mukherjee (1967: 58).

Table A.1.11: Cotton Textile Production for the Domestic Indian Market

Year	*Population (millions)*	*Cotton consumption (m yds)*	*Imports from Britain (m yds)*	*Domestic production (m yds)*
1600	142	1,194	0	1,194
1650	142	1,194	0	1,194
1700	164	1,379	0	1,379
1751	190	1,598	0	1,598
1801	207	1,741	0	1,741
1811	215	1,808	1	1,807
1821	205	1,724	20	1,704
1831	216	1,817	38	1,779
1841	212	1,783	141	1,642
1851	232	1,951	348	1,603
1861	244	2,052	514	1,538
1871	256	2,153	793	1,360

Sources Population: Table 2. Cotton consumption per head: Prakash (1976). Imports from Britain: Sandberg (1974).

Table A.1.12: Indian Textile Exports to Britain, 1665–1831

Year pieces	*Years pieces*
1665	291,666
1665–1669	139,677
1700	868,095
1700–1704	597,978
1751	701,485
1750–1754	632,174
1801	1,037,440
1800–1804	1,355,304
1811	691,640
1810–1814	901,745
1821	758,397
1820–1824	542,117
1831	287,814
1830–1834	192,965

Sources 1665–1761: Chaudhuri (1978); 1761–1834: Bowen (2007).

Table A.1.13: Total Indian Textile Exports, 1831–1871

Year	*Thousand pieces*	*Value of cotton goods (Rs 0000)*
1831	3,000	
1841	2,606	
1851	2,279	7,355
1861		8,716
1871		15,802

Source Piece goods exports from Twomey (1983); value of cotton goods exports from Chaudhuri (1983).

Table A.1.14: Export of Bullion to India, by East India Company (1708–1810)

Years	*Bullion (£)*	*Average per annum*
1708/9–1733/4	12,189,147	420,315
1734/5–1759/60	15,239,115	586,119
1760/1–1765/6	842,381	140,396
1766/7–1771/2	968,289	161,381
1772/3–1775/6	72,911	18,227
1776/7–1784/5	156,106	17,345
1785/6–1792/3	4,476,207	559,525
1793/4–1809/10	8,988,165	528,715

Table A.1.15: Revenue of British India, 1878–1879

Land revenue	£22.5m
Taxation excise	£2.5m
Stamps (judicial and commercial)	£3m
Customs	£2m
Salt	£7m
Assessed taxes	£1m
Court and registration fees	£0.25m
Provincial rates	£2.5m
Total taxation	£18m
Receipts other than taxation Sale of opium	£9m
Productive public works	7m
Post office	1m
Other	7m
Grand total	65m

Source Indian Famine Commission, p. 90. (Figures have been rounded).

War Crimes, Massacres, Crimes Against Humanity, and Genocides Enacted by the British Empire

Proclamation of 1625—30,000 Irish are sold into slavery in the New World.

1641–1652—300,000 Irish sold into slavery (one third were children).

1763 Jeffrey Amherst signs the infamous Smallpox blankets into motion to be used against the native Americans.

1775 Phips Proclamation in Massachusetts, King George II of Britain called for "subjects to embrace all opportunities of pursuing, captivating, killing and destroying all and every of the aforesaid Indians."

1845–1852—Irish Potato Famine—1 million—a population drop of 20–25% Engineered and exacerbated famines in British India and their Death Tolls:

1769–1770 Great Bengal Famine—10 million dead.
1783–1784 Chalisa famine—11 million.
1791–1792 Doji bara famine or Skull famine—11 million.
1837–1838 Agra famine—800,000.

1860–1861 Upper Doab famine—2 million.
1865–1867 Orissa famine—1 million.
1868–1870 Rajputana famine—1.5 million.
1876–1878 Great Famine—5.5 million.
1888–1889 Ganjam—150,000.
1896–1897 Indian famine—5 million.
1899–1900 Indian famine—1 million.
1905–1906 Bombay—235,062.
1824–1908 Tasmania—British settlers kill 15,000 aboriginals via terra nullus The Opium Trade.
1910–1970—over 100,000 aboriginal children in Australia were kidnapped and forcefully assimilated into white society.
1900–1901 Boer concentration camps lead to the deaths of 10% of the population, including 20,000 children. Another 20,000 blacks were worked to death via forced labor. Total civilian casualties for the Boer war number over 48,000.
1919—The Amritsar Massacre, between 500 and 1,000 men and women are shot in cold blood.
1920—10,000 Iraqis are killed during the Iraqi Revolution of 1920.
1943 Bengal Famine—1.4–4 million dead—engineered by policies of Winston Churchill "I hate Indians. They are a beastly people with a beastly religion. The famine was their own fault for breeding like rabbits."—W. Churchill.
1947—Partition of India uproots 10 million Indians, causing mass violence and a death toll between 250,000 and 2 million.
1950s Malaya, half a million locals are forcefully resettled.
1955–1959—3,000 Cypriots are rounded up and tortured.
1950s Kenya–1.5 million Kenyans are placed into concentration camps.
1943—Operation Gomorrah—bombing of Hamburg Germany kills 42,600, wounds 37,000 1945—Bombing of Dresden—25,000 civilians.
1945—Cap Arcona sinking claims the lives of 7,000 Jews and Russian POWs (4 × times the death toll of the Titanic).

Profits Made by the British East India Company Due to Indian Famines

1. 3.9 Million pounds paid by Mir Jafar to East India Company 1757
2. 230000 pounds per annum from Mir Jafar's Successor
3. Annual takling 1,932,900 pounds from Bengal Bihar and Orissa
4. Annual revenue from Bihar alone: 680,000 pounds
5. Famine 1770: 10 million dead, directly due to British policies
6. Annual revenue from Bengal from 1793: 2.68 million pounds
7. Famines in 1783, 1792, 1807, 1813, 1823, 1834 and 1854
8. Famines in 1877, 1878, 1889, 1892, 1897, 1900: 15 million dead. Note how the incidence of famine has increased with the passage of colonial rule…
9. Revenue from Allahabad: pounds 1,682,306 per annum circa 1800s
10. Land Tax: 50% of produce
11. Maratha area: annual revenue 1,500,000 pounds per annum circa 1800s
12. Indian Debt: pounds 51,000,000 in 1857
13. Indian Debt: pounds 97,000,000 in 1862
14. Indian Debt pounds 200,000,000 in 1901
15. 44 Million sterling annual outflow from India to Britain. Multiply this figure alone by around 150 - that is approximate 6600 Million - 6.6 Billion. Now compound by 8%… the number comes to 37 Trillion pounds - or nearly 73 Trillion Dollars. India's external debt as on March 2011 was 345.8 Billion Dollars.. (This last bit - the compounding and the extrapolation of annual revenues over 150 years is my guesstimate; to equal it out I have used a factor 112 years)
16. Just one years revenue earnings to the British amount to 243 Billion Sterling- nearly 480 Billion Dollars even when I compound it by just 8%….. more than our total external debt. Just one years takings…
17. Now just compound the 1.5 Million taking in 1757 for 245 years at 8% - and you get a jaw-dropping number of 232 Trillion Sterling - or 475 Trillion Dollars.

References

Adams, B. (1895/1987). *The law of civilization and decay*. New York: Macmillan.

Alavi, H. (1980). India: Transition from feudalism to colonial capitalism. *Journal of Contemporary Asia, 10* 4, 359–399.

Altes, K. (1994). *Religions and politics*. Hamburg: E. B. Verlag.

Bairoch, P. (1982/1992). *Economics and world history*. Chicago: University of Chicago Press.

Bandyopadhyay, S. (2008). *From Plassey to partition, a history of Modern India*. New Delhi: Orient Longman.

Barber, W. J. (1975). *British economic thought and India, 1600–1858, a study in the history of development economics*. Oxford: Oxford University Press.

Basu, D., & Miroshnik, V. (2016). *Structural revolution in international business architecture*, Vol. 2. Basingstoke: Palgrave Macmillan.

Bayly, C. (1998). The first age of global imperialism, C1760–1830. *Journal of Imperial and Commonwealth History, 26* (2), 28–47.

Bhatia, B. (1963). *Famines in India*. Bombay: Asia Publishing House.

Blackburn, R. (2010). *The making of new world slavery*. London: Verso.

Bordo, M. D., Eichengreen, B., & Irwin, D. A. (1999). *Is globalization today really different than globalization a hundred years ago*. Cambridge: National Bureau of Economic Research.

Bourne, H. R. F. (1903). *Civilisation in Congoland: A story of international wrong-doing*. London: P. S. King & Son.

Bowen, H. (2007). *East India Company, Trade, and domestic financial statistics, 1755–1838*. London: UK Data Archive.

Brezis, E. S. (1995). Foreign capital flows in the century of Britain's industrial revolution. *Economic History Review, XLVII, 1*(6), 46–67.

Broadberry, S., & Gupta, B. (2006). The early modern great divergence: Wages, prices and economic development in Europe and Asia, 1500–1800. *Economic History Review, 59*(1), 2–31.

Cain, P. J., & Hopkins, A. G. (1993). *British imperialism: Innovation and expansion: 1688–1914*. New York: Addison Wesley.

Carey, H. C. (1858). *The harmony of interests, agricultural, manufacturing, and commercials*. New York: Carey & Lea.

Chamberlain, M. E. (2014). *The scramble for Africa*. London: Routledge.

Charlesworth, N. (1982). *British rule and the Indian economy*. London: Macmillan.

Chaudhuri, K. N. (1978). *The trading world of Asia and the English East India Company, 1660–1760*. Cambridge: Cambridge University Press.

Chaudhuri, K. N. (1983). Foreign trade and balance of payments 1757–1947. In D. Kumar (Ed.), *The Cambridge economic history of India: Volume 2: c. 1757–c.1970*. Cambridge: Cambridge University Press.

Chaudhury, S. (1995). *From prosperity to decline: Eighteenth century Bengal*. New Delhi: Manohar.

Chingingsmith, D., & Williamson, J. G. (2008). Deindustrialization in 18th and 19th century India. *Explorations in Economic History, 45*(3), 209–234.

Cook, D. (1995). *The long fuse: How England lost the American colonies*. New York: Atlantic Monthly Press.

Crafts, N. F. (1985). *British economic growth during the industrial revolution*. Oxford: Clarendon Press.

Crouzet, F. (1972). *Capital formation in the industrial revolution*. London: Methuen.

Darwin, J. (1997). Imperialism and the Victorians: The dynamics of territorial expansion. *English Historical Review, 112* (447), 614–642.

Davis, M. (2000/2001). *Late Victorian Holocausts: El Nino famines and the making of the Third World*. London: Verso Books.

Davis, R. (1979). *The industrial revolution and British overseas trade*. Leicester: Leicester University Press.

de Vries, J. (2008). *The industrial revolution: Consumer behavior and the household economy, 1650 to the present*. Cambridge: Cambridge University Press.

Deane, P., & Cole, W. A. (1967). *British economic growth 1688–1959*. Cambridge: Cambridge University Press.

Desai, M., Roy Chowdhury, T., Kumar, D., & Habib, I. (1983). *Cambridge History of India*, Vol. 2. Cambridge: Cambridge University Press.

Dickson, P. G. M. (1967). *The financial revolution*. London: Macmillan.

Dutt, R. C. (1904). *The economic history of India, Vol. I—Under early British rule*. London: Routledge.

Esteban, J. C. (2001). The British balance of payments, 1772–1820: India transfers and war finance. *Economic History Review, LIV*(1), 58–86.

Findley, R., & O'Rourke, K. H. (2003/2007). *Power and plenty, trade, war and the world economy in the second millennium*. Princeton, NJ: Princeton University Press.

Gjersø, J. F. (2015). The scramble for East Africa: British motives reconsidered, 1884–95. *Journal of Imperial and Commonwealth History, 43*(5), 831–860.

Government of India. (1880). *Report of the Indian Famine Commission*. Calcutta: HMSO

Guha, R. (1995). *A rule of property for Bengal, an essay on the idea of the permanent settlement*. Medford, MS: Duke University Press.

Hobsbawm, E. J. (1968). *Industry and Empire*. London: Penguin.

Hobson, J. A. (1902). *Imperialism: A study*. Ann Arbor, MI: Michigan University Press.

Hochschild, A. (2006). *King Leopold's ghost: A story of greed, terror, and heroism in colonial Africa*. London: Pan Books.

Indian Famine Commission. (1901). New Delhi: Agricole Publishing Company.
James, L. (1995). *The rise and fall of the British Empire*. London: Macmillan.
Jenks, L. H. (1971). *Migration of British capital to 1875*. New York: Alfred Knopf.
Keene, H. G. (1887). *The fall of the Mogul Empire of Hindustan*. Oxford: Oxford University Press.
Keith, A. (2003). Agreement between the Nabob Nadjum-ul Dowlah and the Company, 12 August 1765, in Volume 1 of speeches and documents on Indian Policy, 1750–1921. In Harlow and Carter (Ed.), *Archives of empire*. Medford: Duke University Press.
Krishna, B. (1924). *Commercial relations between India and England, 1601–1757*. London: Routledge.
Lambert, S. (1975). *House of Commons sessional papers of the 18th century*. London: HMSO.
Langer, W. A. (1935). *The diplomacy of imperialism, 1890–1902*. New York: Alfred A. Knopf.
Maddison, A. (2006). *The world economy*. Paris: OECD.
Mahalanobis, P. C., & Bhattacharya, D. (1976). Growth of population in India and Pakistan 1801–1961. *Artha Vijnana, 18*(1), 1–10.
Marco, P., & Van Malle-Sabouret, C. (2007). East India Bonds, 1718–1763, early exotic derivatives and London market efficiency. *European Review of Economic History, 11*(3), 367–394.
Marshall, P. J. (1996). *Reappraisal: The rise of British power in the eighteenth century*. Oxford: Clarendon Press.
Marshall, P. J., Ray, R. K., & Bowen, H. V. (1998). *The Oxford history of the British Empire: The eighteenth century*. Oxford: Oxford University Press.
Marx, K. (1957). *India's first war of independence: 1756–58*. Moscow: Progress Publishers.
Mentz, S. (2005). *The English gentleman merchant at work: Madras and the city of London: 1660–1740*. London: Museum Tusculanum Press.
Mitchell, B., & Deane, P. (1962). *Abstract of British historical statistics*. Cambridge: Cambridge University Press.
Mokyr, J. (1985/2018). *The economics of the industrial revolution*. London: Routledge.
Mokyr, J. (1993). *The British industrial revolution: An economic perspective*. Boulder, CO: Westview Press.
Moosvi, S. (2000). *Indian economic experience, 1600–1900: A quantitative study*. New Delhi: Tulika.
Mukherjee, M. (2010). *Churchill's Secret War*. New York: Basic Books.
Mukherjee, R. (1939/1967). *The Economic History of India, 1600–1800*. London: Longman, Green and Company.

Naoroji, D. (1901). *Poverty and Un-British rule in India*. New Delhi: Ministry of Information and Broadcasting.

Nehru, J. L. (1947). *Discovery of India*. New Delhi: Rupa.

Palme Dutt, R. (1939). *India today*. London: Lawrence and Wisert.

Palme-Dutt, R. (1955). *India today and tomorrow*. London: Lawrence and Wisert.

Perlin, F. (1983). Proto-industrialization and pre-colonial South Asia. *Past and Present, 98*, 30–95.

Philips, C. H. (1961). *The East India Company: 1784–1834*. Manchester: Manchester University Press.

Polanyi, K. (1966). *Dahomey and the slave trade*. Seattle: University of Washington Press.

Pomeranz, K., & Topik, S. (1999). *The world that trade created. Society, culture, and the world economy 1400 to the present*. Armonk: M.E. Sharpe.

Prakash, O. (1976). Bullion for goods: International trade and the economy of early eighteenth century Bengal. *Indian Economic and Social History Review, 13*(2), 159–186.

Prakash, O. (2005). *The cultural history of India*. New Delhi: New Age International.

Reinhard, W. (2015). *Empires and encounters*. Cambridge, MA: Harvard University Press.

Richards, J. F. (1997). Early modern India and world history. *Journal of World History, 8*(2), 197–209.

Richards, J. F. (2011). *The finances of East India Company in India, c. 1766–1859*. Working Paper No. 153.11. London: London School of Economics.

Robinson, R., & Gallagher, J. (1962). *'The partition of Africa', in The New Cambridge modern history*. Cambridge: Cambridge University Press.

Robinson, R., Gallagher, J., & Denny, A. (1961). *Africa and the Victorians: The official mind of imperialism*. London: Macmillan.

Roy, T. (2002). Economic history and modern India. *The Journal of Economic Perspectives, 16*(3), 109–130.

Sanderson, G. N. (1974). The European partition of Africa: Coincidence or conjuncture? *Journal of Imperial and Commonwealth History, 3*(1), 1–54.

Sandberg, L. G. (1974). *Lancashire in Decline*. Columbus: Ohio State University Press.

Sen, Amartya. (1981). Ingredients of famine analysis. *Quarterly Journal of Economics, XCVI, 96*(3), 433-464.

Shillington, K. (2005). *History of Africa*. Basingstoke: Macmillan.

Smith, V. (1960). *The Oxford history of India*. Oxford: Oxford University Press.

Southall, R., & Henning, M. (2009). *A new scramble for Africa?: Imperialism, investment, and development*. Durban: University of KwaZulu-Natal Press.

Stern, F. (2011). *The varieties of history: From Voltaire to the present*. New York: Vintage.

Sutton, J. (2010). *The East India Company's maritime service: 1746–1834, Masters of the Eastern Seas*. London: Boydell and Brewer.

Tagore, R. (1997). *Letter to Mrs. Rothbone*. In Krishna Dutta and Andrew Robinson (ed.) *Selected letters of Rabindranath Tagore*. Cambridge: Cambridge University Press.

Tripathi, A. (1957). *Trade and finance in the Bengal presidency, 1793–1833*. Oxford: Oxford University Press.

Twomey, M. J. (1983). Employment in Nineteenth-Century Indian Textiles. *Exploration in Economic History, 20*(1), 37–57.

Visaria, L., & Visaria, P. (1983). *Cambridge economic history of India* (Vol. II). Cambridge: Cambridge University Press.

Von Strandmann, P. (1969). Domestic origins of Germany's colonial expansion under Bismarck, *Past and Present, 42*, 140–159.

Wallerstein, I. (1974). *Rise and future demise of the world capitalist system: Comparative studies in society and history*. Cambridge: Cambridge University Press.

Wallerstein, I. (2011). *The modern world-system I: Capitalist agriculture and the origins of the European world-economy in the sixteenth century*. Berkeley, CA: University of California Press.

Weber, M. (1923). *Essays in economic sociology*. Princeton, NJ: Princeton University Press.

Webster, A. (2007). *The richest East India Merchant: The life and business of John Palmer of Calcutta: 1767–1836*. London: Boydell and Brewer.

Williams, E. (1944). *Capitalism and slavery*. Chappel Hill: University of North Carolina Press.

Williamson, J. G., & Clingingsmith, D. (2004). *India's deindustrialization under British Rule, new ideas new evidence*. Cambridge, MA: National Bureau of Economic Research.

Wilson, H. H. (1848). *History of British India*. London: J. Maddens.

CHAPTER 2

WTO and Its Discontent

The WTO was created out of GATT (General Agreements on Tariffs and Trade) which was created in turn with the spirit of International Trade Organization (ITO), but far away from its original objectives. The ITO designed after the Second World War with the objectives of creating conditions for full employment by reducing tariffs, with workers' rights, promoting competition, helping the developing countries with capital and technology, and promoting trade. The WTO has other objectives: To implement the trade negotiations of the Uruguay Round (1986–1994) among the member countries, and further negotiations on trade, agricultural, manufactured goods, the services sector, and investment to implement 'Washington Consensus' of the IMF, World Bank, and the US Treasury. The WTO works for a global economic policy of total free trade and free market system all over the world (Vander Stichle, 1997).

Let us look at the history. The Multi-Fibre Agreement (MFA) was signed in 1974 and allowed for selective import restrictions on textiles and clothing products. The objective was to allow for protection for textile producers in developed countries against the producers of the developing countries. MFA was abolished after the WTO Uruguay Round Discussion in 1994 and quotas for the developing countries were dismantled in phases (Table 2.1).

WTO members have certain rules regarding trade, investments, and productions (Oxfam report on WTO).

© The Author(s), under exclusive license to Springer Nature Switzerland AG 2021

D. Basu and V. Miroshnik, *The Economic and Political Dangers of Globalization*, https://doi.org/10.1007/978-3-030-79895-6_2

Table 2.1 Schedule for dismantling MFA quotas

I	January 1995	16%
II	January 1998	17%
III	January 2002	18%
IV	January 2005	49%

Source; OXFAM report on WTO.

The agreements on trade in goods are as follows:

- Reductions of tariff and removal of restrictions on imports of industrial products;
- Reductions of restrictions on imports of textile and clothing in the industrialized countries;
- Reforms of marketing and subsidies in agriculture, and government export subsidies.
- Removals of restriction on investment measures (Trade-Related Investment Measures—TRIMs);
- Removals of subsidies, safeguard measures by which a country can restrict imports saying a related industry is in danger of unemployment and anti-dumping measures.

The agreements on trade in services (GATS) are as follows:

- Transparency or making information on laws that concern services easily comprehensible and freely available.
- Foreign companies can have equal access in the service sectors.

The agreement on trade-related intellectual property rights (TRIPs) is as follows:

- Copyrights, trademarks, industrial designs, patents, and trade secrets of a member country must be respected in all WTO member countries.

The WTO is the main contributor for globalization by allowing trade liberalization, removals of subsidies in the domestic economy in terms of enhancement of competition, in the national economy, capital markets, and foreign direct investments.

The WTO's Trade Policy Review Mechanism (TPRM) does not care about workers, consumers, people's lives, and sustainable development, but on WTO rules and trade liberalization. The International Labour Organization (ILO) should take care of labor rights. WTO also has no responsibility for environment. Globalization depends on international trade rules, promoted by the WTO. It encourages non-discriminatory treatment for the trade of goods and services with $19 trillion of goods trade in 2019 alone.

The current global economic and trade system creates an unequal distribution of benefits, but the WTO thinks that these depend on individual countries; the WTO has nothing to do with these inequalities. UNCTAD reports proved, liberalization and globalization increased income inequality within countries. Share of profit and the return on capital went up at a much higher rate (from 12.5% in the early 1980s to 16% in the mid-1990s in G7 countries) than wages in the manufacturing sector. Traders and other intermediaries benefitted more than the farmers in the agricultural sector. Higher profit never promoted investments where these are needed.

In theory, WTO does not allow discrimination between domestic and foreign products, services, and intellectual property rights. It disallows subsidies for agriculture and determines level of environmental protection. It determines compulsory minimum levels of agricultural imports and all non-tariff protections. It prohibited public control on investments, profit repatriation, and quota for domestic factors of production. The WTO through its dispute settlement system can undermine the government at all levels but only for the developing countries. It cannot touch developed countries of Western world, Japan, and China.

Supporters of globalization claimed competitive globalization stimulates export industry and economic growth, by expanding choice for the consumers. It would stimulate employment opportunities for the poor, unskilled, and women. In reality, a complex competition was already established, requiring high technology, highly skilled labor, large marketing outlets, destruction of small business, and public infrastructure. Only the companies from the developed countries can take advantage of these facilities limiting the access for the poor in the developing countries. It has reduced wages, reduced employment opportunities due to automations, abolished rights for the workers, destroyed job security, and pension right but increased the profits of monopolist owners. In agriculture, contract farming would eliminate family-owned land holding as it did in nineteenth-century India and during 1930s in the US and would promote export oriented 'Genetically Modified' (GM) crops instead of natural food crops.

The WTO Contributes to Unequal Competition

The WTO and the Uruguay Round agreements intensified the discriminations of the developed countries against the developing countries with less market access, with higher tariff on clothing, leather, fish, and agriculture. In agriculture, the discrimination was the most intense, while the subsidized farm products of the developed countries and China are set against unsubsidized farm products from the developing countries. Anti-dumping rules are not effective but TRIPS (intellectual property rights) will make medicines and other essential products unaffordable for the poor people of the developing countries.

The World Trade Organization (WTO) undermines the democratic sovereignty of nations, each with their own economic policy, and the well-being of their citizens. In finance, this was promoted by free capital mobility. In trade, the creation of the WTO affects sovereignty of individual countries, with national domestic priorities having to adjust to the needs of globalization. Financial institutions, multinational corporations, and big pharmaceutical companies, in particular, wanted rules that enabled greater market access and greater protection of their interests. The main point of conflict between the US and China is over China's state-subsidized efforts to conquer new market and new technologies. According to Rodrik (2012, 2016), the Trump Administration does not have a coherent trade policy or a systematic approach to reforming the international trade regime; its approach is purely unilateralist and mercantilist.

The Doha Round launched in 2001 was ignored in 2015 due to serious disagreements among the US, Europe, and the rising developing countries like India and China. China's entry into the WTO in 2001 had a surge of exports that contributed to the loss of well-paid manufacturing jobs in the US, Europe, and elsewhere in the world that has fueled a backlash against globalization. President Trump taken out his country out of the Trans-Pacific Partnership (TPP) trade deal and launched a series of tariff protection measures particularly against China.

Most developing countries are not industrialized. There are very few opportunities for people to go away from subsistence farming. Subsistence agriculture is not profitable, but it is sustainable, necessary, and independent of global trends and can reflect actual needs of the farmers. Agriculture is only relegated to secondary status when there are surplus food available.

Reduced Agricultural Protectionism

The Uruguay Round Agreement on Agriculture (AoA) was propagated by the media as the start of a new era in which the withdrawal of subsidies in rich countries would open up new opportunities for poor countries, but the opposite has happened. Agricultural trade has a major influence on efforts to reduce poverty. Approximately three-quarters of the poorest people in developing countries live in rural areas. Subsidies in rich countries diminish export opportunities of poor countries. Smallholder farmers of poor countries cannot compete with imports from the developed countries subsidized by their governments.

In Mexico, maize farmers have been ruined by cheap subsidized imports from the US. Women rice farmers in Haiti are facing similar problems. EU export subsidies are having similar effects in sub-Saharan Africa. The Agreement on Agriculture asked the developed countries to reduce subsidies by 36 percent on agricultural products and tariffs by a similar amount. There has been no real reduction in agricultural subsidies. Governments of the developed countries have avoided any meaningful action. Income transfers are now considered as 'support payments' and 'emergency' payments to US farmers, permissible under the WTO, and have grown rapidly particularly since the outbreak of coronavirus.

Subsidies accounted for almost 40 percent of the value of OECD farm output, the same as it was in 1986–1988. The average tariff imposed by developed countries on agricultural goods from developing countries is close to 20 percent, but the developing countries are told to eliminate all subsidies and to depend on the market price. Tariff rates for groundnuts in the US, and meat and dairy products in the EU, are now about 100 percent. Processed food products have tariffs at least twice as high as those on unprocessed products. These barriers represent a major obstacle for developing countries to expand their exports.

It is an acceptable practice in the WTO rules on agriculture where the practice of dumping, or the sale of items at prices below the cost of production, is allowed. Developed countries are also allowed to use export subsidies. The following Table 2.2 signifies that subsidies are there in most countries.

Table 2.2 Subsidies for farmers, 2019, in US$ Million

China	185.9
India	11.0
EU	101.3
US	48.9
Japan	37.6
Indonesia	29.4

Source Trade vistas, Economic Survey

Absurd Agricultural Policy of India

Indian farmers are at war with the government of Narendra Modi, who otherwise the most popular Prime Minister of India. All non-economic policies of Modi Administration are highly popular and just. However, all economic policies of the Modi government are wrong and unpopular. Demonetization, GST, Abolition of the Planning Commission, and New Agricultural Policy are all unpopular and unjust. When due to economic reform policy implemented by Rao, MM Singh, Vajpayee, massive amount of money, calculated up to 2016, $4600 dollars went away from India to various off shore banks, it is absurd to cancel all existing bank notes in India causing widespread difficulties and even deaths in India to catch the black money. GST has so far caused chaos and loss of revenue for the government and has done nothing good for the people, particularly for the owners of small business. We have no idea where the country is going and what would be plans for the country without the Planning Commission. Lastly, the New Agricultural Policy is rejected by the farmers for whose benefits the government is supposed to implement these.

However, repeal of these new laws regarding agriculture cannot solve the problem when these laws are there to implement the rules of the World Trade Organization. If the Modi government withdraw these new laws, a number of countries, our allies and friends, like Myanmar, Thailand, Brazil, US, and Australia will take India to the WTO for non-implementation of agreed rules of trade negotiations since 1995. As India is one of the developing countries, it got some exemptions for few years not to abolish subsidies and public distribution system, but the time has come for India to implement these now without any delay, according to the WTO system.

Muchkund Dubey in 1995 GATT treaty expressed his objection that the abolition of subsidies and the public distribution system would not benefit India but would take away the long-term protection for both the consumers and producers in India. However, Manmohan Singh had ignored these good advices of Dubey and went ahead to sign the GATT treaty and joined the World Trade Organization in 1995. Since the beginning of the plan period of India, subsidies for fertilizers, and the minimum support prices for two main crops, rice and wheat, were introduced in India to promote investments in agriculture and to protect the farmers from the dangers of the market system, which during the British Rule used to cause famine after famine. British rulers, faithful followers of the Directors of the East India Company, Adam Smith, Malthus, David Ricardo, Bentham, James, and John Stuart Mill, used not to interfere to the market and allowed the natives of the 'rude' country, India to die in millions, as a result. In 1951, when Five Years Plan was introduced in India, the most important task of the planners was to make the people secure in life by providing sufficient supply of food and to provide incentives to the farmers to have fertilizers in affordable price and to cover their cost of production through the minimum support price. These are considered as 'Market Distortions' by the staunch supporters of the market system in the World Trade Organization, World Bank, and the International Monetary Fund, who wanted to abolish these protections for the consumers and producers in the developing countries, although they want to keep these market distortions for the developed countries, and China. China has joined the WTO as a market economy in 2001, certified by the US, although in China all companies foreign or Chinese are under government controls, regarding production, investments, and pricing. These facts about China are ignored by the Western elites, who through the WTO have allowed China to dominate the world trade, and destroy jobs in most countries of the world.

Subsidies are the rules in the Western countries and China for both agricultural and non-agricultural companies, even the social media companies like FACEBOOK, GOOGLE, and BAIDU. Agricultural price support is the foundation of the Common Agricultural Policy of the European Common Market, Japan, and China. However, for India, both agricultural subsidies and minimum support prices are distortionary and must be removed as soon as possible. Modi government is doing just that.

Supports for public companies and opposition to the private companies whether foreign or domestic also create market distortions, according to the WTO. That is the reason for the opposition to the Food Corporation of India and its policy to procure products directly from the farmers and to provide products at affordable price to the consumers. Abolition of the Food Corporation of India was the basic recommendation of the WTO and the World Bank. Thus, the FCI would not be allowed to procure food crops from the farmers at a minimum support price and subsidize the consumers by making food available at affordable prices.

Contract farming is designed to eliminate any discrimination that may exist between private and public companies and between foreign and domestic companies. Thus, state farming that used to exist in Suratgarh in Rajasthan was disallowed, public fertilizer companies were closed down, but multinational foreign companies are invited to invest in Indian agriculture. Contract farming was introduced in 1834 in India during the days of East India Company, to promote the plantations for opium and indigo. That had ruined Indian agriculture and made Indian farmers paupers. The same will be repeated in India again, to produce cash crops instead of food, as recommended by the World Bank.

Minimum Support Price in India

The average monthly incomes of the farmers in Punjab and Haryana are Rs 18,000 and Rs 16,000, respectively, because they have MSP (minimum supply price). In Bihar and West Bengal, these are Rs 3600 and Rs 3800 as they have no MSP (Business Standard, 2021). Eight of the 11 commodities traded on 6 March 2021 were from the list of 23 crops that enjoy MSP. The seven crops were sold below what the Government of India officially assures the farmers to be the minimum price that the farmers must get and the government will support the farmers to secure. This included all the five major crops of that area: Tur, makka, jowar, chana, and bajra. This is what the price table looked like in Ballari on 6 March (Table 2.3):

More or less the same prices were found all over Karnataka markets for most crops. The average February price for bajra and maize was actually lower in the rest of the state than in Ballari. Only tur fetched a better price elsewhere. An average of the last three years (2017–2018 to 2019–2020) by the Karnataka Agricultural Price Commission shows that as much as 72 percent of the agricultural produce in the state sells below the MSP. Farmers of Karnataka lost Rs 3,119 crores last year due to distress sale below MSP.

None of the major kharif (summer) crops, except paddy, fetched anything close to the assured minimum. Paddy did better, it was solely

Table 2.3 Difference between MSP and Market Price

Crop	*MSP*	*Average (Modal) Price*	*Average – MSP*
Bajra	2150	1460	– 690
Chana	5100	4182	– 918
Jowar	2620	1728	– 829
Maize/Makka	1850	1459	– 391
Tur/Arhar	6000	4943	– 1057
Safflower	5327	4010	– 1317
Moong/Green gram	7196	7116	– 80
Urad/Black gram	6000	6166	+ 166

Note All prices in Rs. Per quintal
Source APMC, Ballari

due to the government procurement in many states. Fine varieties of long-grain paddy, which are not covered by MSP, suffered badly and were sold at less than the MSP for ordinary variety. No state other than Haryana, not even Gujarat, procured bajra at the MSP. As a result, Bajra sold around Rs 1,300 against the official MSP of Rs 2,150. During the peak arrivals in the month of November, moong was sold for an average price of Rs 5,556, about Rs 1,600 below the official MSP.

In Ballari, urad was the only exception that fetched a price above MSP. But that was not so in the rest of the country at the time of peak arrivals in November, 2021. In that month, it sold for an average price of Rs 4,789 against the MSP of Rs 6,000. Similarly, tur or arhar sold at around Rs 4,500–5,000 against the MSP of Rs 6,000. The average price for maize was 1,354 against the MSP of Rs 1,850. Wheat, the biggest crop of the season, may get a decent price wherever the state procurement takes place. In other areas, farmers could suffer a loss of Rs 300 to 500 below the official MSP of Rs 1,975. For all other crops, the MSP is the 'maximum aspirational price.' Maize, for example, could get between Rs 1,300 and Rs 1400, much below the MSP of Rs 1850. Barley can get Rs 1,300 against the MSP of Rs 1,600. Jowar can get about Rs 1,000 lower than the MSP of Rs 2,620. Chana or Bengal gram can get between Rs 4,400 and 4,800—that indicates a loss of Rs 300–700 per quintal, since the MSP is Rs 5,100.

MSP is a fraud imposed on farmers, what is called "minimum" price is for all practical purposes a dream price, and that the "support" promised in the support price never arrives. Small farmers are particularly vulnerable to three new laws, which deregulated the agricultural market and weakened the government-established minimum sale price for crops in ways that could put small farmers against big agribusiness firms. India's agriculture problems are severe indeed. Farmers face declining plot sizes, degraded soils, scarce water, and rising debt. In the past 25 years, over 300,000 farmers in the country have committed suicide. However imperfect, India's past agricultural regulations at least ensured that crop sale prices nationwide in India remained close to the price floor set by the government. The group fears the new "era of fragmented and unregulated markets" will be even less "farmer-friendly" than the old system. Under the new laws, problems among the farmers and traders or agribusiness firms would be settled by a new agricultural board, not the local courts as is done now. Poor farmer's access to the legal system in India is already limited. If agribusiness firms file a claim in a far-off jurisdiction, poor farmers who lack access to transport and money to travel would be at an even greater disadvantage, according to Kamdar and Shreyasee Das (2021).

WTO Protocol

Section 9 of WTO Protocol of Accession made it clear that the member countries "*shall allow prices for traded goods and services in every sector to be determined by market forces, and multi-tier pricing practices for such goods and services shall be eliminated.*"

Prices in every sector must be determined by market forces. All subsidies to be notified to the WTO and prohibited subsidies to be eliminated. Under Sect. 15 of WTO Accession Protocol, member countries have the obligation to notify to the WTO any subsidy granted or maintained.

State-owned enterprises (SOEs) will operate free of state influence. Under Sect. 6 of WTO Accession Protocol, and Article XVII GATT 1994, member countries agreed that these SOEs enterprises would make purchase and sales involving imports or exports based solely on commercial considerations such as price, quality, marketability, and availability.

WTO rules suggest that except as otherwise provided for in the Protocol, foreign individuals and enterprises shall be accorded equal treatment that accorded to domestic individuals and enterprises in respect of the procurement of inputs and goods and services necessary. All member countries agreed to joint the *Government Procurement Agreement (GPA)* following accession to the WTO.

Member countries of the WTO agreed to repeal or revise all laws, regulations, and other measures inconsistent with the GATT '*Most Favoured Nation*' ('MFN') and National Treatment rules, with regard to all other WTO members.

According to the WTO rules, all member countries should harmonize in conformity with the Technical Barriers to Trade (TBT) Agreement, all technical regulations, standards, and conformity assessment procedures.

All member countries of the WTO had agreed to remove all trade barriers to open the domestic market to foreign or private companies.

Situation in India

Two-thirds of India's 1.3 billion-strong population depend on farming for their livelihood; however, the agriculture sector makes up only around 17% of the nation's total economic output, amounting to about $2.3 trillion. More than half of India's farmers are reportedly in debt, with 20,638 committing suicide in 2018 and 2019, according to India's National Crime Records Bureau. After Modi came to power in 2014, he promised to double farmers' income by 2022; however, the situation hasn't improved. The government is under pressure to bring private investments to the agriculture sector that has stagnated over the past decades. In September 2020, India's Narendra Modi imposed three bills that eased restrictions on private sector in agricultural markets to confirm to these WTO instructions, remove restrictions on hoarding, remove purchase of the Food Corporation of India to distort the market forces, and remove subsidies on farm prices. The farmers fear losing the MSP (Minimum Support Price) guarantee that they get now under the new laws.

These laws allow big companies to capture the farming, which will harm the small and marginal farmers. These small and marginal farmers own less than 5 and 2.5 acres of land, respectively. In Punjab, and probably for North India, over 50% of farmers hold land of fewer than 5 acres. The Congress Party who was in power from 1947 until 2014 with some gaps for a few years, as it depends on the rural landlords for electoral support in rural areas, was unwilling to implement comprehensive land reforms. It comprised subsidized fertilizers and irrigation, rice and wheat varieties bred to absorb high fertilizer doses, and state-led training programs to assist farmers in transitioning to new practices.

Given the expense, it was rolled out only in a few, well-endowed districts of Punjab and a few other states. Because bumper productions inevitably depress prices, farmers were guaranteed procurement through state-run *mandis* or market yards at MSPs declared in advance. State procurement was therefore crucial to transforming Punjab into India's breadbasket.

Modi introduced the laws as watershed reforms that will usher in a new era of prosperity for farmers backed by corporate investments. On the face of it, they allow private buyers to purchase farm produce outside of the supervision of and without the payment of taxes and fees to *mandis*; limit state intervention in retail prices; and provide a framework for farming on contract to corporations. However, clauses like one that bars farmers—or anyone else—from seeking legal recourse over contractual disputes cement the fear that the laws stack the deck against farmers. Farmers fear that the laws will end the state-regulated procurement at *mandis*. The real agenda behind the laws, farmers allege, is to facilitate corporate control over agriculture and food, and Reliance and Adani Group, two of India's largest business houses, perceived to be close to the Modi government, are blamed by the farmers.

The Minimum Support Price (MSP) is in place to ensure guaranteed prices and to protect farmers from price fluctuations. As this has no legal backing, it could mean that the new laws will also have no provision for it. It is fixed by the central government and is offered for 23 crops based on recommendations from the Commission for Agricultural Costs and Prices (CACP). However, the government is not legally bound to pay these even if open market rates ask for a lower price. MSP is kept at 1.5 times the cost of production but ultimately the price varies. Three formulas are considered by the CACP when it comes to calculating the costs:

- A2: This takes into account money spent by farmers on things such as seeds, fertilizers, and fuel.
- A2 + FL: This is an estimated value of unpaid family labor.
- C2: This considers rent and interest foregone on the land plus if farmers own any machinery.

The government insists that the new reforms are a way to modernize the regulations and have vocally talked about MSP remaining even though it is not a written law. It says it's trying to help, while farmers disagree. The average monthly income for agricultural households is 8,931 Indian rupees, which is £90.36, according to research by the National Bank for Agriculture and Rural Development in 2016. Only 35% of that income is actually from agriculture meaning farmers are forced to earn money from other sources such as rent on building or land, income from interest earned on bank deposits, and interest made from investments. They are worried this could eventually leave them dependent on big corporations and that the government might not step in to help.

India hands out an estimated $32 billion in subsidies to farmers annually, according to the finance ministry, but unsupported by independent observers. With the new ordinance, any corporation can purchase directly from the farmers. Farmers fear that corporates will end up setting prices on their own terms when the state markets eventually become redundant because the corporates have taken over the buying. There is even more reason to be fearful because the MSP clause is absent, and because similar things have happened before in other industries.

On the second ordinance, the concern is that allowing the corporates to engage in contract with the farmers puts farmers at the mercy of corporates. If there is a flood situation, and the farmers cannot produce top quality products, the corporates may not pay the farmers. This means that with this ordinance, farmers have less security on payments.

With the final ordinance, that corporates are given the liberty to store as much as they want in their warehouses. Previously, in India, there was a law that prohibited buyers from storing for more than what is required, because these are essential items. Now, with this ordinance, corporates could sell the produce on their own terms during shortages, causing inflation. Every year, farmers from Punjab and Haryana sell almost their entire produce to the FCI at MSPs thanks to well-developed market yards and efficient procurement centers, very different from Bihar's underdeveloped grain procurement infrastructure. Average monthly income of the farmers in Punjab and Haryana is Rs 18,000 and Rs 16,000 in 2013, but it is only Rs 3600 in Bihar. There is no MSP in Bihar.

While Punjab and Haryana sell almost their entire rice and wheat output to FCI, the government agency's procurement in Bihar has remained at less than two percent of the state's total production. The Food Corporation of India (FCI), the main state-run grain procurement agency, buys only rice and wheat at those prices due to a lack of storage and funds. After buying rice and wheat from farmers at MSPs, the FCI sells the staples at highly subsidized prices to the poor. The government compensates the FCI for its losses. All these are against the WTO rules and have to go. The two top Indian billionaires, who the farmers point to as poised to benefit from the Farm Bills, are Ambani (who became 4th richest person in the world in 2020, up from 40th in 2014) and Adani (who grew to be 40th richest in the world in 2020 up from 609th in 2014); both are in the business of food and agriculture, including in marketing-related infrastructures such as ports and retails.

There is a National Food Security Act. It had the aim to ensure food security for all. The state should protect rights of small and marginalized farmers and provide land reforms, minor and small irrigation systems, remunerative prices, affordable power, and crop insurance. The state should provide also provisions for procurement, storage, and movement-related interventions toward decentralized procurement. These three new Farm Bills ignore that act and shift the responsibility of state for the big corporations, without any protection for the farmers. The Farm Bills will also undermine India's public distribution system. Hunger is widespread in India. According to the India Food Bank, about 15% of the population is undernourished, while an estimated 34.7% of children are stunted. At the same time, roughly a third of food is wasted in the country due to inefficiencies in the agricultural system. The changes in the Essential Commodities Act will make basic food items unaffordable, as the big corporations will determine prices by hoarding.

These policies, embedded in the US Farm Bill, have resulted in the number of US small and medium-scale farmers dwindling and farm-consolidation increasing, with agribusiness having a strong grip over farmers and farmworkers lives, and agribusiness determining much of what the people eat in the US. The result in the US is clear: A crisis in public health, ecological health, and for rural communities. All three laws are pro-corporates. Farmer's organizations are unanimous in the demand that the only solution is to repeal the laws. Despite decades of economic growth, up to half of India's population relies on growing crops on small areas of land, typically less than 3 acres, and farmers worry that without guaranteed prices they will be forced to sell their land and lose their livelihoods.

The Modi reforms were motivated by a well-organized effort of the World Economic Forum (WEF) and its New Vision for Agriculture, part of Klaus Schwab's Great Reset, the corporate side of the UN Agenda 2030. According to William Engdahl (2007, 2008), Todhunter (2019a), and Brown (2019), the new Modi laws are measures the IMF and World Bank have been demanding since the early 1990s to bring Indian agriculture and farming into the corporate agribusiness model pioneered in the US by the Rockefeller Foundation decades ago. It allows corporations to buy farmland for the first time nationally by large companies, food processing firms, and exporters, who can invest in the farm sector. Against them, a small farmer has no chance to survive. Here, we find the WEF and the Gates Foundation's radical globalized agriculture agenda.

WEF and the Corporations

William Engdahl (2007, 2008, 2020), Todhunter (2019a, b, c), and Brown (2019) explained that these laws are a direct result of several years' effort of the World Economic Forum and its New Vision for Agriculture (NVA) initiative. For more than 12 years, the WEF and its NVA have pushed a corporate model in Africa, Latin America, and Asia. The "big target" has been India, where resistance to corporate takeover of agriculture has been fierce ever since the 1960's Green Revolution. For the WEF Great Reset, better known as the UN Agenda 2030 for "sustainable agriculture," India's traditional farm and food system must be broken. Its smallholder family farmers must be forced to sell to large agribusiness conglomerates and regional or state-level protections for those farmers eliminated. It will be "sustainable," not for the small farmers, but rather the giant agribusiness groups.

To advance that agenda, the WEF created a powerful group of corporate and government interests called the NVA India Business Council. Its website at the homepage of the WEF states, "The NVA India Business Council serves as an informal, high-level leadership group to champion private sector collaboration and investment to drive sustainable agricultural growth in India." The WEF's NVA India Business Council in 2017 includes Bayer Crop Science, one of the world's largest purveyors of agriculture pesticides and now of Monsanto GMO seeds, Cargill India Pvt. of the giant US grain company, Dow Agro Sciences, GMO seed and pesticide producer, GMO and agrichemical firm DuPont, grain cartel giant Louis Dreyfus Company, Wal-Mart India; India Mahindra & Mahindra (world's largest tractor maker), Nestle India Ltd, PepsiCo India, Rabobank International, State Bank of India, Swiss Re Services, the world's largest re-insurer, India Private Limited, a chemicals maker; and the Adani Group of Gautam Adani, the second richest man in India and major financier of Modi's BJP party. There is no presence of any Indian farmer organizations.

In addition to top Modi backer, Gautam Adani on the WEF-NVA India Business Council, Mukesh Ambani, sits on the Board of Directors of Klaus Schwab's World Economic Forum. Ambani, another top Modi backer, is Chairman and Managing Director of India's largest conglomerate, Reliance Industries, and Asia's second wealthiest person worth some $74 billion. Ambani is a strong advocate of the radical farm reform as Reliance stands to reap huge gains. It is clear that the interests and welfare of India's estimated 650 million farmers are not the priority. On 26 November 2020, a nationwide general strike began that involved approximately 250 million people in support of the farmers. Transport unions representing over 14 million truck drivers have come out in support of the farmer unions. The fact the government refuses to back down suggests it will be a bitter battle or a great defeat of the farming community. Modi deregulation corresponds to the UN 2021 Food Systems Summit.

AGRA and the UN Food Systems Summit

According to William Engdahl, indication of the agenda in store for India's farmers is the upcoming September UN Food Systems Summit. UN Secretary General Antonio Guterres in 2019 announced the UN will host Food Systems Summit in 2021 with the aim of maximizing the benefits of a "food systems approach" consistent with UN 2030 Sustainable Development Goals. He named Agnes Kalibata of Rwanda as his Special Envoy for the 2021 Food Systems Summit. The summit's founding statement pushes "precision farming" such as GPS, Big Data and robotics, and GMO, as solutions (Brown, 2019; Todhunter, 2019a, b, c).

AGRA, the Alliance for a Green Revolution in Africa, was created by the Gates and Rockefeller Foundations to introduce GMO patented seeds and related chemical pesticides into African agriculture. A key person Gates put in charge of the AGRA, Robert Horsch, spent 25 years as a senior Monsanto executive. The Bill & Melinda Gates Foundation is also a "Contributing Partner" of the WEF. After nearly 15 years and some $1 billion in funds from Gates, Rockefeller, and other large donors, AGRA has failed to lift farmers into a better well-being. Farmers are forced by their governments to buy seeds from commercial suppliers, often tied to Monsanto and other GMO companies, as well as commercial fertilizer. The result is debt and often bankruptcy. The farmers cannot reuse the commercial seeds and instead, are forced to abandon traditional seeds, which they could reuse.

AGRA's focus on "market-oriented" means the global export market controlled by Cargill and other major grain cartel giants. In the 1990s, under pressure from Washington and agribusiness, the World Bank demanded African and other governments in developing countries end their agriculture subsidies, but at the same time, the US and EU agriculture remains heavily subsidized. The cheap subsidized EU and OECD imports drive local farmers bankrupt, which was planned. A 2020 report on AGRA, False Promises, concluded, "yield increases for key staple crops in the years before AGRA were just as low as during AGRA. Instead of halving hunger, the situation in the 13 focus countries has worsened since AGRA was launched. The number of people going hungry has increased by 30 percent during the AGRA years... affecting 130 million people in the 13 AGRA focus countries." Gates' AGRA has made African food production more globalized and dependent than ever on the will of global multinationals whose aim is cheap inputs. It forces farmers into debt and demands specific "cash crops" like GMO corn or soya, be grown for export.

Gates Foundation's confidential Agricultural Development Strategy 2008–2011 mentioned its strategy:

> *"Smallholders with the potential to produce a surplus can create a market-oriented agricultural system... to exit poverty...The vision of success involves market-oriented farmers operating profitable farms...this will require some degree of land mobility and a lower percentage of total employment involved in direct agricultural production."*

"In 2008 Rajiv Shah was the Gates Foundation's Director of Agricultural Development, and led the Foundation's creation of the AGRA together with the Rockefeller Foundation. Today Shah is President of Rockefeller Foundation, Gates' partner in AGRA, which foundation also financed the creation of GMO patented seeds back in the 1970s, the creation of seed banks with the World Bank. Rajiv Shah is also an Agenda Contributor at the World Economic Forum. The fact that the President of AGRA is heading the September 2021 UN Food Systems Summit exposes the links between the UN, the Gates and Rockefeller Foundations, the World Economic Forum and their web of global corporate mega companies."

India, with 1.4 billion people, perhaps half in agriculture, is the last bastion where global agribusiness has been unable to dominate the production of food. The OECD has been globalized by industrial agribusiness since decades. China has opened up and is a major player in the GMO world with Syngenta, as well as the world's largest producer of glyphosate. China's industrial pork factory farms such as Smithfield Farms, where the recent African Swine Fever is believed to have originated, are on the way to wipe out small-scale farmers there. "The central role of the Gates-Rockefeller AGRA in the UN 2021 Food Systems Summit, the major role of the WEF in the world "food systems" reset, and the pressures in recent months on the Modi government to implement the same corporate agenda in India as in Africa, are all no accident" (William Engdahl, 2020).

India Farming Protests Resonate with US Agriculture

The dispute raises questions not only about agriculture but about dwindling populations in rural India where small communities are already struggling to survive—an issue mirrored in the parts of the US. The images of farmers marching through New Delhi recall similar scenes in Washington, D.C., during the farming crisis of the late 1970s and early 1980s, when hundreds of trucks and tractors flooded the National Mall. Thousands of farmers lost their land, in part because of government policies that caused soaring interest rates as demand for their products plunged, leading to falling land values.

In Iowa, one of the hardest hit states, there were about 500 farm auctions a month in 1983 when families had no choice but to sell. Just as feared by those protesting in India, the American farmers lost their livelihoods and sense of identity. Rural economies in the Midwest that had been declining for decades were devastated by the farm crisis. But while many farmers who survived emerged more prosperous, the communities near them continued to struggle. There are fears that the same could happen in India if New Delhi refuses to repeal the law that favors corporate farming. India has not had a substantial industrial base to absorb the large population into gainful industrial or urban employment. Instead, vast number of rural migrants are integrated into the low-end urban and construction economy. The challenges facing India are common to many developing countries in Asia, where farmland has been gobbled up, often for factories and property development, leaving hundreds of farmers without a proper livelihoods. In countries including Myanmar, Cambodia, and China, many ended up on the fast industrializing cities, doing low-paid work in service sector in massage parlors and delivery services that provide no social benefits or security.

What are the solutions? Repeal of new agricultural laws to reform Indian agriculture cannot provide any solution as these are recommended by the WTO and India government alone will be unable to rectify these unjust rules of the WTO. Withdrawal from the WTO and its replacement by bilateral trade negotiations with the major trade partners of India should be examined seriously. India has only a handful of countries as serious trade partners. The US, the UK, European Common Market, Russia, Japan, Australia, and the Arab Gulf Co-Operation Council member countries are the important trade partners of India. It will not be difficult to have trade treaties with these countries and other countries will follow up these treaties. In that case, India's special requirements regarding subsidies and price supports can be considered. Trade with China and Pakistan can be eliminated completely, which cannot be done at present under the WTO rules.

WTO and Textiles and Garments Industry

During the Uruguay Round, industrialized countries agreed to phase out the Multi-Fibre Agreement in four stages by 2005. Industrialized countries have found various ways to comprehensively ignore its spirit. Despite the commitments made in the Uruguay Round, there are still excessive trade barriers in textiles and garments with the developing countries facing restrictions on 80 percent of their exports. "The average industrial-country tariff on textiles and clothing imports from developing countries is 11 per cent – three times higher than the average industrial tariff.

Bangladesh, one of the world's poorest countries, faces tariffs as high as 20 per cent on its key exports to the US and Canada."

These measures are having a serious effect on many developing countries. Textiles and clothing are one of the most important areas of export activity for developing countries, accounting for around 10 percent of total exports. Lost markets mean lower wages and fewer jobs in textile and garment industries which employ millions of vulnerable people. Women account for the vast majority of workers in this sector.

WTO and the Least Developed Countries

At the 1996 Singapore Ministerial Conference, governments agreed to "a Plan of Action, including provision for ... duty free access aimed at improving the overall capacity of Least Developed Countries to respond to opportunities provided by the international trading system." As in other areas, there has been no real progress.

There are 49 countries classified by the UN as Least Developed Countries (LDCs). And they are among the poorest in the world with about half of their population live below the poverty line. They contribute for less than one percent of world trade. Yet their exports face very serious obstructions in the developed countries. In the US and Canada, only around one-tenth of all tariffs are pitched at levels above five percent; however, half of LDC exports have to pay tariffs higher than this. Exports from the LDC countries face tariffs 15 percent more in the developed countries with trade barriers highest in items where LDCs have trade advantage. Sugar exports face very high restrictions in the EU and clothing and footwear exports from the LDC face tariff restrictions in both the US and Canada. Eliminating duties and quotas on LDC exports would create new jobs in the LDC countries. However, these opportunities are now denied to them. For example, reduction of tariffs on rice and sugar is being postponed, although these items could earn huge foreign exchange earnings for the LDC.

WTO and Africa

Immense problem is facing Africa. With 12 percent of the world's population, it contributes less than one percent of exports, its share went down since 1970s due to serious decline of the price of its export items with poverty increased since the 1990s. Globalization has practically no effects on it. The decline of the commodity prices in the world affected Africa very badly. Primary commodities account for three-quarters of Africa's exports. The objective of the International Trade Organisation (ITO) proposed in 1948, alongside the IMF and World Bank, was to provide 'such [commodity] prices as are fair to consumers and provide a reasonable return to producers.' WTO failed to provide these. The issue of commodities was not there in the WTO agenda. Debt is another problem which needs money to be diverted from crucial areas like health, education, and infrastructure. Failure to tackle Africa's debt problems is another source of the region's trade problems.

WTO's Patent Rules and Public Health in Poor Countries

The application of the Trade-Related Aspects of Intellectual Property Rights (TRIPS) agreement to pharmaceutical products was one of the most dangerous and debatable parts of the WTO. Developing-country governments are concerned most stringent patent protection on the affordability of vital medicines to the poor and on development of vaccines generally. Recently, India and South Africa jointly on behalf of the developing countries appealed to the WTO to relax this law regarding TRIPS during the coronavirus outbreak but it was opposed by the major pharmaceutical companies of the US and EU.

Article 8 of the agreement acknowledged these concerns by allowing governments to 'adopt measures necessary to protect public health.' Article 7 stipulated that the agreement should help contribute to technology transfer in a manner conducive to social and economic welfare, and a later article committed industrialized countries actively to encourage such transfers (Promise 8). These are only words, and the developed countries ignored these laws to increase the profits of their pharmaceutical companies.

The TRIPS agreement, which provides a minimum 20-year period of patent protection, has figured in two high-profile disputes. In South Africa, 39 drug companies began a court action to prevent the South African government from importing cheap generic copies of patented HIV/AIDS drugs. This case was followed by the US decision to take Brazil to a WTO dispute panel. The aim of the complaint was to prevent Brazil from producing generic copies of vital drugs (Oxfam report).

The TRIPS agreement created a threat because it has raised the cost of medicines. Patented medicines frequently cost more than ten times the price of generic equivalents. Developed countries have in order to support their pharmaceutical companies to apply the most strict interpretation of the TRIPS agreement. The US had used the threat of trade sanctions to demand that the patent claims of US companies should be honored. Diverse countries like India, Brazil, Argentina, the Dominican Republic, Vietnam, South Africa, and Thailand have all been threatened under the 'Special 301' provision of US trade law. However, at the same time, the US and Canadian governments had threaten to override patents at home when faced with bio-terrorist threats to their own citizens and the threat of purchasing low-cost generics was successfully used to bargain down prices for pharmaceutical companies of the developing countries. Thus, there is discrimination in the application of TRIPS rules in favor of the developed countries.

Aid and Technical Assistance to Developing Countries

For most developing countries, the cost of implementing the Uruguay Round agreements is huge and places a huge burden on the limited resources of the developing countries. The WTO has provided insufficient financial supports to meet the requirements. As a result, poor countries failed to participate in negotiations that determine important industrial, agricultural, investment, and services policy which can affect the future of these poor countries. Thus, they could not direct policies which would affect their interests.

The preamble to the agreement establishing the WTO says: 'There is need for positive efforts designed to ensure that developing countries ... secure a share in the growth in international trade commensurate with the needs of their economic development.'

However, WTO agreements restrict governments from adopting policies that might help their countries to gain the benefits of integration into the world market.

"These included the selective protection of domestic industries, targeted subsidies for domestic firms, restrictions on foreign investors, the copying of patented technologies, and requirements on foreign investors to link with the local economy."

The TRIPS agreement is an example. By providing more stringent royalty system to patent protection, TRIPS will provide profits for patent holders on new technologies which will create benefits to developed countries. Industrialized countries contribute and obtained for over 90 percent of research and royalty. Contrary to its stated promise, the TRIPS agreement has failed to promote technology transfer to poorer countries. The increased cost of royalty payments is the huge cost for developing countries to gain new technologies. By pushing up the cost of technology transfer, TRIPS will restrict access to the new technologies. It is important to notice that no developed country had an intellectual property regime, during the period of their own development as strict as that demanded by TRIPS. TRIPS is creating a situation that is restricting the spread of new technologies.

The WTO Trade-Related Investment Measures (TRIMs) agreement, concluded in 1994, poses similar problems. It restricts the right of governments to use 'local content requirements'—a requirement to source factors of production from local industry. Countries like South Korea and Taiwan have developed dynamic linkages between the export sector and domestic firms. Today, these two countries account for over one-third of medium- and high-technology exports from developing countries. Yet the policies that created the success are now prohibited by the WTO. The General Agreement on Trade in Services (GATS) is another area of concern. Supported by both the EU and the US, WTO is demanding radical liberalization, including the sectors like financial and technical services, utilities such as electricity, water, and education. Companies in developing countries are not equipped to compete with multinational companies in areas such as finance and insurance. Free-market principles cannot act efficiently to manage basic services such as water, health, and education. There is a real danger that these WTO agreements will turn developing countries into a dependency position in the global system.

The WTO, during the Singapore Ministerial Conference in December 1996, accepted that the globalization had the risk for the least developed countries that they would be ignored. There are 48 least developed countries, with one-half of one percent of total world merchandize trade with some specific characteristics that per capita GNP of 456 US$ in 1993, 32 of them are in sub-Saharan Africa. The General System of Preferences allows unilaterally to reduce tariffs from them. In 1996, the WTO asked the developed countries to eliminate all tariffs against these countries but the US and the EU refused. "LLDCs representatives are excluded from participation in informal meetings where the big trading powers take crucial decisions. They also have little capacity to participate in formal WTO meetings because of lack of staff and knowledge. The result is that concerns of the LLDCs are not given due attention" (Vander Stichle, 1997).

How the WTO Deals with Indigenous Peoples' Rights

The WTO is the one of the major instruments to implement the Washington Consensus of neoliberal globalization. Several WTO Ministerials, such as the Doha Development Round in 2001, collapsed due to continuing disagreements over subsidies on agricultural products, market access, and special safeguard mechanisms, and massive peoples' protests. Later in its 9th Ministerial Conference, the WTO made decisions on ignoring the objections of a number of developing countries such as the Agreement on Agriculture (AoA), Trade-Related Aspects of Intellectual Property Rights (TRIPS), Trade-Related Investment Measures (TRIMS), and General Agreement on Trade in Services (GATS), and forged new multilateral agreements with wide range of implications for the poor people. The agreement for the Bali Package has pushed for greater liberalization in agriculture, acceleration of LDCs in the WTO, and expedites trade facilitation through restructuring of GATT articles on imports-exports and trade costs. The Bali Package, along with post-Bali issues on International Technology Agreement (ITA) and Trade in Services Agreement (TISA), is labeled by developed countries as the solution to the stalled Doha Round to pursue intensified trade liberalization.

Since colonization, after the invasion of American continents by Columbus and India by Vasco da Gama, neoliberal policies have intensified the sufferings of the Indigenous Peoples. Their lands, territories, and natural resources have been exploited recently by unsustainable development projects, such as mono-cultural chemically intensive plantations, extractive industries such as mining, oil drilling, hydro projects, and other environmentally destructive "renewable" energy projects. They were driven out from their 'Indigenous lands' and territories. All of this has happened for the sake of globalization and is bound to get worse as the WTO decides more agreements and policies.

"The AoA has forced many developing countries to favor transnational agricultural companies like Monsanto and compelled impoverished Indigenous Peoples to use high yielding varieties (HYV) seeds without being informed of the negative effects. The AoA pushes for commercial agricultural production, replacing traditional plant varieties with genetically altered species marketed by agriculture companies, and chemical-laden foods." The WTO demands reduction of subsidies on price support, while capitalist countries refuse to apply this in their own economies; this is the root cause of the farmer's movement in India. This has damaged livelihoods resulting in bankruptcy of farmers, as they are unable to compete with subsidized and cheaper imports from abroad.

Indigenous are denied rights and control over Indigenous medicines, which are taken over by big pharmaceutical corporations as their intellectual property rights under WTO. WTO allows the patenting of life forms including extraction of genetic information under its TRIPS. Bill Gates treat Indigenous Peoples as valuable and vulnerable targets for medical research and experiments in which thousands were sterilized or made cripple with polio vaccines of Gates.

Trade agreements on services have further marginalized and impoverished indigenous people. WTO allows foreign corporations to own and operate educational and health institutions leading to profit-oriented and corporate-owned services that are available only to the few who have the means to pay. Globalization has even destroyed the biological and cultural diversity, ecosystems, values, and traditional knowledge of the Indigenous Peoples. The WTO in its Bali conference has pushed more new deals that would intensify the misery of Indigenous Peoples, humanity, and Mother Earth.

A Membership That Pays Off

The US, China, and Germany are the countries that benefit the most worldwide from their accession to the WTO. For the US, income gains amount to about 87 billion US dollars (measured in gross domestic product, GDP). The Chinese generate income gains of about 86 billion US dollars and the Germans about 66 billion US dollars. These are the results of a recent study commissioned by the Bertelsmann Stiftung, for which the authors Felbermayr, Larch, Yotov, and Yalcin (2021) calculated the wealth effects of WTO membership for 180 countries worldwide, including all 164 member states.

The whole of the WTO membership achieved a total increase in prosperity of around 855 billion US dollars. EU members benefit together with 232 billion and OECD countries with a total of 480 billion US dollars. But the success story also has its downsides: Countries that are not members of the WTO are losing out due to the greater economic integration of WTO members. According to the analysis, nations with strong exports and production are the main beneficiaries of membership. This is true for Germany and South Korea (around USD 31 billion in GDP growth) as industrial and innovation locations, but also for Mexico (around USD 58 billion in GDP growth) and China.

China and the WTO

China became a member of the WTO in the middle of this process, in December 2001. With its WTO entry, textile exports of China were subject to immediate quota removals on product groups that would have been liberalized between 1995 and 2002 (the first three phases of quota removals), while the remaining product groups would be liberalized in 2005. Therefore, in 2002 and 2005, India was faced with the removal of import quota on their own exports, but also on Chinese exports. Thus, India lost its import quota and it has to face competition on its export markets from China. Due to the dismantling of the MFA, increased Chinese export competition was particularly significant in the textiles sector. Between 2000 and 2005, China's share of US and EU textiles imports doubled (increased by 5123% in the US and by 98% in the EU). In 2013, China accounted for 29% of global textile exports (WITS, World Bank, 2014). Confidence on the WTO is undermined due to its failure to control trade practices of China. WTO is complicit on China—that caused suspicions on the effectiveness of the WTO.

According to the World Bank, global wealth increased by nearly two-thirds from 1995 to 2014, to more than $1.1 trillion. The share going to middle-income countries such as China and India grew from 19 to 28%, while the advanced economies of the West saw their share fall from 75 to 65%. The global great convergence, however, coincided with a great divergence within the wealthy countries and many developing countries as well (Alden, 2019). American companies have enormous choice—workers who demand more wages can be replaced, either by cheaper workers in some developing countries or by robots at home. In the two advanced economies, the US and the UK, inequalities are the gravest and public backlash against globalization is also greatest.

Since it has joined the WTO, China has gained maximum economic advantage but it has no regards for the rules and obligations of WTO membership. "It has heavily subsidized industry after industry, used discriminatory regulations to disadvantage foreign companies and favor its own national champions, and engaged in a broad campaign of technology acquisition using every tactic from forcing foreign investors to share technology with Chinese competitors to outright cyber-theft" (Alden, 2019). For many years, it devalued and kept the exchange rate of Yuan low, to gain competitive advantage. These are the issues which have caused trade dispute between the US and China. China is spending more on its state industries, trying to control foreign multinational companies, and using debt as a control mechanism for smaller countries who took loans from China. The tariffs against China are far more popular in the US. There is little confidence that US sanctions and bilateral pressure will produce changes in Chinese behavior.

China: A "Rule Shaker" or a "Rule Maker"?

Valbona Zeneli and Michael R. Czinkota (2019) wrote that the West's open invitation for China to join the WTO in 2001 paved the way for its rise to a global economic power. Since then, the balance of power at the WTO has changed dramatically. Chinese outward investment in the global economy has increased 30-fold, from $7 billion (making up only one percent of the global FDI) to almost $200 billion (13 percent of the global FDI).

China entered the WTO as a "rule taker," evolved into a "rule shaker," and now aims to become a "rule maker." In fact, economic relations between China, the US, and the EU define many of the agreements and disputes at the WTO. Xi Jinping's "China Dream" of national rejuvenation could be seen as a way to reshape the international economic system, putting China at the center. Initial optimism that China would turn toward a free market economy has yet to be fulfilled. With the existing WTO rule book, it is difficult to hold China accountable. Due to high trade deficits, the US is pushing for WTO reforms, increasing tariffs, and blocking the nominations of seats on the WTO's appellate body (where the US is a major player in the dispute resolution process) as leverage. Desired reforms aim to regulate market distortions caused by government interventions, simplifying the process of gathering information on unfair trade and investment practices, broadening the scope of banned subsidies, and setting boundaries to proportionate retaliations.

According to Lori Wallach (2019), "The World Trade Organization is not mainly about *trade*. Rather the organization has the primary task of carrying out what the Harvard economist Dani Rodrik calls hyperglobalization—the worldwide imposition of one-size-fits-all rules, favored by global financial markets and three important institutions in Washington, the US Treasury, IMF and the World Bank, which restricts sovereignty of the national governments' ability to control the economy to satisfy their societies' needs."

If countries do not comply, they are subject to millions of dollars in trade penalties. Of the 242 completed W.T.O. cases, in only 22 did the domestic policies, many unrelated to trade, survive challenged. Thus, the country-of-origin labels on meat that we relied on in American grocery stores were eliminated after the W.T.O. classified them as "illegal trade barriers" and authorized $1 billion in sanctions. The US was also forced to weaken regulations under the Clean Air Act, dolphin protection laws, and Endangered Species Act rules.

The US has filed 49 challenges against other countries, with rulings against Indian policies promoting access to seeds for poor farmers and European limits on genetically modified foods and a ban on artificial growth hormones in meat. The US has used threats to pressure Thailand, Brazil, and South Africa to reverse policies on access to AIDS medication and other lifesaving drugs. The US won a case against a solar-power program in India.

Trade negotiations have been dominated by corporate interests, while labor, consumer, and environmental groups are ignored. The WTO does not care about labor or environmental requirements, limit pollution, or about consumer safety standards. It also does not care about monopolistic mega-corporations distorting global markets or China doing currency manipulations and creates unfair trade advantages. It does not care that China is not a market economy, but a fascist dictatorship controlling every business organizations in the way it wants. American workers and workers in most countries do not believe in great gains from free "trade" agreements. During the WTO era, developed and developing countries have lost millions of manufacturing jobs, since China joined in 2001. Income inequality between rich and poor countries, and within countries, went up greatly (Wallach, 2019).

Valbona Zeneli and Michael R. Czinkota (2019) wrote, there is the issue of China in influence in the WTO. In September 2018, the US together with the EU and Japan expressed doubt about the future of the WTO, questioning its validity as the forum for multilateral trade. China would not accept any reforms at the WTO, or any level, as that would affect its own economic plan. China wants to preserve the existing global trade order. It is the rule that state-led economic systems are incompatible with membership in the WTO but there are pressures from China that changes in the WTO rules are necessary to accommodate countries like China.

The shift of manufacturing from advanced countries and many developing nations to China was very destructive. However, a vast majority of multinational companies protectionism, however popular. Under article 24 of the WTO, regional trade agreements are possible, and in 2019, 291 regional trade agreements were concluded. The EU, NAFTA, and ASEAN free trade agreements have been especially successful in supporting regional production networks and accelerating industrialization but have nothing much to do solution of poverty of the nations.

Why the WTO Has Not Worked for the World's Poor

If rich countries gave market access and fair treatments at the World Trade Organization (WTO), globalization would produce benefits for reduction of poverty. However, developed countries are maintaining trade policies that discriminate against the poor countries and so far the WTO could do nothing about that. Since 1994, the developed countries collectively reneged on every commitment they made. According to the United Nations, developing countries have to forgo around US$100bn a year because of unfair protectionist policies of the developed countries and China. Tariff barriers in developed countries are four times higher for poor countries than for industrialized countries. It is near impossible to enter the Chinese market unless China wants it. Developed countries have increased agricultural subsidies, instead of cutting them, to US$350bn a year. Barriers to agricultural trade cost developing countries US$20bn a year. China's agricultural subsidies are more than $100 million per year. The world's poorest countries, the least developed countries, got to overcome some of the highest tariff barriers for their exports to the developed countries. Intellectual property and investment rules are being applied in a manner that go against the social and economic welfare in poor countries. Even during the COVID-19 pandemic, EU and the US refused to relax the TRIPS rules for the developing countries.

Developed countries have used the IMF and World Bank to force trade liberalization through loan conditions. China used its loans to force the debtor countries to import from China exclusively. At the same time, developed countries have maintained exceptionally high trade barriers and other health-related restrictions. These barriers cost developing countries each year approximately twice the amount they receive in aid. Far from supporting poor countries, developed countries are actively discriminating against them.

For manufactured goods, tariffs facing developing-country exports to high-income countries are on average four times higher than those facing exports by industrialized countries. Between them, the US and the European Union have launched 234 anti-dumping cases against developing countries since 1994. Unbalanced liberalization is denying poor countries the opportunity to share the benefits of globalization, if there is any.

Indian Government, if it wants to be popular, should come out of WTO and World Bank as these are nothing but obstacles on the way to promote India's national interest. Bangladesh has demonstrated that World Bank is not only alternative when the World Bank refused to finance the bridge over the Padma River. Recommendations of the World Bank and the rules of the WTO, now controlled by China, are harmful for India. The minimum support price should be extended to all kinds of agricultural products to eliminate the possibility of suicide of the farmers. A revival of the economy can be taken place under a planned investment program eliminating Chinese and other foreign imports.

Illegal Transfer of Money from India Since Privatization

In March 2018, it was revealed that the amount of Indian black money currently present in Swiss and other offshore banks is estimated to be US$1.5 trillion, a lot of these were transferred to other off shore accounts since then. When India started privatization since 1993, and particularly after 1995 to make India market economy, to qualify for the membership of the WTO, some politicians and businessmen took that opportunity to take over the vast public assets and sold a part of these to the foreigners and illegally send the money to foreign bank accounts to avoid paying taxes and to hide illegal transactions with the foreign companies.

Size of India's Black Economy

There are no official estimates of India's black economy. In 2011, the government had commissioned a joint study to estimate Indian entities' unaccounted wealth both at home and abroad. The final report has not been submitted. India ranked fifth largest exporter of illicit money between 2002 and 2011, with a total of $343.04 billion. India is 5th in the world on illicit outflows.

Other Estimates

$462 billion: According to Global Financial Integrity (GFI), a Washington-based think tank, Indians send away $462 billion in overseas tax havens between 1948 and 2008.

$500 billion: Money stashed away in tax havens by Indians, according to former CBI director AP Singh.

$500 billion and $1.4 trillion: Parked in undisclosed overseas accounts, according to a BJP task force report of 2011 (Tables 2.4 and 2.5).

The latest report from Global Financial Integrity (GFI), a Washington-based think tank, estimates as much as $510 billion has flowed out of India illicitly between 2004 and 2013, of which $332 billion went out between 2010 and 2013. In 2013, for instance, about $83 billion was estimated to have been siphoned out of the country, and the only comfort was that it was significantly lower than the $93 billion taken out of the country in 2012. The think tank has estimated that over $1 trillion was siphoned out of developing nations in 2013 alone and over $7.8 trillion in the decade up to 2013.

Some the main findings of the report are:

- India lost a total of $462bn in illegal capital flows between 1948, a year after Independence, and 2008.
- The flows are more than twice India's external debt of $230bn.
- Total capital flight out of India represents some 16.6% of its GDP.
- Some 68% of India's capital loss has happened since the economy opened up in 1991.

Table 2.4 Liabilities of Swiss Banks toward Indians

Year End	*Exchange Rate*	*Liabilities of Swiss Banks toward Indians*	*Liabilities toward All Countries*	*Liability toward Indian (Fiduciary Business)*	*Liability toward All Countries (Fiduciary Business)*	*Total Liabilities toward Indians*	*Total Liabilities toward all Countries*	*Liabilities toward Indians as % of Total Liabilities*
2010	47.79	1.66 Billion CHF (Rs. 7,924 crore)	1349.24 Billion CHF	0.29 Billion CHF (Rs. 1,372 crore)	145.18 Billion CHF	1.95 Billion CHF (Rs. 9,295 crore)	1,494.42 Billion CHF	0.1302
2009	45.19	1.39 Billion CHF (Rs. 6,286 crore)	1335.98 Billion CHF	0.57 Billion CHF (Rs. 2,594 crore)	179.03 Billion CHF	1.97 Billion CHF (Rs. 8,879 crore)	1,515.01 Billion CHF	0.1297
2008	45.52	1.59 Billion CHF (Rs. 7,214 crore)	1,739.90 Billion CHF	0.82 Billion CHF (Rs. 3,710 crore)	280.23 Billion CHF	2.40 Billion CHF (Rs. 10,924 crore)	2,020.13 Billion CHF	0.1188
2007	34.79	2.92 Billion CHF (Rs. 10,168 crore)	2,070.44 Billion CHF	1.38 Billion CHF (Rs. 4,811 crore)	364.33 Billion CHF	4.31 Billion CHF (Rs. 14,979 crore)	2,434.77 Billion CHF	0.1769
2006	36.17	4.99 Billion CHF (Rs. 18,041 crore)	1,900.27 Billion CHF	1.47 Billion CHF (Rs. 5,332 crore)	328.26 Billion CHF	6.46 Billion CHF (Rs. 23,373 crore)	2,228.53 Billion CHF	0.2900

- "High net-worth individuals" and private companies were found to be primary drivers of illegal capital flows.
- The share of money Indian companies moved from developed country banks to "offshore financial centres" (OFCs) increased from 36.4% in 1995 to 54.2% in 2009.

Table 2.5 Illicit Flow, GFI Report, December, 2011

Rank	*Country*	*Illicit outflow (billions of USD)*
1	China	2,467
2	Mexico	453
3	Russia	427
4	Saudi Arabia	366
5	Malaysia	338
6	Kuwait	269
7	United Arab Emirates	262
8	Venezuela, BR	171
9	Qatar	170
10	Poland	160
11	Nigeria	158
12	Kazakhstan	123
13	Philippines	121
14	Indonesia	119
15	India (US$104 billion)	104
16	Ukraine	92
17	Chile	84
18	Argentina	83
19	Islamic Republic of Iran	66
20	Egypt	60

Source Global Financial Integrity

The author of the Global Financial Integrity Report, Dev Kar, a former International Monetary Fund economist, said that almost three-quarters of the illegal money that comprises India's underground economy ends up outside the country.

India's underground economy has been estimated to account for 50% of the country's GDP—$640bn at the end of 2008. This is the list of 28 'Nationalist' business men who looted money from Indian Banks:- (1) Vijay Mallya, (2) Mehul Choksi, (3) Nirav Modi, (4) Nishan Modi, (5) Pushpesh Baidya, (6) Ashish Jobanputra, (7) Sunny Kalara, (8) Arti Kalara, (9) Sunjay Kalara, (10) Varsha Kalara, (11) Sudhir Kalara, (12) Jatin Mehta, (13) Umesh Parikh, (14) Kamlesh Parikh, (15) Nilesh Parikh, (16) Vinay Mittal, (17) Eklavya Garg, (18) Chetan Jayantilal, (19) Nitin Jayantilal, (20) Dipti Bein Chetan, (21) Saviya Saith, (22) Rajiv Goyal, (23) Alka Goyal, (24) Lalit Modi, (25) Ritesh Jain, (26) Hitesh Nagenderbhai Patel, (27) Mayuriben Patel, and (28) Ashish Suresh Bhai.

Total looted amount stands at Rs.10,000,000,000,000/- (only Rupees Ten Trillion).

In comparison, the total funds held by all foreign clients of Swiss banks rose about 3 percent to CHF 1.46 trillion or about Rs 1000 billion in 2017, according to the official annual data released today by Swiss National Bank (SNB), the central banking authority of Switzerland. According to the SNB data, the total funds held by Indians directly with Swiss banks rose to 999 million Swiss franc (Rs 6,891 crore) in 2017, while the same held through fiduciaries or wealth managers increased to CHF 16.2 million (Rs 112 crore). These figures stood at CHF 664.8 million and CHF 11 million, respectively, at the end of 2016.

As per the latest data, the Indian money in Swiss banks included CHF 464 million (Rs 3,200 crore) in the form of customer deposits, CHF 152 million (Rs 1,050 crore) through other banks, and CHF 383 million (Rs 2,640 crore) as 'other liabilities' such as securities at the end of 2017. The funds under all three heads have risen sharply, as against a huge plunge across all categories in the previous year, the SNB data showed. The funds held through fiduciaries alone used to be in billions till 2007 but began falling after that amid fears of regulatory crackdown. The total funds held by Indians with Swiss banks stood at a record high of CHF 6.5 billion (Rs 23,000 crore) at 2006-end, but came down to nearly one-tenth of that level in about a decade (1 Crore is equal to 100 million).

Swiss Banking Association Report

2006 details bank deposits in the territory of Switzerland by nationals of following countries:

Top five.

India	*$1,456 billion*
Russia	$ 470 billion
UK	$390 billion
Ukraine	$100 billion
China	$ 96 billion

India has more money in Swiss bank than all the other countries combined. Second best Russia has 4 times lesser deposit. US is not even there in the counting in top five.

India has around 450 billion dollar of coal deposit and 170 billion of iron ore deposit, looted by state politicians. According to Indian Government, there are around 1 lakh places in India where people doing illegal mining. Dishonest persons, scandalous politicians, and corrupt IAS and IPS officers have deposited in foreign banks in their illegal personal accounts a sum of about $ 1500 billion, which have been misappropriated by them. This amount is about 13 times larger than the country's foreign debt. With this amount, 45 crore poor people can get Rs 1,00,000 each. This huge amount has been appropriated from the people of India by exploiting and betraying them.

According to the latest SNB (Switzerland National Bank) data, funds parked by Indian individuals and enterprises in Swiss banks, including through India-based branches, fell by 5.8% in 2019 to 899 million Swiss francs (₹6,625 crore). The data is for 'total liabilities' of Swiss banks toward Indian clients takes into account all types of funds of Indian customers at Swiss banks, including deposits from individuals, banks and enterprises. This also includes data for branches of Swiss banks in India, as well as non-deposit liabilities.

According to the latest SNB data, funds parked by Indian individuals and enterprises in Swiss banks, including through India-based branches, fell by 5.8 percent in 2019 to 899 million Swiss francs (Rs 6,625 crore). The list included close to 2,600 dormant accounts when it was first made public in December 2015, which had around 45 million Swiss francs (over ₹300 crore) lying unclaimed since at least 1955. There were also nearly 80 safety unclaimed deposit boxes when the list was first made public for claims from the real owners or their heirs.

A viral message on social media claims that WikiLeaks has released a list of top black money holders in Swiss banks. Incidentally, all the individuals named in the list are Indians. "*Undigestible news: Indians black money in Swiss bank is Rs. 358,679,863,300,000 (estimated to be 1.3 trillion dollars) this money belongs to 2000 indians who have kept there to evade from tax, This money is enough for India to become 10 America and become one of the most powerful developed country in the world for next 100yrs*" reads the concluding para of the message.

WikiLeaks published 1st list of black money holders in Swiss bank; the top most 30 members are all politicians (money is in crores; 1 crore is equal to 100 million; as in 2019).

1. *Asadudhin Ovaisi (568,000)*
2. *Moidin Bava (7800)*
3. *U T Khadar (158,000)*
4. *Siddaramayya*(82,000)
5. *Sonia Gandhi* (155,040)
6. *Mallikarjun Karge*(28,900)
7. *Roshan Beg* (9000)
8. *Mohammed Haris Nalpad (15,000)*
9. *Pranav Mukharjee*(75,000)
10. *Manishankar Ayyer*(50,000)
11. *Shashi Taroor*(5900)
12. *Ahmed Patel*(220,000)
13. *Aajam Khan*(76,888)
14. *K J George* (582,114)
15. *Ambika Soni(19,800)*
16. *DK Shivakumar*(135,800)
17. *Chidambaram*(8200)
18. *Manmohan Singh*(14,500)
19. *Lalu Prasad Yadav*(28,900)
20. *G Parameshwarappa* (9000)
21. *Kalanidi Maran(15,000)*
22. *A Raja(35,000)*
23. *Kanzhimoli*(5900)
24. *Rahul Gandhi*(189,008)
25. *Mayawathi*(168,009)
26. *Mamatha Benarjee* (257,500)
27. *Akhikesh Yadav* (300,089)
28. *Digvijay Singh* (220,060)
29. *Sashi Kala*(154,700)
30. *Karunanidhi*(12,870).

WikiLeaks published another list of black money holders in Swiss bank, as in 2019. The top most 24 members are as follows: (money is in crores; 1 crore = 100 million); they are all businessman.

1. *Ambani(568,000)*
2. *Adani(7800)*
3. *Amit Shah(158,000)*

4. Rajnath Singh(82,000)
5. *Arun Jaitley(15,040)*
6. Smriti Irani(28,900)
7. Yadiyurappa(9000)
8. *Ravi Shankar Guruji(15,000)*
9. Baba Ramdev(75,000)
10. Janard jana Reddy(50,000)
11. Nalin Kohli(5900)
12. Devendra Fadnavis(220,000)
13. Lalit Modi(76,888)
14. Sushma Swaraj(582,114)
15. *Narendra Modi(19,800)*
16. Harshad Mehta(135,800)
17. Ketan Parekh(8200)
18. Katta Subramanya Naidu(14,500)
19. Lalu Prasad Yadav(28,900)
20. J. M. Scindia(9000)
21. *Kalanidi Maran(15,000)*
22. *Karunanidi(35,000)*
23. Vasundhara Raje(5900)
24. Raj foundation(189,008)
25. N. Chandrbabu(168,009).

Another report from the highly reliable Bank of International Settlement in Switzerland said the following Table 2.6.

The data from the BIS is available from the year 1996. Going by this data, the liabilities of Swiss banks toward Indian non-banks had reached a peak of USD 8885 million in the year 2007, just before the global financial crisis. But following the global financial crisis, these liabilities had continuously decreased ever since except in the year 2013 when they increased marginally.

Contribution of Mauritius

In February 2008, R. Prasad, the then chairman of the Central Board of Direct Taxes (CBDT), led a team of tax sleuths to Port Louis, the capital city of Mauritius. Backed by a team from the ministry of external affairs, Prasad made an attempt to convince Mauritius officials to re-negotiate the

Table 2.6 Money in the Swiss banks from India (Millions of US$)

1996	5211
1997	4863
1999	5985
2004	5088
2005	5766
2006	7223
2007	8885
2008	8257
2011	3393
2012	2566
2013	2648
2014	2234
2015	1448
2016	800
2017	524

Source BIS, 2019

double tax avoidance agreement (DTAA), which was resulting in massive tax losses to India. Prasad's attempt was unsuccessful, but what he discovered in the process was startling: A handful of persons acted as directors for about 30,000 companies located in that island nation. Also, companies there exist only on paper, as addresses of many of those begin with a mere post box number.

Mauritius and many other tax havens act as buffers to bring back India's black money as white. Now, the Supreme Court-appointed Special Investigation Team (SIT) on black money wants such tax treaties to be redrafted. The government had to hand over to the apex court a complete list of 627 Indians who have accounts in HSBC Bank, Geneva.

While tax havens like Mauritius will help black money come back into the country as white, Indians continue to send illicit money abroad. This is done through various methods, 'Hawala' transactions—where money is transferred abroad without any real movement of funds—being one of them although, according to a finance ministry white paper on black money released two years ago, 'Hawala' transactions have actually dwindled over the past decade.

The classic example of such a hurdle is seen in the case of Pune-based stud farm-owner Hasan Ali Khan, who was raided by the I-T department seven years ago. Documents and data in his laptop established that he had a Swiss bank account with a whopping $8 billion in deposits. Ali was sent to jail, but the ED that probes money laundering cases found out from the Swiss authorities that Ali's accounts had been emptied (Table 2.7).

The maximum amount of money associated with a client connected to Mauritius was $24.2 million. Total amount from Swiss Bank HSBC was $141 million (Source: World Bank). Mauritius has been the biggest source of Foreign Domestic Investment in India over the last 15 years. In fact, Mauritius accounted for one-third of all inflows of investment into India over the last 15 years. In the same time, the US only accounted for 6.2% of investment.

Table 2.7 Top countries with dollar accounts in Swiss banks

1	Bahamas	$7B
2	Cayman Islands	$4.3B
3	India	$4.1B
4	Luxembourg	$2.9B
5	Panama	$2.8B
6	Liechtenstein	$2.6B
7	Guernsey	$2B
8	Monaco	$2B
9	Jersey	$2B
10	Suriname	$722.3 M
11	Bermuda	$609.1 M
12	Seychelles	$506.4 M
13	Isle of Man	$317.1 M
14	Antigua & Barbuda	$288.1 M
15	Mauritius	$141 M
16	St. Vincent	$48.7 M
17	Dominica	$40.9 M
18	Dominican Republic	$34.3 M
19	St. Kitts & Nevis	$19.5 M
20	Anguilla	$16 M
21	Réunion	$10.3 M
22	Macau	$8.8 M
23	Jamaica	$3.9 M
24	Guadeloupe	$3.6 M
25	Cape Verde *	$2 M
26	Turks & Caicos	$1 M
27	Guyana *	$64.8 K
28	Cook Islands	$215

Source BIS, HSBC; as in 2019; * means estimated

Why Mauritius Is more Important than Switzerland

Black money sent abroad is not the same as black money *held* abroad. Funds are moved out of India not to be stashed away in Swiss banks but to be brought back as foreign investment. In the case of India, this mostly happens through sham corporations registered in Mauritius. While the money comes back as investments, the earnings on such investments are not taxed in India because India and Mauritius have a double tax avoidance treaty.

The primacy of the small island to the subcontinent is apparent from this statistic: Between 2000 and 2012, 38% of the foreign direct investment in India came from Mauritius, while only 6% came from the US. Mauritius accounted for $8,059 million of $18,286 million of FDI in India in 2012–2013. If the government were serious about tackling the black economy in India, it would achieve more by closing the loopholes in the Mauritius route.

Forty percent of the total FDI coming into India comes from Mauritius. There is no taxation on capital gains in Mauritius, so that if an entity sets up a paper company there, our Double Taxation Avoidance (DTA) Agreement becomes in fact a double non-taxation agreement. Income Tax Department had the power to examine and verify whether the resident status of a company in Mauritius was genuine or not. The BJP government withdrew that power by Circular 789 of April 2000, under which a simple certification from the Mauritius government is now accepted. This means that India no longer has the power to question the residential status of a company there.

Mauritius-based funds investing in India get a tax breather. They have now been virtually exempt from the indirect transfer provisions of the income tax law.

The Finance Ministry has now specified 'Mauritius' as an eligible country for its funds to be registered with SEBI as category I foreign portfolio investor. The budget had exempted category I foreign portfolio investor from the ambit of indirect transfer provisions under income tax law. This move will benefit both regulated and unregulated funds domiciled in Mauritius.

Singapore has become an alternative to Mauritius. Shifting to Singapore will allow category II FPIs to escape the higher tax liability imposed on them in Mauritius. Foreign funds are making changes to their structures to reduce their tax outgo. India-focused funds that use Mauritius for favorable tax treatment are planning to route their funds through Singapore, another tax haven, to escape higher tax liability after the Union budget removed some exemptions for those based in Mauritius.

Shifting to Singapore will ensure that category II FPIs are not saddled with higher tax liability as the city state is still exempt from indirect transfer provisions. Mauritius made in 2019 ₹4.37 trillion worth of portfolio investments into India.

While a majority of foreign funds were exempted from indirect transfer provisions in 2017, the Finance Bill of 2020 has removed exemptions for category II FPIs, which include hedge funds, and funds that are set up in countries not compliant with the Financial Action Task Force (FATF) norms to combat money laundering and terror financing. Mauritius is not an FATF jurisdiction. The other big issue is the retrospective nature of the provisions. Investments made between September 2019 and 1 February 2020 by FPIs that don't fall in category I will also attract indirect transfer tax provisions.

The UK's Role

Investments routed through Mauritius are estimated to have cost India between $10bn and $15bn over the last 20 years in lost capital gains tax, dividends tax, and tax on interest and royalty payments. The system has been used by foreign investors, but also by Indian nationals, who essentially send their funds on a round trip.

Britain's overseas territories have topped a list of the world's most significant tax havens ahead of Switzerland, the Netherlands, and Luxembourg. The British Virgin Islands were ranked as the "greatest enabler of corporate tax abuse," with the Cayman Islands in second place and Bermuda third.

The United Arab Emirates (UAE) was a new entry into the top 10 after an investigation found it had benefited from $250bn (£180bn) of multinational funds routed through the Netherlands. The report said the UAE had emerged as a new destination for multinational corporations operating in Africa and the Middle East. South Africa was highlighted as one of the biggest losers from firms shifting profits to the low-tax UAE (Table 2.8).

Table 2.8 Top 10 biggest enablers of global corporate tax abuse (as in 2019)

1	British Virgin Islands (British overseas territory)
2	Cayman Islands (British overseas territory)
3	Bermuda (British overseas territory)
4	Netherlands
5	Switzerland
6	Luxembourg
7	Hong Kong
8	Jersey (British crown dependency)
9	Singapore
10	United Arab Emirates

Global Alliance for Tax Justice wrote, "the biggest economies in the world were helping companies avoid $245billion in tax," and "to trust the OECD in light of its findings is like trusting a pack of wolves to build a fence around your chicken coop." OECD countries were responsible for 39% of the world's corporate tax abuse risks. Their territories and former colonies—such as the UK's independent territories and Jersey, Guernsey and the Isle of Man, which are crown dependencies—were responsible for 29%. Countries graded by the OECD as "not harmful" are responsible for 98% of the world's corporate tax abuses risks. Britain's overseas territories and crown dependencies continued to facilitate capital flight from many of the world's poorest nations, allowing multinational corporations to avoid legitimate claims on their profits (Fig. 2.1).

The total amount of black money deposited in foreign banks by Indians is unknown. Some reports claim a total of US$1.06–$1.4 trillions is held illegally in Switzerland (in Wiki leak); other reports, including

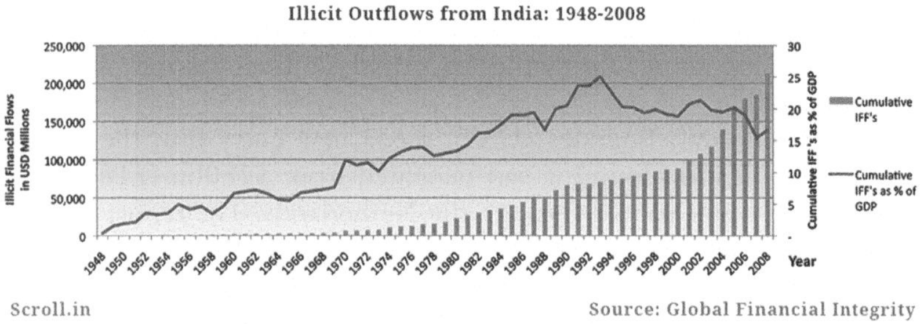

Fig. 2.1 Illicit outflows from India: 1984–2008

those reported by the Swiss Bankers Association and the Government of Switzerland, claim these reports are false and fabricated, and the total amount held in all Swiss bank accounts by citizens of India is about US$2 billion. In February 2012, the director of India's Central Bureau of Investigation said that Indians have US$500 billion of illegal funds in foreign tax havens, more than any other country. In March 2012, the Government of India clarified in its parliament that the CBI director's statement on $500 billion of illegal money was an estimate based on a statement made to India's Supreme Court in July 2011. In March 2018, it was revealed that the amount of Indian black money currently present in Swiss and other offshore banks is estimated to be US$1.5 trillion. As per data released by the Department of Industrial Policy and Promotion (DIPP), two of the topmost sources of the cumulative inflows from April 2000 to March 2011 are Mauritius (41.80 percent, US$54.227 billions) and Singapore (9.17 percent, US$11.895 billions). It is obvious that tax evaders routed through these money in order to conceal from revenue authorities.

Investment in the Indian stock market through participatory notes (PNs) or overseas derivative instruments (ODIs) is other ways in which the black money generated by Indians is re-invested in India. The investor in PNs is legally held by the Foreign Institutions Investors, like Foreign Pension Funds, Gold imports through official channel and smuggling is a major conduit to bring back the black money from abroad and convert into local black money as the gold commands high demand among the rural investors particularly. Also fictitious high value round trip transactions, by diamonds and precious stones exporters and importers, are a channel for transactions. Also, fictitious software exports can be booked by software companies to bring black money into India.

In February 2015, balances for the year 2006–07 in HSBC's Geneva branch were obtained by French newspaper Le Monde and included the names of several prominent businessmen, diamond traders, and politicians. The balance against the 1195 names stood at US$3.6 billion.

The 2016 Panama Papers were obtained by International Consortium of Investigative Journalists, originally from Mossack Fonseca, a Panama-based law firm with offices in more than 35 countries. The list had names of 500 Indians such as Amitabh Bachchan, Aishwarya Rai, Niira Radia, K. P. Singh, Garware family, Harish Salve, and others.

WTO-induced privatization of public assets generated these gigantic flows of illegal monies from India. However, India is not the only country in this matter. One has to blame corruptions, lax administration, and implicit support from the developed countries along with the drive to comply with the WTO's agenda for a market economy.

Role of Dubai and the UAE

While the vast majority of financial, business, and real estate transactions in Dubai are not associated with illegal activity, part of what underpins Dubai's prosperity is a steady stream of illicit proceeds borne from corruption and crime. Dubai is now a major gold trading hub. Meanwhile, both Emirati leaders and the international community continue to turn a blind eye to the problematic behaviors, administrative loopholes, and weak enforcement practices that make Dubai a globally attractive destination for dirty money (Cornwell, 2020a, b).

Corrupt and criminal actors from around the world operate through or from Dubai. Afghan warlords, Russian mobsters, Nigerian kleptocrats, European money launderers, Iranian sanctions-busters, and East African gold smugglers, all find Dubai a conducive place to operate. Dubai's property market is a magnet for tainted money. Built to attract foreign buyers, the emirate is dominated by towers of upscale flats and man-made islands studded with luxury villas. Now, one of the world's largest gold hubs, Dubai is also a place to launder illegally mined gold, especially from conflict-prone parts of East and Central Africa. Opaque business practices and regulatory loopholes allow this laundered gold to enter world markets on a massive scale. With approximately thirty free trade zones, Dubai is a haven for trade-based money laundering. Operating with minimal regulatory oversight or customs enforcement, these zones allow businesses to disguise the proceeds of crime via the over- and under-invoicing of goods, multiple invoicing, and falsifying of other trade documentation (Vittori, 2021).

The Central Government of the United Arab Emirates (UAE), Dubai officials, and Emirati law enforcement agencies largely possess the technical knowledge and capacity to tackle these challenges. Emirati regulators, officials, and law enforcement agents are aware of how Dubai is being used as a conduit for illicit financial transactions. Dubai and the UAE are strategically important to the US, UK, and other countries. In its April 2020 report on the UAE, the intergovernmental Financial Action Task Force (FATF) specifically called out Dubai for its limited number of money laundering prosecutions and convictions. The European Commission said in 2020 that it would place the United Arab Emirates on the EU's anti-money laundering and counter-terrorist financing list if it has not made significant progress in the fight against money laundering and terror financing by June 2021. Currently, the UAE is in a probationary period after the European Financial Action Task Force (FATF) identified several shortcomings.

We provide below a typical example of these illicit activities. Members of the royal families of Saudi Arabia, Kuwait, and the United Arab Emirates reportedly helped launder funds from the Malaysian MDB (Malaysia Development Berhad) through their sovereign wealth funds and state-owned enterprises, apparently with help from certain Western banks. Chinese officials then allegedly offered to help bail out the Malaysian prime minister at the center of the scandal, Najib Razak, in return for Chinese stakes in various railway and pipeline projects—a charge the Chinese government denies. Moldova is the poorest country in Europe, and yet between $20 billion and $80 billion allegedly was laundered through its banks from 2010 to 2014. According to reporting by the Organized Crime and Corruption Reporting Project (OCCRP), shell companies were created in the UK, Cyprus, and New Zealand in which a fake "lender" company would use a Moldovan court to collect debts from a defaulting fake Russian "debtor." The Russian shell company would then allegedly wire the money through a Moldovan bank to accounts of the "lender" in a bank in Latvia; from there, the funds were wired to 5,140 companies in 96 countries. Although the US, UK, and European Union could have done more to help prevent this immense theft, it nonetheless demonstrates how weaker jurisdictions like Moldova and Latvia can be used for massive money laundering scenarios (Ford, 2020).

WTO and Inequality

Illegal money transfer is the direct result of privatization and the drive to create a market economy as desired by the WTO. That has caused extreme in equality. In India, privatization has started in 1993 under the instruction of IMF-World Bank, and it was intensified after the WTO was created. The WTO wants to create a worldwide market economy as a part of the Washington Consensus. Market system automatically creates inequality, as the market is ruthless to distribute resources to them who by any means can control the resources in a fully privatized economy.

The result can be extreme inequality. In India, 10 percent of the people control 77 percent of the resources of the country. In the US, 1 percent can control more than 90 percent of the resources. The dominance of large corporations in global markets has implications for how trade policy affects inequality. The gains from international trade are most frequently captured by large corporations, often at the expense of small enterprises, women entrepreneurs, rural agriculturists, and fisheries. Such small organizations face various obstacles to gain from the international trade, including limited information, lack of financing, prohibitive entry costs, and underrepresentation in trade policy decision-making. Small firms are thus often unable to compete with larger foreign corporations, as the latter have the capacities to overcome such obstacles by influencing the politicians to monopolize competitive advantages.

Trade policy also increases inequality through market access and entry conditions. International trade is increasingly regulated through non-tariff measures, like legal restrictions, which affect most traded goods and have a greater influence on trade than tariffs. Product standard based on health criteria restricts exports from countries that lack quality control and appropriate infrastructure. Such non-tariff measures influence international trade and can have serious effects on inequality, both within and between countries.

International trade can further affect inequality by promoting structural transformation. It has been instrumental in the transformation of many unplanned countries in East Asia from agricultural to manufacturing economies. This process has contributed to the creation of a thriving middle class in many emerging newly industrialized countries but at the same time destruction of the rural economies. Farmers became unskilled workers in the city often doing menial works. This has further intensified within country income inequality. A planned economy in place of a market economy would be the solution, but the WTO is totally against planning.

Today, developing countries have been completely ignored by the economic and political interests of global powers. We provide below some examples.

Cotton: It is well known that subsidies paid to rich-country producers in the past 10 years has created obstacles for the 15 million cotton farmers across West Africa trying to trade their way out of poverty, and how 5 million of the world's poorest farming families have been forced out of business and into deeper poverty because of those subsidies. Cotton farmers in India often commit suicides as they cannot get the price to cover their cost of production.

Agricultural subsidies: WTO members have failed to reduce the huge subsidies paid to rich farmers of the developed countries, whose overproduction continues to threaten the livelihoods of farmers in the developing countries. Yet these developed countries insist to eliminate public subsidies and price supports in country like India, where the government is trying to introduce market system in agriculture by eliminating all public supports.

Trade agreements: The WTO has allowed the developing countries to be manipulated by the developed countries. In Africa, in negotiations with the EU, countries are forced to eliminate tariffs on up to 90% of their trading items because there are no clear rules to protect them.

Medicine: The poorest in developing countries are unable to have affordable medicine because members have refused to relax TRIPS agreement even in protect public health during the recent pandemic to protect the intellectual property rights of pharmaceutical companies. India, South Africa, and 100 other developing countries made an appeal recently in view of coronavirus to the WTO to relax the TRIPS rules but are disappointed.

Legal costs: In the first 15 years of dispute settlement under the WTO, 400 cases have been initiated. No African country had any access. Only one least developed country filed a claim.

Protectionist economic policies: The WTO has failed in its global economic policy-making, as it could do nothing against the highly protectionist China and some developed countries in Europe.

Natural disaster: The WTO fails to support developing countries during and after a natural disasters.

Decision-making: The WTO makes most of its decisions by consensus and achieving consensus between 153 countries is nearly impossible. Small and poor developing countries have hardly a voice in the trade negotiations.

The WTO has failed to control China, which ignores most of the rules and the WTO is unable to do anything about that. The WTO should not insist on a market economy while a number of countries do not follow the rules of the market economy in spirit. Planning, social action, and public policy also should be allowed to have their role to create one of the genuine cooperations, not ruthless heartless competition.

Comments

Since the end of the Uruguay Round, developed countries and China have refused consistently to deliver on their reciprocal response to the developing countries. As a result, the multilateral trading system is full of double standards that favor the business interests of the developed countries and China undermining the economic and social development requirements of the developing countries. Doha declaration in 2001 provided an opportunity for the WTO and the developed countries to demonstrate that they are serious about poverty reduction. The developed countries should have addressed the incomplete agendas of the Uruguay Round rather than expanding the WTO agenda to include new issues on investment, patent laws, and competition policy. However, the Doha declaration failed because the developed countries have not changed their attitude. Bali declaration of 2014 was a total victory for the developed countries. Although the declaration was opposed by some of the developing countries, their objections were ignored. Hypocrisy and double standards in the WTO have prevailed over the concern for poorer countries. This has undermined the efforts of poorer countries to apply trade for development. It threatens the credibility of the multilateral trading system as designed by the WTO, where privatization and market system dominate.

Appendix

Globalization and Killing Through Vaccines

Bill Gates is one of the very important supporters of globalization and of China. However, recently, he became a hate figure despite of his self-advertised charities. At present, he is in a minority elite group, but given their power and money, in future, this group can be very influential. The purpose is to reduce the world population.

Climate change movement is part of it. The argument is that given the limited resources of the world, if the population can be reduced, there will be less demand for resources and climate can be protected. It is a part of the Eugenics movement, to reduce those people who are undesirable, like tribal, non-white, non-Christian, and uneducated. Bill Gates and his like-minded people in the Davos, Switzerland-based World Economic Forum, have the same objectives. Bill Gates is developing vaccines, which will not work but will create more diseases, which cannot be cured but definitely can kill people or turn them into vegetables.

In India

In 2012, Kalpana Mehta and others took a criminal complaint against Bill Gates, World Health Organization, Gates Foundation, PATH (Program for Appropriate Technology in Health), and GAVI (Global Alliance for Vaccines and Immunization).

The petition states: BMGF, PATH, and WHO were criminally negligent trailing the vaccines on a vulnerable, uneducated, and under-informed population, school administrators, students, and their parents who were not provided informed consent or advised of potential adverse effects or required to be monitored post-vaccination.

A report published in the Economic Times, on August 2014, said that in 2009 tests were carried out on 16,000 tribal schoolchildren in Andhra Pradesh, India, using the human papilloma virus (HPV) vaccines named Gardasil. Many of the children fell ill and 5 of them died. In Vadodara, Gujarat, another HPV vaccine, Cervarix, manufactured by Glaxo-Smith-Kline was used on another 14,000 tribal children, where 2 of them died afterward. Consent forms were obtained illegally where consents were given by the wardens of the hostels where these girls were staying or by thumb impressions by their illiterate parents.

A government organization, SAMA, had investigated and found out that the effects of these vaccination were heavy bleeding, severe menstrual cramps, and deaths among these girls, which were dismissed by some state government investigation committees as unrelated to the vaccination program (Washington Post, article by J.Rogin, 30 April, 2020).

The WHO, BMGF, International Federation of Gynecology and Obstetrics, and the Federation of Obstetrics and Gynecological Societies of India have all recommended these vaccines as effective preventive measures for cervical cancer. These vaccines are licensed in India, as said by the BMGF.

In Africa

In December 2012, about 500 children in a village named Gouro, in Chad, were forced to accept Meningitis vaccine without any consent from their parents. Within hours, they started suffering from vomiting, convulsions, and paralysis. Because the village is remote, doctors came after one week but they could do nothing. Each family of these children was given $1000 as compensation. This was reported in a local newspaper La Voix. That project was organized by BMGF. According to it, Menafrivac was a tremendous success in Africa. WHO and PATH supported this program (Daily News, article by D.Mathews, 15 April, 2020).

In Pakistan

According to a government investigation, published in Express Tribune, the vaccination program created by BMGF and GOVI was causing death and paralysis. These vaccines are polio vaccine and Pentavalent vaccine. These vaccines were untested but used in Pakistani villages (Huffington Post, article by Kathryn Joyce, 12 May, 2020).

Dr. Neetu Vashist and Dr. Jacob Piliyel of Department of Pediatrics of St. Stephens Hospital in New Delhi, in Pharmabiz.com, wrote that incident of non-polio acute flaccid paralysis (NPAFP) increased many folds in areas where many doses of vaccine were used. NPAFP is not distinguishable from polio paralysis but twice as deadly. It was considered as unethical by the Indian Journal of Medical Ethics (War on Want, report 17 April, 2014; Economic Times, article by N. Kumar, 31 Aug, 2014).

References

Alden, E. (2019, May/June). *Global governance & global gains: What went wrong?* Japan Spotlight.

Baldwin, R. (2016). *The great convergence*. Cambridge: Harvard University Press.

Brown, E. (2019, April 29) *Monsanto, Bayer, and the push for corporate cannabis*. Counter Punch. http://www.counterpunch.org.

Cornwell, A. (2020a, April 29). UAE doing to little to stem money laundering and terrorist finance: Watchdog. *Reuters*. https://www.reuters.com/article/us-emirates-financing/uae-doing-too-little-to-stem-money-laundering-and-terrorist-finance-watchdog-idUSKBN22B3CF.

Cornwell, A. (2020b, April 30). *United Arab emirates' measures to combat money laundering and terrorist financing*. http://www.fatf-gafi.org/publications/mutualevaluations/documents/mer-uae-2020.html.

Culter, W., & Doyle, K. (2019, January 21). China's developing country status in the WTO: time for an upgrade? *East Asia Forum*. http://www.eastasiaf

orum.org/2019/01/21/chinas-developing-country-status-in-the-wto-time-for-an-upgrade/.

Engdahl, W. (2007). *Seeds of destruction*. Wiesbaden: Global Research.

Engdahl, W. (2008, June). The seed barons. How big AG, big oil & big government are Hijacking the world's food supply. *Acres USA a Voice for Eco-Agriculture*, 38, no. 6.

Engdahl , W. (2020). *AGRA and the UN food systems summit*. New Eastern Outlook. https://journal-neo.org.

Felbermayr , G., Larch, M., Erdal, Y., & Yoto, Y. (2020). *On the heterogeneous trade and welfare effects of GATT/WTO membership* (School of Economics Working Paper Series 2020–12), Drexel University, Chicago.

Ford , M. (2020). *Dubai's free trade zones under examination by GFI*. https://gfintegrity.orgt/free-for-all-zones-the-case-of-Dubai.

Kamdar, B., & Das, S. (2021, March 13). *Women and Indian new agricultural laws*. The Conversation.

Lamy, P., & Mehta, P. S. (2019). https://www.thewire.in/trade/what-should-the-role-of-g-20-countries-be-in-reforming-the-wto.

McKinsey Global Institute. (2019). *Globalization in transition*. New York, USA: McKinsey.

Oxfam Report on WTO, Eight Broken Promises, file:///G:/WTO%205%20OXFAM%20report.pdf.

Rashish, P., & Tamura, A.. (2018). *Mitigating the adjustment costs of international trade*. http://www.economics-ejournal.org/economics/discussionpapers/2018-49.

Rashish, P., & Tamura, A. (2019). *Crisis in world trade*. Tokyo: Asian development Bank.

Rodrik, D. (2016). *Straight talk on trade*. New York: WW Norton.

Rodrik, D. (2012). *The globalization paradox*. Oxford: Oxford University Press.

Todhunter, C. (2019a, April 29). On independence day, India's new rulers are the World Bank, IMF, WTO and Monsanto. *The Ecologist*. http://www.theecologist.org.

Todhunter, C. (2019b, April 29). *Poisoned agriculture: Depopulation and human extinction*. Counter Punch. http://www.counterpunch.org.

Todhunter, C. (2019c, April 30). *Monsanto In India: Meet the new boss—Same as the old boss?* Counter Currents. http://www.countercurrents.org.

UNCTAD. (2017). *Trade and development report*. New York: UNCTAD.

Vander Stichle , M. (1997). *Globalisation, marginalisation and the WTO*. Transnational Institute.

Vittori, J. (2021). *Illicit financial flows in authoritarian states*. Washington, DC: Carnegie International.

Wallach, L. (2019, November 28). What should replace it? Two decades after Seattle, it has failed to deliver on its promises. *The New York Times*.

World Bank. (2014). *World Integrated Trade Solution*. Washington, DC: The World Bank.

Zeneli, V., & Czinkota, M. (2019, February 11). WTO as a reflection of emerging 'new' world order. *The Diplomat*.

CHAPTER 3

Empire of China

The winner of the new international business order is China, which has dominated the markets of most of the developed countries. The result of that victory also has promoted Chinese imperialism in Asia. This chapter analyzes the history of some of the victims of China.

China's geopolitical strategy is to use their competitive advantage of soft power to out-maneuver the US, and other countries such as India, Japan, Vietnam, or the Philippines, in acquiring natural resources and to allow for continued growth of their economy while gaining political influence in various countries and regions throughout the world.

China's application of unrestricted warfare is apparent when the security and military aspects of China's involvement in Afghanistan are examined. China enjoys protection of its projects in Afghanistan because of its close relationship with Pakistan. This implies that Pakistan's national intelligence agency, Inter-Services Intelligence Directorate, or ISI, exerts its influence over the Taliban to allow the Chinese projects to continue unimpeded. While Chinese workers in Afghanistan have been attacked, the level of violence is very low when compared to attacks on the US, India, and UN personnel and facilities.

It is unlikely that there will be peaceful development of China overall, as there appears to be no desire for peace and stability, but rather a development of good, old-fashioned militarism and imperialism. In the first place, the economic 'miracle' of the Chinese economy is based on the

© The Author(s), under exclusive license to Springer Nature Switzerland AG 2021

D. Basu and V. Miroshnik, *The Economic and Political Dangers of Globalization*, https://doi.org/10.1007/978-3-030-79895-6_3

fierce exploitation of its working class and farmers, and on an export drive to destroy the manufacturing capacity of most of the countries of the world by offering cheap debt facility and cheaper manufactured products. The economic colonization accompanied by a strong geopolitical strategy to project Chinese power, both military and financial, is the building blocks for the new Chinese empire, in which the new international business order is facilitating the Chinese expansion.

Since China resumed its threats against Taiwan, India, Vietnam and the Philippines, and increasingly threatened Japan, both France and Germany have been trying to overturn the arms embargo on the People's Liberation Army for purely commercial reasons. That demonstrates the influence of Chinese finances and the lure of the Chinese markets for the European powers.

To the south of China, the country is largely underwriting the construction and development of a 1850 km network of roads, rivers, and ports in Vietnam and Laos, circumventing the natural defensive barriers of the foothills of the Himalayas in India, which will directly connect Chinese Kunming to Thailand. That facilitates the movement of the Chinese military to the South East Asia region whenever it needs and provides markets and natural resources for the Chinese economy.

Around India and Pakistan to the west of China, within the framework of Chinese imperialism major development is also occurring. As the US and India enjoy an increasingly warmer relationship, Pakistan will probably look closer to China for technical and military assistance. China already supplies Pakistan with nuclear technology, including nuclear weapons.

According to the Asian Studies department at the Brooking Institute, the nuclear program in Pakistan is essentially the result of Sino–Pakistani relations. Some news agency reports suggest that Chinese security agencies knew of the transfer of nuclear technology from Pakistan to Iran. Worldanalysis.net shows that one of the most significant recent projects is the construction of a major port complex at the naval base of Gwadar on the Arabian Sea, giving China strategic access to the Persian Gulf and a naval outpost on the Indian Ocean.

Relations between China and India deteriorated after India gave refuge to the Dalai Lama in 1959, followed by India's humiliating defeat in the 1962 war over a disputed border, and Chinese aid to Pakistan. India still claims that China occupies 38,000 square kilometer of its territories and, for its part, Beijing still lays claim to the northeastern Indian province of Arunachal Pradesh.

China's recent demand that Arunachal Pradesh of India is a part of China has provoked a very adverse reaction from the government of India and the Indian media in general. Once again, India has failed to turn the tables against China. India should have said, China has no border with India at all, but Tibet has. By not recognizing the fact that China is occupying Tibet illegally India has once again, in practice, accepted the Chinese occupation of Tibet, Manchuria and Eastern Turkistan or the Pakistani occupations of Baluchistan and NWFP (North West Frontier Province).

There is no evidence that Tibet was a part of China before China colonized it in 1949. The same is true of Taiwan and Eastern Turkistan. If the Manchus are not Chinese, as Sun Yat Sen declared in 1911, Manchuria, which China received as a gift from Stalin in 1950, was never a part of China either. However, the world has ignored this Chinese imperialism, and even gives recognition to China as being one of the five controlling powers of the world affairs as a permanent member of the UN Security Council.

China has no continuous history as a nation-state. Before 1279, only the central part of what is China today was pure Chinese—that is, inhabited by the Han Chinese tribe. During 1279–1368, China was a part of the Mongol empire and it ceased to exist as a sovereign state. From 1368 to 1644, China had the Ming Dynasty of the Han Chinese tribe, but was occupied by the Manchus in 1644 until 1911.

Chinese Empire of Tibet

Tibet has a history of at least 1300 years of independence. The first recorded contacts between Tibetans and Chinese date back to the seventh century, following the unification of Tibet under King Songtsen Gampo and the marriage of a Chinese princess to Songtsen Gampo in 641. This marriage alliance was sought after Tibetan armies had captured towns in Sichuan province. In 821, a treaty recognizing them as two independent nations ended almost 200 years of war between China and Tibet.

During the thirteenth and fourteenth centuries both China and Tibet came under the influence of the Mongol empire. The Mongol's militarily conquered China while the Tibetans and the Mongols established the historically unique 'priest patron' relationship, also known as CHO-YON. The Mongol aristocracy had converted to Buddhism and they sought spiritual guidance and moral legitimacy for the rule of their vast empire from the Tibetan theocracy. As the patrons of Tibet, the Mongols promised to protect Tibet against foreign invasion. The Mongol empire came to an end in the mid-fourteenth century. Today parts of Mongolia, which is not occupied by China, is an independent country, not a part of China and Mongols are not Chinese. By the fifteenth century, political authority in Tibet had passed into the hands of contending religious hegemonies that were eventually replaced by a system of rule under the Dalai Lamas. In China, the native Ming Dynasty overthrew the Mongols. During the Ming Dynasty both Tibet and China existed as separate and fully sovereign states.

Tibet and the British

The British, after 1911, convened a tripartite conference to discuss Tibet's border with the British India in Simla in 1914 (Aitchison, 1929). The Tibetans arrived at the conference with written proof of Tibet's historical independence. The Chinese delegation—present only to witness the treaty between Britain and Tibet—argued that Tibet's subjugation by the Mongols and the Manchus became an integral part of China, and should therefore be ruled as part of the new Republic of China of Sun Yat Sen from Peking. That was also the beginning of the border dispute between China and India. However, although Tibet was not really subjugated by the Mongols and Manchus, it was certainly influenced by them. Neither Mongols nor Manchus were Chinese. In fact, China itself had been occupied for a long time by both the Mongols and the Manchus (van Walt van Praag, 1987).

The fact that both Tibet and China came under Mongol political influence does not indicate unification of the two countries, as China claims. Iraq, Turkey, most parts of Russia and Eastern Europe, the Indian subcontinent, northern Burma, north Vietnam and Korea were all part of the vast Mongol empire. Would that mean these areas belong to China? British India included Burma until very recently. The British Empire also used to control Sri Lanka, Malaysia, Iraq, and Burma. Does that mean India should now legitimately claim Sri Lanka, Iraq, Malaysia, and Burma as its integral parts? Such is the absurdity of the Chinese claim. The most important point is that Manchus, like Mongols, are not ethnic Chinese and suggestions that Tibet became an integral part of a 'Chinese' empire during the Manchu empire are just absurd. Tibet continued to conduct itself as a fully sovereign nation, recognized by the British empire until its occupation by Communist China in 1949 (van Walt van Praag, 1987).

Today however, China disputes the legal status of the Simla Convention and the resultant McMahon line—the border between India and Tibet accepted by the British, the true significance of which lies in its recognition of Tibet as an independent nation with which binding agreements such as the Lhasa Treaty of 1904 could be negotiated. Throughout the Nationalist (Kuomintang) period from 1912 to 1949, no Chinese government was able to exert any influence over Tibet. During the Second World War, Tibet remained neutral, despite strong pressure from the US, Britain, and China to allow the passage of raw materials through the country. When Nepal applied for membership of the UN in 1949, it cited its treaty and diplomatic relations with Tibet to demonstrate its full international personality (van Walt van Praag, 1987).

Chinese Invasion of Tibet

The invasion of Tibet by troops from the People's Liberation Army in 1949–1950 is described in official Chinese histories as a 'peaceful liberation'. The Seventeen-Point Plan for the Peaceful Liberation of Tibet (1951) was signed between the Communist Government and Tibetan officials in May 1951, which apparently 'enjoyed the approval and support of the people from every ethnic group in Tibet' (Information Office of the State Council of The People's Republic of China, 1992). If Tibet was part of China, then there was no need for the agreement, which was forced upon the Tibetan delegation in China for signature, and then China announced to the world that Tibet was liberated.

Human Rights Violations in Tibet by China

> In fact, discrimination and the suppression of traditional practices in eastern Tibet drove hundreds of Tibetans up into the mountains to conduct guerrilla warfare, while thousands more fled west to Lhasa to escape Chinese persecution. In March 1959, growing Tibetan resistance exploded in an uprising against the Chinese occupation. The 14th Dalai Lama fled into exile in northern India, and the subsequent Chinese crackdown in Tibet

> was brutal. ... Tibetan sources suggest as many as 430,000 were killed in the Uprising and subsequent years of guerrilla warfare (Tibet Support Group, 1994).

From 1951 to 1959 China broke every promise that it made toward Tibet, resulting in the Tibetan uprising against China in March 1959. The Dalai Lama and 100,000 Tibetans escaped into exile. From that day onward, Tibet effectively became an occupied country.

Despite promising not to get involved with the existing system of government and society in Tibet by signing the Seventeen-Point Plan for the Peaceful Liberation of Tibet, China did interfere in eastern Tibet—reneging on the treaty altogether in 1959. China has renamed two of Tibet's three provinces as parts of the Chinese provinces of Qinghai, Gansu, Sichuan and Yunnan, and has renamed the remaining province of U' Tsang as Tibet Autonomous Region (TAR). On October 28, 1991, US Congress under a Foreign Authorization Act passed the resolution wherein they recognized 'Tibet, including those areas incorporated into the Chinese provinces of Sichuan, Yunnan, Gansu and Qinghai, AN OCCUPIED COUNTRY under the established principal of international law'. The resolution further stated that Tibet's true representatives are the Dalai Lama and the Tibetan government in exile as recognized by the Tibetan people (US State Department Authorization Act, 1991).

Some 1.2 million Tibetans are estimated to have been killed by the Chinese since 1950. Reprisals for the 1959 National Uprising alone involved the elimination of 87,000 Tibetans by the Chinese count, according to a Radio Lhasa broadcast of 1 October 1960. Tibetan exiles claim that 430,000 died during the Uprising and the subsequent 15 years of guerrilla warfare. In its 1959 and 1960 reports, the International Commission of Jurists concluded that 'there was a prima facie case of genocide committed by the Chinese upon the Tibetan nation'. These reports consider events before the Cultural Revolution of Mao-Tse-Tung, during which much of Tibet's own cultural assets were destroyed and thousands of Tibetans killed (Tibet Support Group, 1994).

Up to 260,000 people died in prisons and labor camps between 1950 and 1984. Since September 1987, approximately 3,000 people are believed to have been imprisoned for political offenses such as giving out leaflets, writing letters, or talking to foreigners about the Tibetans' right to independence. From March 1989 to May 1990, the Chinese administered a campaign of torture against Tibetan dissidents in prison.

During 1994–1995, three nuns died shortly after release from custody as a result of ill treatment and torture in detention. Beatings and torture are still regularly used against political prisoners today. Detainees are held in sub-standard conditions, malnourished, forbidden to talk, denied medical treatment, and often held in solitary confinement. According to the Tibet Support Group (1994), 'The Chinese have refused to allow independent observers to attend so-called public trials. Prison sentences are regularly decided before the trial. Less than 2% of cases in China are won by the defense'.

Tibetan was replaced by Chinese as the official language and despite official pronouncements there was no practical change in this policy. It is difficult for Tibetans to gain employment in the state sector without proficiency in Chinese. Secondary school children are taught all classes in Chinese. Religious practice was forcibly suppressed until 1979, and up to 6,000 monasteries and shrines were destroyed. In 1995 the Chinese authorities rejected the child recognized by the Dalai Lama as the rebirth of the Panchen Lama, and installed their own candidate. There are an estimated 300,000 troops stationed on Tibetan territory and three nuclear missile sites. Near Lake Kokonor, the largest lake on the Tibetan plateau, there is a 20-square kilometer dump for radioactive pollutants and China has admitted depositing nuclear waste (Tibet Support Group, 1994).

Demographic Change in Tibet

China is filling up Tibet with ethnic Han Chinese in an attempt to destroy the ethnicity of the Tibetans. This policy has much more potential to destroy Tibet as a nation than the millions who have died from Chinese policies, the destruction of more than 6,000 Buddhist monasteries, the arrest and torture of Tibetan monks, the destruction of Tibetan forests, and the stationing of nuclear weapons and waste dumps in Tibet.

Samdhong Rinpoche, the Prime Minister of the Tibetan government in exile, estimates that seven million ethnic Chinese now live in Tibet, where there are only 2.3 million Tibetans. In towns like Lhasa and Chengdu, 75 percent of the people are ethnic Chinese. According to the Tibet Support Group (1994), it was this influx of Chinese nationals that destabilized the economy. Forced agricultural modernizations in Tibet were the cause of extensive crop failures and the country's first recorded famine (1960–1962), in which 340,000 Tibetans died. Tibetan farms and grazing lands have been confiscated and incorporated into collectivized and communal farms.

The resettlement of Chinese migrants has led to Tibetans becoming the minority in many areas, including Lhasa. This in turn has created high unemployment among Tibetans. Official figures put the number of non-Tibetans in the TAR (Tibet Autonomous Region) at 79,000. Independent research puts the figure at 250,000–300,000, and for the whole of Tibet 5–5.5 million Chinese to 4.5 million Tibetans. In Kham and Amdo the Chinese outnumber Tibetans many times over.

As with previous railways built by China in Mongolia and East Turkistan, the more recently built Tibet railway would greatly speed colonization of the area. The railway will improve China's military maneuverability, enable rapid troop deployments, and facilitate the expansion of People's Liberation Army bases and increases in nuclear weapons stockpiles and missile deployments on the Tibetan plateau (Terril, 2003).

China's Empire in East Turkistan

East Turkistan, another colony of China, is bordered by Kazakhstan to the north, Tibet and India to the south, and Afghanistan and Pakistan to the West. It is China's largest province of 640,000 square kilometers—one-sixth of the present Chinese territory. However, it was not a part of China until 1949 and the people of that land are not Chinese either. About 96 percent of its population are Turkic peoples of Tajik, Kyrghyz, Uzbek, or Kazakh, similar to their relatives in the former Soviet Union, commonly known as Uyghurs. The invasion of East Turkistan by the Han Chinese started in 104 BC, and the country was occupied several times by Chinese soldiers, but none of these occupations lasted for long. There were six invasions from 104 BC to 751 AD, but during that period the Chinese invaders sustained their control for only 157 years. Arab, Turkic, and Tibetan forces repulsed the Chinese occupiers in 751 AD. East Turkistan later became a part of the Mongol empire briefly. In 1876, the Manchu empire occupied East Turkistan. The people in the southern part of East Turkistan established an Eastern Turkistan Islamic Republic in 1933 and then, in 1944, established the second Eastern Turkistan Republic (Castes, 2003; Yu, 2018).

East Turkistan was occupied by China in 1949 and its name was changed to Xing Kiang in 1955. Communist China has been exercising a colonial rule over the land since then. The people there, just like the people in two other colonies of China in Tibet and Manchuria, have to undergo unimaginable suffering and have been subjugated to inhuman conditions under the repressive alien rule. The year 1999 saw mass arrests and murders of the people of East Turkistan become most widespread. This policy was especially sinister in the regions of Hotan, Kashgar, Aksu, and Ili. As recently as 1999, somc 2500 were killed. According to Amnesty International, currently at least 250,000 people are in prison.

Chinese Empire of Manchuria

In 1639, the 5th Dalai Lama established another CHO-YON relationship with the Manchu Emperor, who, driven out of Manchuria by the Russians, occupied China and established the Manchu Dynasty in 1644. Manchu officials or *Ann bans* were stationed in Tibet from 1728 until the fall of the dynasty in 1911. *Ann bans* were instructed not to interfere in the internal policies of Tibet and to refrain from exploitation. In 1911, Sun Yat Sen declared Manchus to be foreigners, deposed the Manchu Emperor of China Pei Wei and proclaimed China to be a republic.

Manchuria had been a Russian territory since the sixteenth century. Russia had developed industrial cities like Harbin in Manchuria and Port Arthur in Korea. The settlement of Han Chinese in Manchuria was prohibited until late into the nineteenth century. In 1905, Japan according to the Portsmouth Treaty took over Manchuria from Russia but allowed some pro-Japanese warlords of China to rule over it from 1918. In 1931, Japan took complete control over Manchuria, renamed it Manchuko, re-established Pei Wei as the sovereign Emperor of China and in his name they tried to occupy the rest of China. The Soviet Union took over Manchuria in 1945 after the surrender of Japan to the US, but gave it away to China in 1950 without any consideration for the wishes of the people in Manchuria. Despite claims of Chinese propaganda, millions of non-Chinese people living in areas presently under the People's Republic of China suffer all kinds of discrimination. The most disturbing effect of Chinese policy toward people in these areas is the demographic transformation that has been imposed upon them. In virtually every area, new Chinese immigrants have become the majority community. Manchuria has been completely absorbed and the distinct Manchu culture that was vibrant until 1949 does not exist at all anymore.

China's False Claim on Formosa

In 1949, Kuomintang forces of Chiang-Kei-Seik defeated by Mao-Tse-Tung invaded Formosa. They massacred the local population, who are not ethnic Chinese but a mixed population of Japanese, Chinese, Portuguese, and the indigenous proto-Malays (Schaeffer & Tuttle, 2012). However, now China claims that Formosa, renamed as Taiwan, is an inalienable part of China and China wants to reclaim it as soon as possible. History cannot support that Chinese claim.

From 1368 to 1644, China had the Ming Dynasty of the Chin or Han Chinese tribe. At that time, Formosa was occupied first by the Dutch and then by the Portuguese. For a brief period from 1645 to 1662, a half-Japanese general of the Ming Dynasty, Tei Seiko, after being driven from China by the invading Manchus from the north, occupied that island. However, the Portuguese soon regained control of the island, which they had renamed as Formosa, or the beautiful island. The Machu empire only ruled Formosa for eight years between 1887 and 1895, but Manchus were not Chinese either.

The Manchu empire of China managed Formosa for just that brief period of time and, in 1895, gladly ceded it to Japan. After that, China had forfeited its rights to the island permanently or until the signing of another international treaty. The present-day Beijing government claims that the 1943 Cairo Declaration and the 1945 Potsdam Declaration recognized China's sovereignty over Formosa. That is not factually correct. The Cairo Declaration had nothing new on the question of Chinese territorial sovereignty over Formosa. Furthermore, both the Cairo and Potsdam Declarations were not valid international treaties but, to quote Justice Radha Binod Pal, a 'victor's justice' (Ushimura, 2003), where Japan never took any part.

The People's Republic of China, which came into being in 1949, was at war with the UN in 1951 over Korea and wasn't invited to sign the San Francisco Treaty in which Japan formally renounced 'all right, title and claim to Formosa'. The Republic of China or Kuomintang was unable to represent China in that treaty. Accordingly, to follow the UN principle of self-determination, Formosa belongs only to Formosans, not to China.

The history of Tibet, Manchuria, East Turkistan, and Formosa, dating back more than two thousand years, has been one of independence from China. At no time, since the founding of the nation in 127 BC, have the Tibetans conceded their sovereignty to a foreign power. East Turkistan was occupied from time to time, but those periods of occupation were brief. Manchuria was not occupied by China until 1950. Formosa, except for seven years, was never a part of China.

Chinese Empire in Vietnam, the Philippines and Indonesia

China has no limit to its demands on lands, islands, rocks, and reefs in the South China Sea, disregarding any international laws and conventions. China only recognizes might, not logic. Legitimate claims by other nations of East Asia have no meaning in the dictionary of China. China has claimed sovereignty across most of the South China Sea. It grants itself rights that cannot apply to an international shipping route. In fact, China imposes its demands by building military structures on uninhabited archipelagos, islets, rocks and reefs that are already possessed by other countries in the region, including Japan, Vietnam, the Philippines, Malaysia, and Indonesia. Chinese citizens are encouraged to fish everywhere under the protection of China's coastguards, and to engage in prospecting for oil, with the installation of a drilling platform off the coast of Vietnam. In a direct head to head with Vietnam, Malaysia, Brunei and the Philippines, Taiwan and Japan, Beijing claims possession of the Paracel and Spratly Islands, the Scarborough Shoal and the Senkaku Islands. It also appears to be extending its own territorial waters so much that there is practically nothing left for the rest of South-East Asia (O'Neill, 2018).

In April 2012, there was a clash between China and the Philippines over Scarborough Shoal, one of the Spratly Islands in the South China Sea. The confrontation between the naval vessels of the two countries continued for almost two months and in the middle of this the US and the Philippines carried out a joint military drill in the vicinity. Japan, Australia, and South Korea all sent their personnel to participate in this drill.

China deployed an armada of 80 military and civilian ships, along with support aircraft, to install a billion dollar oil rig on Vietnam's continental shelf well within its 200 mile exclusive economic zone (EEZ). According to Rodis (2012):

> When Vietnam responded by dispatching 30 of its ships to defend its sovereign territory, China used high-powered water cannons to disperse them and even rammed its vessels straight into Vietnamese ships causing damage to the Vietnamese ships and injury to those on board. Vietnam

> may have the will to fight but clearly lacks the 'suitable' might to defend itself against China.
>
> Vietnam is mindful about what happened on March 14, 1988 when four ships of the Chinese People's Liberation Army Navy [PLAN] landed on Vietnam's Johnson South Reef and faced Vietnamese defenders on the reef who refused to leave. The Chinese ships fired at will at the sailors and pounded the reef with heavy shells. When the dust settled, several Vietnamese ships were destroyed and 64 Vietnamese sailors lay dead. The Johnson South Reef Massacre was recorded by the Chinese Navy and shown all over China as an example of China's might.

China's attack against the Philippines was initiated when China moved a giant oil rig to the Recto Bank—just 85 nautical miles from Palawan. The US Energy Information Administration (USEIA) has estimated that there could be approximately 11 billion barrels (bbl) of oil reserves and 190 trillion cubic feet (tcf) of natural gas reserves in the West Philippine Sea. Ayungin is the gateway to the Recto Bank and China intends to occupy Ayungin Shoal (Robis, 2014).

China's occupation of the Philippine mining industry is another issue. One of China's mining companies is operating in the Philippines 'located near the Scarborough Shoal in the coastal town of Masinloc where China's Wei-Wei Group has set up a US$100 million nickel processing plant. In nearby Botolan, Zambales, China's Jiangxi Rare Earth and Rare Metals Tungsten Group Company Limited operates a US$150 million nickel exploration and cobalt processing project' (Rodis, 2012).

There is an estimated US$1 trillion in untapped mineral resources in the Philippines. Chinese mining companies, many of them operating illegally, have been exporting precious minerals such as gold and nickel out through the island country's porous coastal ports, where there are no customs officials. If China can occupy the Scarborough Shoal, smuggling precious metals from the Philippines to a Chinese base will be easy. In 1996, China occupied the Mischief Reef—75 miles from Palawan. Vietnam, Malaysia, and the Philippines have separately protested against Chinese land reclamation at numerous reefs in the Spratly Islands. The fear is that they could be used for air, naval, or logistic bases to strengthen China's territorial claims a long way from its mainland (O'Neill, 2018).

Around the Great Natula Island, in Indonesia there is a growing of alarm, over China's claim to maritime rights in the sea surround the island. In February 2021, China allowed the coast guards to enforce the Chinese rights on the island using all kinds of weapons. That area has fishing resources and a possible natural gas reserve. Natula Island is located 1800 km south of China's mainland. This island is located within the so-called Nine-Dash line drawn by China itself to demonstrate its claim. In January, 2021, about 50 Chinese fishing boats operated inside the exclusive economic zone of Indonesia. Indonesia objected to the United Nations, but without any effects. The Natuna archipelago has a population of about 80,000. Japan is providing assistance to Indonesia worth about 830 million Yen to construct docks, so that Indonesia can build up a fisheries zone free of Chinese occupation. Thus, after Vietnam and Philippines, Indonesia is now a victim of Chinese colonialism.

China and the Asian Financial Crisis on 1998

After 1998, IMF-World Bank tried to hide China under a strange argument of crony capitalism. If that would be the correct analysis, then the crisis would be repeated every year. However, that was not the case. The countries affected by that crisis changed their trade pattern to survive from the Chinese attack on their economies. They used to be export-oriented economies. Now they, since 1998, became the suppliers of raw materials and primary products to China.

To analyze that history, we can start from the background of that crisis. Between 1970 and 1996 the 'Tiger' economies of South East and East Asia through their industrial and trade policies narrowed the gap between output per person in the those countries and that of the most advanced countries. Between those years, the gross national product per head in South Korea went up by 11- fold, of Hong Kong by four fold and that of Thailand went up by 3.5 fold. In 1970, Korea's real income per head, at the purchasing power parity, was only 15 percent of the US level. By 1995, it became 40 percent of the US level. Thailand's income per head has risen from 11 to 28 percent of the US level over the same period. The instruments used to achieve these very positive results are high rate mass education, prudent industrial policies, high savings rate, promotions of exports, realistic exchange rates, and appropriate intervention in the market. East Asian economies with currencies linked to the US Dollar enjoyed high levels of competiveness particularly against Japan. The Thai economy expanded at an average rate of 8.4 percent a year between 1990 and 1995. Rapid growth initiated high inflows of foreign capital. Thailand had a current account deficit of about 7 percent of its GNP between 1990 and 1995 financed by these capital inflows.

In 1994, China devalued its currency by about 50 percent. As a result, South East and East Asian countries lost their competiveness and started to have declining growth rates of their economies.

The Asian economic crisis started in the middle of 1997 when a large conglomerate of South Korea defaulted in its debt repayment and the stock market of Thailand started collapsing along with its currency. Very soon, one country after another was experiencing a combination of mass depreciation of their currencies, sharp downfall of stock prices, floods of outflows of foreign capital, and bankruptcies of big and small companies. Within a year the so-called Tiger economies of East Asia were reduced to countries with mass unemployment, social upheavals, political disturbances, and were begging for assistance from the IMF and the rich developed countries. By the end of 1996, sharp depreciation of currencies has caused rise in the price of imports, increased foreign debts in local currencies for the corporations and banks. Authorities increased rates of interest to stop outflows of capital. The result is reduction of consumption and investments and deep economic downturns. Reductions of money supply and public expenditure as suggested by the IMF as the prices of economic assistance led to the reductions of investments and consumptions. Financial and credit functions became paralyzed and the currency crisis became an economic crisis.

As these countries of East and South East Asia are closely interlinked through trade and investments during the era of high-speed economic growth, economic crisis spread from one to other quickly. Real economic growth in South East Asia in 1998 was reduced to -6.9 percent, compared with 8.2 percent in 1995, and 7.1 percent in 1996. Inflation was 21.0 percent in 1998 in South East Asia, compare with 5.6 percent in 1997 and 6.6 percent in 1996. South Korea, Indonesia, Thailand, Malaysia all had negative growth rates in 1998. There were growing non-performing loans in the banks as the companies depend on the banks rather than the stock markets. Asian countries have liberalized their capital accounts of the balance of payments and relaxed restrictions of their financial markets. That had caused significant inflows of foreign institutional funds of short-term nature. By the end of 1996, the share of short-term liabilities to total liabilities was above 50 percent and the ratio of short-term external liabilities to foreign reserves was above 100 percent in South Korea, Indonesia, and Thailand. However, anticipations of future bailout provided international banks strong incentives to take on even more risks.

The ratio of short-term debts to foreign reserve was 54 percent in 1994 in South Korea, 177 percent in Indonesia in 1996, 100 percent in Thailand in 1996, 79 percent in the Philippines, 41 percent in Malaysia in 1996 but only 24 percent in 1996 in China.

The ration of short-term debt and debt service to foreign reserve was 85 percent in 1994 in South Korea, 294 percent in 1996 in Indonesia, 137 percent in 1996 in the Philippines, 123 percent in Thailand in 1996, 69 percent in 1996 in Malaysia but only 38 percent in China.

China also protected its balance of payment capital account against any sudden outflows. Ratio of foreign liabilities to assets in 1996 reached 1103 percent in Thailand, 375 percent in South Korea, 424 in Indonesia, 172 percent in the Philippines, 148 percent in Malaysia, but 120 percent in China. In the presence of rapid currency depreciation if foreign banks refuse to extend the credit lines to domestic banks, these imbalances may cause serious financial problem and that had happened in 1997 in South East Asia. Since 1990, China was devaluing its exchange rate and in 1994 it devalued Yuan by about 50 percent, which along with its policy export subsidies drove out exports from the ASEAN countries. In 1997 and 1998, China's exports were growing at some fantastic rates. The following table demonstrates how China destroyed the export market of the ASEAN countries causing the 1998 financial crisis (Tables 3.1 and 3.2).

From 1996 to 1997, the nominal GDP per capita dropped by 43.2% in Indonesia, 21.2% in Thailand, 19% in Malaysia, 18.5% in South Korea, and 12.5% in the Philippines. Hong Kong, Mainland China, Singapore, and Japan were also affected, but less significantly.

Besides its economic impact, the Asian Financial Crisis also resulted in political repercussions. The Prime Minister General of Thailand, Yongchaiyudh, and the President of Indonesia, Suharto, resigned. An anti-Western sentiment was triggered, especially against George Soros, who was blamed for triggering the crisis with large amounts of currency speculation by some individuals.

The impact of the Asian Financial Crisis was not limited to Asia. International investors became less willing to invest in and lend to developing countries, not only in Asia in other areas of the world. China gains from that. Oil prices also fell due to the crisis. As a result, some major mergers and acquisitions in the oil industry took place to achieve economies of scale. Russia was seriously affected.

The IMF generated several bailout packages for the most affected countries during the financial crisis. It provided packages of around $20

Table 3.1 Trade Destruction Caused By China (US$ million) (Categories of Goods whose Exports to the US fell by over US$1 million in 1995–1996 and whose exports by China to the US increased)

Categories of Goods Exported	*Decrease*	*Increase in China*
Malaysia		
Skirts, Knitted, Synthetic fibers	3130	2230
Nightshirts, pajamas, of cotton	5040	43,230
Clothing for infants, synthetic fibers	3820	4810
Men's or boys overcoats, car coats	2170	31,960
Women's overcoats, car coats	1180	11,640
Tin alloys	3600	7560
Fittings for loose-leaf binders	7740	22,120
Lamps	1110	121,160
Thailand		
Frozen fish	5180	22,890
Silicon dioxide	1340	7380
Tubes, pipes, hoses, of plastic	1980	2440
Gloves	3810	13,860
Footwear	2310	28,780
Soles of footwear	1790	12,700
Seats etc	1720	19,210

Source MITI and JETRO, Japan

Table 3.2 Export Growth Rates in East Asian Economies (%)

	1997							*1998*		
Months	*6*	*7*	*8*	*9*	*10*	*11*	*12*	*1*	*2*	*3*
South Korea	9.6	19.3	14.0	13.4	5.2	3.8	1.7	– 0.3	19.9	6.6
Thailand	– 5.1	0.7	0.7	9.9	10.7	– 0.5	– 1.4	– 11.8	– 4.9	– 10.5
Malaysia	1.2	4.5	2.5	0.9	– 2.6	– 2.4	– 11.0	– 23.2	8.9	– 12.9
Indonesia	6.8	12.7	8.8	8.7	1.9	5.0	0.5	– 2.2	– 6.5	11.5
China	25.3	25.1	13.4	23.4	17.1	23.0	4.7	8.4	23.5	9.5

Source JETRO, Japan

billion to Thailand, $40 billion to Indonesia, and $59 billion to South Korea to support them, so they did not default.

The bailout packages are structural-adjustment packages. The countries that received the packages were asked to reduce their government spending, allow insolvent financial institutions to fail, and raise interest rates aggressively. The purpose of the adjustments was to support the currency values and confidence over the countries' solvency. However, it has nearly destroyed the affected countries in their economies and their trade patterns. They became dependent to China more and more as China took over their export markets and they were reduced to supplier of raw materials or semi-finished products to China.

Comments

China's aim to make Asia's seas its exclusive property, keeping Japan at bay and excluding US military presence, is just one part of a greater mission. China intends to extend its military power through Burma, Africa, and Pakistan up to the Arabian Sea, on to the Persian Gulf and into the Middle East and Africa. China's defense budget is second only to that of the US, giving it great purchasing power and increasing military capabilities (Green & Hicks, 2017).

Recent outbreak of coronavirus and resultant thousands of death all over the world is blamed on China that either China has developed this virus in its laboratory in Wuhan or it suppressed the information so that other countries could not take action beforehand. The result is worldwide shutdown and mass unemployment and bankruptcy. Most companies are having the problem of very low demand and falling share price. China is taking advantage of that. It is buying up companies after companies everywhere particularly in the developing countries.

Every nation in the world talks of peace. Throughout the twentieth century, countries have enthusiastically praised the virtues of 'stability', 'peace', and 'good relations', yet they have all been caught up in the irrationality of actively prepared for and fomented war. Among growing economic chaos, there is unlikely to be a 'peaceful rise' to Chinese imperialism—just preparations for war to expand China's economic interest through its militarism.

China recently created a new type of imperialism. In the name of Belt and Road Initiative, it is giving huge loans to a number of countries for infrastructure projects at very high interest rates. All materials for these projects including labor force would come from China, although the recipient countries could supply most of these particularly the labor forces to reduce the borrowings. When the country will be unable to pay back these loans, China will take very long-term lease of important ports, airports, mines, or islands. Recently Sri Lanka when unable to repay its loan to China gave lease of an airport, Humbantota, for 100 years to China. Maldive has taken from China a loan of $250 million, which is the same as its GDP. Kenya gave up Mombasa port to China, after failing to repay its debt to China.

In Africa, similarly, a number of countries leased out their mines. China has a plan to invest $60 billion in Africa, 75 percent of that in oil related industries. Sudan has taken $6.4 billion, Kenya has taken $8 billion, Republic of Congo has taken $7.3 billion, Ethiopia has $13.5 billion loan from China, and Angola has taken $25 billion from China. These are nothing when we consider Pakistan, which has taken $40 billion loan from China with a guaranteed rate of return of 30 percent, which it cannot repay. Therefore, Pakistan has given away Gwadar port in Balochistan for a joint military base with China. This is imperialism in another name (Kesling & Emont, 2019; Terril, 2003; Toh, 2017).

Big corporations in the western world control the mass media. For example, Wall Mart, the biggest retail chain stores in the US, which receives most of its supplies from China, is owned by Rupert Murdoch, who also owns some of the most important newspapers and television channels in the US, UK, Australia, India, and East Asia. The result is a continuous pro-Chinese propaganda in the media, which is blaming the democratically elected Taiwanese leaders for provoking China by not accepting the Chinese colonialism. When the interests and ambitions of the Kuomintang Chinese and China have now merged, it will not take long for the US to discard Taiwan to its fate in order to please China and to protect the commercial interests of the American companies in China.

Both China and the US thus correspond to the classical pattern of colonialism. They both want to capture territories to promote their business interests. In the case of American Empire the desire is to protect its overseas investments and particularly the oil industry worldwide. It can correspond somehow to the theory of Lenin. Chinese empire does not correspond to the theory of Lenin at all. China wants to capture resources of the world to promote its industry in future as a matter of national honor and prestige to wipe out 'the century of humiliation'.

References

Aitchison, C. U. (1929). *A collection of treaties, engagements, and sanads* (Vol. XIV). Calcutta: Government Printing Office.

Green, M., & Hicks, K. (2017). *Countering Coercion in Maritime Asia*. Washington, DC: Center for Strategic and International Studies.

Information Office of the State Council of The People's Republic of China. (1992). xinhuanet.com/english/2021-05/c_139959978.htm

Kesling, B., & Emont, J. (2019). How the U.S is countering China's Empire Building Plan, Wall Street Journal, 9 April.

O'Neill, D. (2018). *Dividing ASEAN and Conquering the South China Sea*. Hong Kong: Hong Kong University Press.

Rodis, R. (2012). *China's mining occupation of the Philippines, Philippines Daily Inquirer, December 12.*

Rodis, R. (2014). *What did Estrada and Arryo promise China, Philippines Daily Inquirer, March 21.*

Schaeffer, K. R., & Tuttle, G. (2012). *Tibetan history reader*. New York: Columbia University Press.

Toh, H. S. (2017). *Is China an Empire?* Singapore: World Scientific.

Terril, R. (2003). *The New Chinese Empire*. New York: Basic Books.

Tibet Support Group. (1994). www.dalailama.com.

US State Department Authorisation Act. (1991). archives.gov/research/guide-led-records/groups/059.html

Ushimura, K. (2003). Beyond the judgment of civilization: The intellectual legacy of the Japanese War Crimes Trials, 1946–1949. International House of Japan.

van Walt van Praag, M. (1987). *The status of Tibet, history, rights, and prospect in international law*. London: Wisdom.

Yu, M. M. (2018). China's Final Solution in Xinjiang, The Caravan, issue1819. Palo Alto, CA: Hoover Institute.

CHAPTER 4

Expanding Empire of China

After occupying Tibet, East Turkestan, Inner Mongolia, and Manchuria, China now is trying to occupy the entire South China Sea and the islands in it. At the same time, it is threatening Taiwan continuously that sooner or later China will occupy it. Although none of the countries in the U.N supports the claim of China, but China does not care. It does not allow Vietnam or Philippines to explore oil and gas in those islands and sometimes it gives warning to passing ships that they are entering Chinese territories.

China wants to dominate the world. It has a long-term strategy. It first wants the world dependent on it by removing all competitors in the supply line of the world. With the money it earns it buys all politicians, all journalists, all judges, and all industrial leaders. The steps are as follows:

1. It has started its campaign first in Asia, by creating the Asian financial crisis in 1998.
2. It then tried to take care of all Western countries.
3. By joining WTO, it got the legitimacy to control the World.
4. Trump made an attempt to stop that plan, but he lost the game as by that time China has total control on the media, the judges and politicians in the US and other Western countries and some of the parts of the United Nations itself.

© The Author(s), under exclusive license to Springer Nature Switzerland AG 2021

D. Basu and V. Miroshnik, *The Economic and Political Dangers of Globalization*, https://doi.org/10.1007/978-3-030-79895-6_4

When China joined the WTO, it was forced to change some of its law but there was not any genuine commitment, but China never observed those commitments in reality only signed the Protocol of Accession to the WTO. The objective of these commitments was to transform China into a market economy but in reality, China is still a controlled economy. Supachai Panitchpakdi, Director General of WTO from 2002 to 2005 and Mark Clifford, former editor of Business week, wrote a book, 'China and the WTO' where they asserted that WTO has created a set of rules for China to transform itself to market economy like the other members after it would join WTO. However, China has violated all premises of a market system (Ezell & Atkinson, 2015). China joined the WTO in 2001 in Doha Conference of the WTO. WTO is based on the so-called Washington Consensus, which promotes non-discrimination, transparency, the primacy of rule based, market-based rules, in accordance to the theory of comparative advantage. China on the other hand developed a policy regime based on mercantilism, which is against the policy of the WTO.

In the following Table 4.1, we summarize the violations of China (Ezell & Atkinson, 2015; Oxfam Report on WTO, 2019; Webster, 2013):

Currency manipulations to keep of the exchange value of Yuan low promotes export subsidies and helped China to have a massive trade surplus. In its policy of 'innovative mercantilism,' it discriminates against foreign firms and provides supports for the domestic firms. It induces foreign firms to collaborate with the Chinese forms to promote technology transfer.

In a document, '*National Medium and Long Term program for Science and Technology Development 2006–2020*,' China identified 402 key technologies intelligent automobiles to integrated circuits and high-performance computers where foreign companies are encouraged to transfer technologies in exchange for market access and contracts. That was extended for aircraft, missiles, and multiple target nuclear missiles as well. In the '*National Guideline for Development and Promotion of the Integrated Circuit Industry*,' China had a plan to invest at least $100 Billion in the semiconductor industry to create a closed loop system where design, manufacturing, assembly, packaging, all activities will be combined in a planned size of $140 billion by 2020. China wants to eliminate the US semiconductor industry within 20 years from 2006. China wants to combine invisible hand of the market with the visible hand of the government. In its '*National and Regional IC Funds*,' China already allocated at least $100 billion to invest first in state-owned forms which in turn will

Table 4.1 Conditions of the WTO and China's behavior

Conditions of the WTO	*China applied this rule to itself*
Technology transfer as a Condition for market access	No
The Government Procurement agreement	No
State industries purchases based on pure commercial considerations	No
Reduction of Share of the State industries in the economy	No
Foreign banks receives same treatment as domestic banks	No
Telecommunication market open to foreign producers	No
Foreign film distribution liberalized	No
Substantial reduction of export subsidies	No
Progress toward the implementation of Washington Consensus	No
Reductions of intellectual property theft and violations	No
Removal of technical barriers to trade agreements	No
Non Manipulation of technology Standards	No
No currency manipulations	No

invest in private equity firms, particularly to buy foreign semiconductor firms. One major example is China Tsinghua Unicorn Groups purchase of Micron Technology in 2015 for $23 billion. For economic development, China embraced industrial policy, State-Owned Industries, and Techno Nationalism. China ignores the core principle of the WTO, it does not accept non-discrimination toward foreign companies, ***most-favored nation*** status to charge the minimum possible tariffs for WTO member countries and transparency. If a company uses at least 60% Chinese components, it receives government subsidy. China as conditions to join the WTO that it would not put any condition of Research and development on new investment, but in new investments in automobile and steel sector, these conditions regarding research and development are still there. China does not care about the WTO standard but has its own standard regarding all information technology products (ABC News, 2018, 2019).

Ezell and Atkinson (2015), Oxfam report on WTO and Webster (2013), mentioned a number of commitments, which China disregarded.

Commitment No 1: Prices in Every Sector Must Be Determined by Market Forces

Section 9 of China's WTO Protocol of Accession provides that China "*shall allow prices for traded goods and services in every sector to be determined by market forces, and multi-tier pricing practices for such goods and services shall be eliminated.*"

Exceptions to this requirement are quite limited and are set out in Annex 4 of the Protocol. The products covered in Annex 4 are certain agricultural products, certain pharmaceuticals, natural gas, and processed oils. Except these, China committed to allowing prices to be set by the market immediately in 2001. Even today in 2021, many key prices are being determined by the government in China.

Commitment No 2: All Subsidies to be Notified to the WTO and Prohibited Subsidies to be Eliminated

Under Section 15 of WTO Accession Protocol, China agreed to notify to the WTO any subsidy granted by China. China also committed itself to eliminate all subsidy programs. These obligations are disregarded by China. Subsidies are not revealed at all or inadequate publicity of subsidies is given. China still provides export subsidies and subsidies to use of local products. China committed to make available to all other WTO Members, all laws, regulations, and other factors affecting trade in goods, services, TRIPS, or the control of foreign exchange. Unfortunately, China has disregarded those obligations it committed to join the WTO.

Commitment No 3: State-Owned Enterprises (SOEs) to Operate Free of State Influence

Under Section 6 of China's Accession Protocol, and Article XVII GATT 1994, China agreed that these SOEs organizations would imports or exports based on market conditions on prices, quality, marketability, and availability. However, China has disregarded this rule of the WTO. There are government subsidies, which are illegal under the WTO rules, for the SOEs. Overcapacities in the SOEs resulted in a flood of exports of steel, glass, cement, and other building materials to other countries in the excuse of the *Belt and Road Initiatives*.

Commitment No 4: Non-Discrimination in Procurement

WTO rules suggest that foreign individuals and organizations shall be treated equally to domestic individuals and organizations regarding the procurement of inputs and goods and services. China disregarded this rule and refused to accept the *Government Procurement Agreement (GPA)*. FIEs face discriminations in public procurement unless they have Chinese partners. FIEs cannot bid for public contracts in certain sectors important for China, like railways, constructions, steel, engineering, and design sectors. Tenders are not publicly announced. There is discrimination against foreign equipment and technology through *the Steel and Iron Industry Development Policy,* and China encourages the use of local companies and local technology.

Commitment No 5: Non-Discrimination in General

China, when it has joined the WTO, has agreed to change all laws which are inconsistent with the GATT '*Most Favoured Nation*' ('MFN') and National Treatment rules. China in *the Strategic Emerging Industries* encourages innovation in high technology areas and discriminate against foreign firms and products.

Commitment No 6: Technical Barriers to Trade (TBT)

China disregarded the TBT rules of the WTO. China has not harmonized technical regulations, standards, and conformity evaluation procedures, which creates difficulties for foreign companies to enter the Chinese market. China does not use international standards.

Commitment No 7: Intellectual Property Rights (IPR)

China violates these TRIPS rules totally; it does not accept intellectual property rights of foreigners and foreign companies.

Commitment No 8: Market Access

In China, there are still restrictions for foreign companies to enter the Chinese market. There are prohibition to invest in certain strategic sectors, requirements for local content and joint-venture. Steel companies and mining sector are prohibited for foreign investment.

Commitment No 9: Non-Tariff Measures

Foreign business organizations in order to enter the market in China must transfer its technology to the Chinese partner company. There are also requirement to balance trade and foreign exchange by which a foreign company must export similar in value to its import requirements.

Commitment No 10: Judicial Review

The judicial system in China is biased against foreign companies. According to the WTO rules, China must implement all administrative actions relating to the implementation of laws, related to Article X:1 of the GATT 1994, and the TRIPS Agreement; China has never respected its commitments to the WTO.

Commitments for Specific Areas

Automotive Sector

In China, industrial plans of foreign companies require substantial investments in R&D facilities in China with local contents, which are not allowed in the WTO regime.

Banking Sector

According to the WTO rules, China should treat foreign banks in the same way as it treats domestic banks. However, it is not doing that.

Telecommunications

China should have opened its telecommunications sector to foreign companies but it has not done. It has many restrictions for foreign companies like very high level of capital investments, and Chinese partners and technology transfer requirement. These are not allowed under the WTO rules but so far China ignored these requirements.

The Film Industry

China has not liberalized the distribution of foreign films.

Agriculture

China has today more than $100 billion subsidies for agriculture sector including domestic subsidies, export subsidies. It does not allow free market access. It has arbitrary import restrictions, although India has introduced its three new agricultural laws to be in line with the WTO rules. China refuses to do so.

Retail Industry

China has restriction of foreign retail outlets, which are against the WTO rules.

Legal Services

In China, foreign legal services are restricted, which is against the WTO rules.

The Fertilizer Industry

In China, there are discriminatory tax and import controls, which are against WTO rules.

Import and Export Regulations

In China, there are still export control, import controls, and deliberate dumping efforts to promote exports.

Unfair Trade Practices

China ignored rules fair trade and reciprocal treatment in international trade. For year after year, China used dumping subsidies, exchange rate manipulations, industrial planning, forced technology transfer, discriminations against foreign companies, and got away with. "China's average tariff rate is nearly three times higher than the average United States rate. The United States charges a 2.5% tariff on Chinese cars, while China charges a 25% tariff on cars from the United States" (Ezell & Atkinson, 2015). President Trump imposed 25% tariff on Chinese exports, but now a pro-Chinese Biden was installed as the President of the US and most tariffs are expected to be removed.

In 2018 alone, the Trump Administration had found dumping or unfair subsidies on 13 different products, including steel wheels, cold-drawn mechanical tubing, tool chests and cabinets, forged steel fittings, aluminum foil, rubber bands, cast iron soil pipe and fittings, and large diameter welded pipe. In January 2018, the Trump Administration found that China's overproduction of steel and aluminum. Belt and Road program of China is nothing but to export these excess products of China. The US has a $375 billion deficit Balance of Trade in 2017 alone (Asia Maritime Transperancy Initiative, 2020; Bandeira & Tsiropoulos, 2019).

Colonization of the Indian Economy by China

India is very similar to China and therefore it is more affected by the Chinese competition, since China has entered the WTO. India, where its textiles and clothing sector plays a substantial economic role and was accounted for 8.2% of Indian manufacturing value added in 2009. The Multifibre Agreement (MFA) was signed in 1974 and most textiles exports from developing to developed countries were subject to import quotas under MFA. China's quota was 4 times of that of India and quota of 4 Chinese-oriented countries (China, Taiwan, Hong Kong, and Singapore) was 8 times of that of India. There was a definite pro-Chinese bias in the MFA and it was carried forward in the WTO as well since 2001. Therefore, in 2002 and 2005, India was faced with the removal of a secure import quota in the markets of the developed countries, but Chinese exports have no restrictions in the markets of the developed countries. Thus, India is affected badly twice. China's WTO membership intensified competition for developing countries on their traditional export markets. Due to the dismantling of the MFA, increased Chinese export competition was particularly destructive in the textiles sector. Between 2000 and 2005, China's share of US and EU textiles imports doubled, increased by 5123% in the US and by 98% in the EU. In 2013, China accounted for 29% of global textile exports. That had nearly destroyed export markets of all non-Chinese countries, India was the main victim (Chin & Gallagher, 2019; Dhar, 2018, 2019a, b, 2020; Dhar & Reji, 2019; FT.com, 2020).

India-China Conflict in Trade

India-China bilateral trade in the year 2019 has reached US$ 92.89 billion. India'ds exports to China were US$17.97 billion, and India's imports from China were US$74.92 billion. One can easily see the difference. India rejected China's demand to grant its market economy status, with the background of near-war situation between the two armies along the Line of Actual Control (LAC). New Delhi will continue to treat its neighbor as a non-market economy, which allows it to impose steep anti-dumping duties on imports from China. World Trade Organization (WTO) members are allowed to apply anti-dumping measures on any company if it exports a product at a lower price than its home market, and if the product threatens to affect badly the local industry. So far, at least 50% of the manufacturing job in India were destroyed by Chinese exports to India.

"China joined the WTO in December 2001 after years of negotiations on the condition that it will be treated as a non-market economy by other member countries for anti-dumping proceedings. A non-market economy refers to a country which has a complete or substantially complete monopoly of its trade and where all domestic prices are fixed by the state. While the 15-year period ended in December 2016, the European Union and the US have desisted from granting market economy status to China, citing wide-ranging price control on export commodities by China" (Horn et al., 2019). After the expiry of China's accession to WTO, it must be treated in same way as any other WTO member and, regardless of the domestic law of that particular member, imports from China PR must be demonstrated on the basis of Chinese prices and costs. India, however, said since Chinese producers failed to file relevant information to prove the market economy status; it will continue to treat it as a non-market economy. Jayant Dasgupta, former Indian ambassador to the WTO, said, "If 80% of the companies are directly or indirectly controlled by the state and the banks are controlled by the Chinese Communist Party, then how can China claim that its trade partners should give it market economy status" (Dhar, 2020).

India initiated 18 anti-dumping proceedings in 2019, most of them against China, according to the WTO website. However, China remains one of India's largest trading partners and a major source for intermediate products for its industry. India's exports to China rose to $17.1 billion in 2019, while imports to $68.3 billion. Imports from China began expanding quite rapidly from 2003–2004. In 2019–2020, China accounted for nearly 14% of India's imports and was by far its largest source of goods imports (Khosla, 2020) (Table 4.2 and Fig. 4.1).

India depends on China in two product groups, namely telecom and electronics products, and pharmaceutical intermediates (Active Pharmaceutical Ingredients). India imports more than 90% of the APIs for several antibiotics and vitamins from China; three other sectors are important. The first is the motorcycle industry, which in 2018–2019 sourced 85% of its imports of parts and components from China. More than 90% of imports of silicon wafers and solar lanterns in 2019–2020 were from China. The third sector is textiles in which synthetic and artificial woven yarn. India's imports from China are mainly capital goods, railway equipment, and power plants. Although India produced these but private

Table 4.2 India's imports from China ($ billion)

China	
2014–2015	66
2015–2016	67.8
2016–2017	69.5
2017–2018	87.1
2018–2019	88.3
2019–2020	82.2

Source Economic Survey, 2021

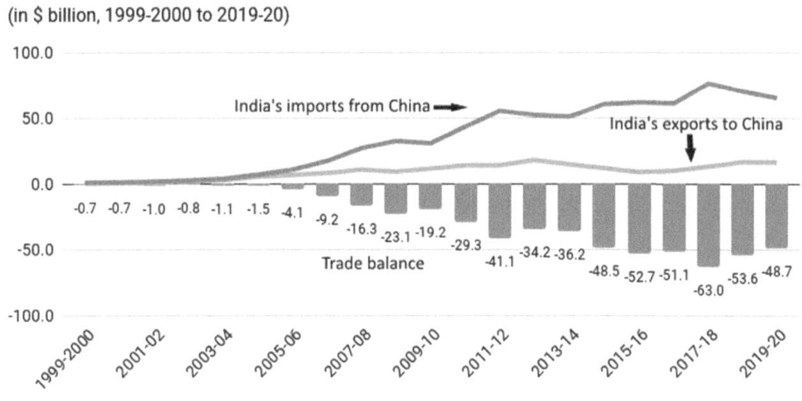

Fig. 4.1 India-China trade

sector of India imports these because of their low costs. Indian imports include consumer durables. Imports of intermediates like APIs have also been sizeable. The share of imports of these products from China as a proportion of total imports increased to 57% in 2017 from 37% in 2003. The share of intermediate goods imports from China, including APIs, but increased by nearly 34% in 2019. India is critically dependent on China in many areas and that this dependence cannot be reduced quickly. India's exports are mainly raw materials and intermediates while capital and consumer are insignificant. Thus, it has the colonial pattern in trade (Dhar, 2020; Khosla, 2020; Glosserman, 2019; Rai, 2020) (Figs. 4.2 and 4.3).

The pattern of India's imports (classified by technology content) from China that high and medium technology products dominated imports

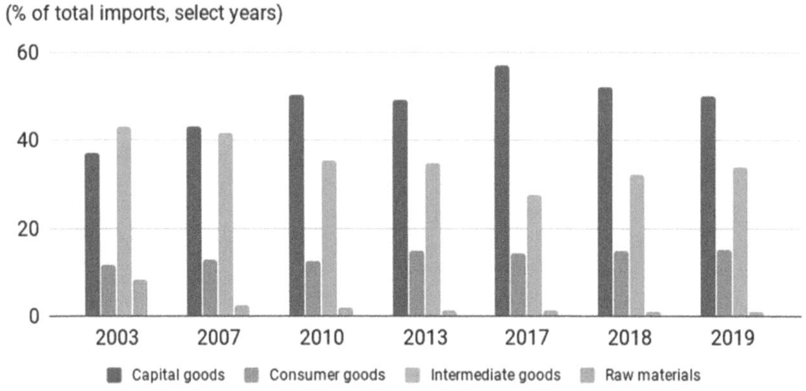

Fig. 4.2 Composition of India's imports from China (*Source* UN comtrade database)

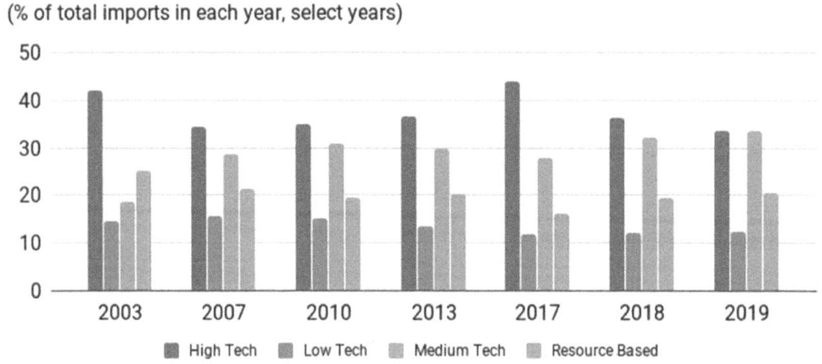

Fig. 4.3 Technology content of India's manufactured imports from China (*Sources* UN comtrade database)

in 2019, accounting for more than 67% of the total. Only 12% of the manufactured products that India imported from China in 2019 were low technology. The reason is the privatization and liberalization of import-tariff. The average import duties on industrial products decline to below 9% in 2008 from 33% in 2000 under WTO instructions. India also had to remove all the quantitative restrictions on imports, such as import licensing, in 2001. More important reason is the faith in the Government of India on the marketplace. The public sector companies that were established to produce capital goods and ingredients of generic medicines APIs neglected, and Indian government is now privatizing even profitable public sector companies and banks. Some of the biggest importers from China are close friends of the Prime Minister Modi and his financiers. Successive governments have deepened import liberalization through free trade agreements (FTAs). India's three major FTAs, with the Association of Southeast Asian Nations (ASEAN), Korea, and Japan, respectively, have resulted in a widening trade deficit (Dhar, 2018, 2020). Trade with China constitutes more than 40% of India's total trade deficit. India's anti-dumping duties on Chinese goods are being evaded by misclassification of products by the officers of the Government of India, thus there are Chinese agents in very powerful positions in India (Dhar, 2019a, b).

Impact on micro, small and medium enterprises (MSMEs): Very poor quality Chinese products dominate the unorganized retail sector. This sector comprises domestic industries producing better quality products. The solution is to use anti-dumping measures to promote these industries, which used to provide massive employment but now at least 50% of the jobs were destroyed by Chinese exports to India (Khosla, 2020).

Textile Industry: Goods and Services Tax (GST) on synthetic fibers of 18% has increased the import of similar fabrics from China. Chinese fabric is manufactured into garments in Bangladesh and imported at cheap rates into India. It is difficult to impose any tariffs on imports from Bangladesh. However, actions can be taken on the brand names of some Western companies who buy from Bangladesh. That requires withdrawal from the WTO.

Bicycle Industry: There are preference for cheap Chinese bicycles over Indian ones mainly because of the price advantages. The government can use the Public Procurement (Preference to Make in India) Order, 2017.

All these and more industries were defeated by cheap low quality imports from China; reducing manufacturing units into importers; destroying jobs in India. India freed imports thereby strangling its domestic industry. The tariffs on finished goods were often less than those for intermediate inputs. This discourages manufacturing industry and employment in manufacturing. Many now believe service industry jobs can replace industrialization. However, with 12.5% annual growth between 2007 and 2016, services added only 3% to India's employment. On the contrary, growth of services sector creates inequality of incomes and shifts employment for the highly educated section of the population. India's attractive domestic demand with a large market has attracted FDI. 60% of FDI inflows are in the service sector, where few jobs can be created. Nearly, half of FDI have taken over local industry. They downsized these industries, reduced employment to increase efficiency. 92% of FDI in pharma and 60% in chemical sector was 'Merger & Acquisitions' driven (Dhar, 2020; Glosserman, 2019).

Chinese steel companies also have big plants in India. A majority of power companies in India use China-made power-equipment, and TBEA, one of the biggest equipment exporters, has set up a China-dedicated industrial park in Gujarat. One key example is China's overwhelming presence in India's mobile-phone market, where four out of the top five brands are Chinese. Xiaomi, the market leader, has seven factories in India and plans to invest more than $ 500 million to expand its retail presence here. Xiaomi's rival, BBK Electronics, which sells phones under three different brands—Oppo, Vivo, and OnePlus—has two factories in UP. Chinese share in India's imports grew from 11.6% in 2013–2014 to 16.6% in 2017–2018. In a decade to 2017–2018, China's imports in India rose by $50 billion. India registered a trade deficit of $157 billion in 2017–2018. Chinese government gives an effective rebate of 17% to its exporter companies (Dhar & Joseph, 2019). This results in Chinese goods being 5–6% cheaper than their Indian counterparts, making it lucrative for Indian importers. On account of costlier energy, finance, and logistics, Indian goods are costlier by about 9% in the global market. Chinese industry gets loans at 6%, compared to 11–14% in India. Logistics costs are 1% of the business in China, compared to 3% in India. Of the 803 licenses provided by the Bureau of Indian Standards (BIS) to foreign manufacturers selling in India under the Foreign Manufacturer Certification Scheme (FMCS), 294 licenses for 55 products have been granted to Chinese manufacturers. A similar scheme has also provided 9,274 registrations for information technology and electronics products. Of this, 5857, or 64%, registrations have been granted to Chinese manufacturers. As much as 75% of the APIs (Active Pharmaceutical Ingredients) used in the formulations of essential drugs in the National List of Essential Medicines

(NLEM) are sourced from China (Dhar, 2019a, b, 2020; Rao, & Dhar, 2018).

Cheap Chinese imports have resulted in 35% closure of power looms in Surat and Bhiwandi. Bicycle imports from China saw a rise of 58% in volume and 47% in value in April to October 2017 over the previous year. Further, under-invoiced bicycles constitute 85% of the total bicycle imports from China in 2017–2018. Apart from affecting bicycle manufacturers, it is gradually killing the unorganized industry of small bicycle parts manufacturers who provide employment to many skilled and unskilled workers (Impact of Chinese Goods on Indian Industry, 145th report of Parliamentary standing committee on commerce; Rao & Dhar, 2018).

India, particularly the politicians, officers and the business community have surrendered to China already and only look at their profit by being an economic colony of China. So far India has not taken any serious efforts to reduce imports from China but have gone to the extreme to implement the WTO rules, which will only benefit China and open the economy for further colonization by China.

Belt and Road Initiative (BRI)

Belt and Road initiative (BRI) or China's effort to develop infrastructure in the developing countries is an attempt to extend China's empire throughout the world by fair means or foul. China uses BRI funds to drown the developing countries in debt and then take over ports, land, mines, and other strategic assets. BRI was started in 2013 and became the foreign policy strategy of Xi Jinping. In 2017, BRI was written into the constitution of the Chinese Communist Party and 138 countries and 30 international organizations have agreed to participate, with declared Chinese investments to some $8 trillion (Dezenski, 2020; CSIS.org, 2020; Chatham House, 2020; Brazys & Vadlamannati, 2018; Asia Maritime Transperancy Initiative, 2020; ABC News, 2018; Dornan & Brant, 2014; Duncan, 2016; Dziedzic, 2018, 2019; Export Finance Australia, 2018).

There are many examples of corruption in the Belt and Road. Bangladesh shut down a highway project, contract of which was given to the China Harbour Engineering Company but then it was revealed that the company reputedly offering a Bangladeshi official a bribe. The US arrested the representative of China's CEFC Energy Company for illicit payments to officials in Chad and Uganda. A 2017 McKinsey survey found that at least 60–80% of Chinese companies in Africa admitted to paying bribes (Gibson & Nero, 2007; Graue & Dziedzic, 2018; Hillman, 2018; Horn et al., 2019; CSIS.org, 2020).

In much the same way, Djibouti in East Africa lost control of a container terminal built as part of BRI projects, after the project had debt equivalent to 88% of its GDP of $1.72 billion. Similarly, Venezuela owes China around $20 billion, according to estimates by China's Commerce Ministry.

BRI is a vehicle to expand China's military capability beyond its geographical limits in a very clever way. China has the management control of Haifa port in Israel; it means that the US Mediterranean fleet cannot go to the port of Haifa. China is about to build a rail line connecting Haifa with the Red Sea as an alternative to the Suez Canal.

The China-led Asia Infrastructure Investment Bank, or AIIB, is the vehicle to finance OBOR(One Belt One Road). So far, it has provided $1.73 billion to support infrastructure projects in seven countries, including Pakistan, Bangladesh, Tajikistan, Indonesia, Myanmar, Azerbaijan, and Oman. Apart from AIIB, China also has a $40 billion Silk Road Fund and a New Development Bank to fund the OBOR initiative.

"Chinese aid activity in the Pacific region has been predominantly in infrastructure development, fuelled largely by loans rather than grants. Pacific countries are among the most vulnerable countries in the world to potential debt sustainability problems and by extension possible 'debt trap' diplomacy" (Cerutti & Zhou, 2018). Three small Pacific economies, Tonga, Samoa, and Vanuatu, are among those most heavily indebted to China. Regarding the global debt sustainability issues of Chinese projects, the Pacific islands are very important, as they also changed their diplomatic relations from Taiwan to China in return for massive bribes (ABC News, 19 November 2018; Dziedzic, 2019; Riordan, 2018; Whiting et al., 2019; Wroe, 2018).

The Pacific islands, in 2017, the Pacific received aid equal to 5.2% of its gross national income; sub-Saharan Africa received only 3% of their gross national income. Pacific islands have limited scope to grow their way out of any existing debt. China is an important creditor to all four. In 2011–2018, China made official loan commitments totaling US$6 billion (about 21% of regional GDP) (ABC News, 7 August 2019; CSIS.org, 2020; Dornan & Brant, 2014).

Africa and China

In Africa, BRI projects are designed to expand Chinese colonies in resource-rich countries. Elaine Dezenski analyzed a vital connection between Chinese capitalism and large-scale corruption; she argues that BRI exports "corruption, opacity, and waste" (Dezenski, 2020). All projects have delays, financial implosions, and negative public sentiment. "A large portion of these deals were being made with countries that had credit ratings classified as "junk." Making big deals with countries like Pakistan, Sri Lanka, and Malaysia showed the initial propensity of the Belt and Road to emphasize quantity over quality, expediency over transparency (Hurley et al., 2018; Riordan, 2018).

There are growing fear among African countries over the 'debt trap.' Djibouti is said to have debt to China, which is the equivalent of 75% of its GDP. China owns 72% of Kenya's external debt, which stands at US$50 billion (Bandiera & Tsiropoulos, 2019).

Kenya is the country, which was one of the first to sign a memorandum of understanding with China under its Belt and Road Initiative and has benefited from being a recipient of its funds. Kenya owes $6.5 billion to China, 21.9% of its total external debt. It is already using a third of its revenue to service that borrowing.

Kenya's standard gauge railway (SGR) connecting Mombasa to Nairobi, the biggest investment in Kenya since its independence, is a flagship BRI project in east Africa. It is also a textbook example of the kind of early BRI lending that is credited with fueling budget deficits that pushed the nation's debt to 61.7% of GDP at the end of 2019, up from 50.2% at the end of 2015, according to the IMF—from a manageable debt level to an unsustainable debt problem.

Over the next three years from 2020, Kenya has to pay US$60 billion to the China Exim Bank alone. For the Mombasa port and the standard gauge railway (SGR) connecting to Nairobi, the Kenyan government borrowed Sh227 billion from China. Kenya may lose the control of Mombasa port if it defaults on the SGR loans from the China Exim Bank (Horn et al., 2019).

African states spent $100.8 billion on infrastructure in 2018. Approximately 38% came from the African governments themselves, while 25.7% came from China. Some countries have already started to push back on the terms of Chinese lending. Bagamoyo in Tanzania was going to be the biggest port in east Africa, but the agreement, signed in 2013 with China

Merchants Holdings International, has stalled. Although China accounts for a relatively small share of Tanzania's external debt, Beijing has been among the largest investors in Tanzania in recent years. Tanzania owes around $2 billion to China, 9% of its total external debt. In Uganda, several Turkish companies have opened manufacturing plants and other businesses, while the government have drawn up a short list of companies from China, France, Portugal, Turkey, Austria, and South Korea to begin work on its Kampala–Jinja smart motorway.

African countries canceling or postponing now BRI projects over rising debt concerns. Zambian government has revoked a Chinese company's license to operate coalmines. Ugandan government has postponed the construction of the Kampala-Entebbe Expressway. Sierra Leone government canceled the US$318 million Mamamah International Airport project under the BRI. Tanzanian government has postponed lending from China for its new Bagamoyo port project (Dezenski, 2020; Hurley et al., 2018; Knowledge@Wharton, 2020).

Of the 49 countries that China claims have signed Memorandums of Understanding (MOUs) of officially expressed support for the BRI, 34 (nearly 70%) are located along the coast of Africa—16 in the West, eight each in the North and East, and two in the South. These include, it says, Djibouti Port, three Egyptian ports—Port Sudan, Port Said-Port Tewfik, Port Ain Sokhna–Zarzis Port in Tunisia, and El Hamdania Port in Algeria. An oil refinery in the north of Sudan is located close to the railway line connecting Port Sudan and Dakar Port. Gabes, a hub for petrochemical and phosphate industries in Tunisia, has been connected by rail to the port of Zarzis. An industrial park in Ethiopia is located near the Addis Ababa–Adama highway, which connects with the Addis-Djibouti rail line connected to Djibouti port. This enables China to use the maritime route to transport raw materials such as phosphate, copper, cobalt, gold, iron ore, cocoa, bauxite, coal, lithium, steel, granite and marble back to the mainland, and finished goods and Chinese labor to Africa (Brazys & Vadlamannati, 2018; Dezenski, 2020).

Recipients of BRI cash would lose control of assets if they could not repay their debts. Countries rich in natural resources, like Angola, Zambia, and Republic of the Congo, or with strategically important infrastructure, like ports or railways such as Kenya, are most vulnerable to the risk of losing control over important assets in negotiations with Chinese creditors (Brazys & Vadlamannati, 2018; IMF, Debt Limits Policy, 2015; Smith, 2020; World Bank, 2018) (Table 4.3).

Table 4.3 General government gross debt (% of GDP)

	2015	*2016*	*2017*	*2018*
World	80.6	83.6	83.1	82.8
MICs	44.5	47.4	48.6	49.8
Mongolia	62.1	87.6	85.3	89.0
Montenegro	76.8	78.0	79.7	80.9
Pakistan	65.7	70.0	69.1	67.6
LICs	36.1	40.4	41.9	41.6
Maldives	73.1	83.1	96.5	109.0
Djibouti	72.1	86.6	88.1	87.5
Laos	65.8	67.8	69.0	70.3
Kyrgyzia	65.0	62.1	64.2	65.5
Tajikistan	33.4	44.8	51.8	56.8

Source UNCTAD

China and Asia

In BRI, most of its investment contracts have been negotiated in secret. It is called "debt trap diplomacy." When Sri Lanka defaulted on the loan to build Hambantota Port and a Chinese company got a 99-year lease in return, the evidence of China's strategic designs became clear. Center for Global Development, in Washington D.C., warned that "23 of 68 countries benefiting from Belt and Road investments were significantly or highly vulnerable to debt distress," and identified eight countries—Djibouti, Kyrgyzstan, Laos, Mongolia, Montenegro, the Maldives, Pakistan, and Tajikistan—to be particularly at risk. "concern that debt problems will create an unfavorable degree of dependency on China as a creditor. Increasing debt, and China's role in managing bilateral debt problems, has already exacerbated internal and bilateral tensions in some BRI countries" (Hillman, 2018). However, a new study from Chatham House, the very biased pro-Chinese British think tank, blames Sri Lanka's IMF bailout; Chinese investment was "not used to repay port-related debt, but to pay off more expensive loans, generally to Western entities" (Chatham House—International Affairs, 2020).

According to the World Bank, between 2010 and 2016 nearly $36 billion was given to Malaysia by Chinese state-owned firms. Multiple infrastructure projects, including the East Coast Rail Link project and a massive port city called Melaka Gateway, were started, Chinese firms bought up multiple Malaysian ports, and mega-projects, such as the $100 billion, were being built with Chinese direction and financial backing. Then it was discovered that over $7.5 billion of government money had disappeared. Via Belt and Road projects, China had tried to help the embattled prime minister to cover evidence of financial irregularities by artificially inflating the costs of infrastructure projects so the excess could be justified for other reasons. In return, Malaysia was to give Chinese companies big shares in national railway and pipeline projects and to give permission for the Chinese navy to use two Malaysian ports (World Bank, IDA Lending Terms; World Bank, 2018).

Laos is among the poorest countries in Southeast Asia, though it has been expanding rapidly with GDP growth averaging 8% over the past decade. Since 2013, the IMF has been raising doubts about the ability of Laos to service its debts if it moves ahead with its plans to build the China-Laos railway, in addition to other major capital projects. The financial terms for many elements of the project remain a secret, although one source has reported that a $465 million loan from China Exim Bank for the joint company building and operating the railway would be provided. The Laotian government has also reportedly signed a $600 million loan agreement with China Exim Bank for a hydropower project (Smith, 2020; Rai, 2020; Chin & Gallagher, 2019).

For Mongolia, China Exim Bank agreed in early 2017 to provide financing under its $1 billion line of credit at concessional rates for a hydropower project and a highway project from the airport to the capital. However, the hydropower project has stalled. If reports that China would provide $30 billion in credit to BRI-related projects over the next five to ten years, then the prospect of a Mongolia default is extremely high, regardless of the concessional nature of the financing (Bandiera & Tsiropoulos, 2019).

Tajikistan is evaluated by the IMF and World Bank as a "high risk" country regarding debt. Despite this, it is planning to borrow from China to pay for infrastructure investments in the power and transportation sectors. Most significantly, a $3 billion portion of the Central Asia-China gas pipeline (Line D) will pass through Tajikistan, financed through Chinese foreign direct investment (FDI). Most recently, Tajikistan issued $500 million in Eurobonds to pay for a new hydropower generating facility. China is Tajikistan's single largest creditor, accounts for almost 80% of the total increase in Tajikistan's external debt over the 2007–2016 period (Horn et al., 2019).

Kyrgyzstan is a poor country with significant new BRI-related infrastructure projects under construction, financed by loans from China. By the end of March 2017, public and publicly guaranteed debt amounted to roughly 65% of GDP, of which external debt represented about 90% of the total debt. China's Exim Bank is the largest single creditor; roughly, 40% of the country's total external debt belongs to it. Kyrgyz and Chinese authorities have plans for construction of a chain of hydropower plants, a China-Kyrgyzstan-Uzbekistan railway, additional highway construction, and completion of the Central Asia-China gas pipeline, with loans from China (Bandiera & Tsiropoulos, 2019).

The most high profile of the BRI ventures in Pakistan is the Gwadar Port project. It is the main feature of the $62 billion China-Pakistan Economic Corridor (CPEC), with at least $33 billion of this amount would be invested in energy projects. China will reportedly finance roughly 80% of that amount. China is charging high interest rate for the loans taken by Pakistan. That could lead to public debt ratios well above 70%. The CPEC is a road link between Pakistan's Gwadar port near Karachi to Xinjiang in China, and a stretch of it passes through the Gilgit-Baltistan region, which Pakistan invaded and occupied in 1947. India cannot join Belt and Road because it would mean accepting that parts of Kashmir that Pakistan occupied is essentially Pakistan (Horn et al., 2019).

In the Maldives, there is a similar concern that Beijing is using debt-trap diplomacy to build a strategic advantage in the region. Chinese investors due to China's unbalanced economy are eager to invest in Sri Lanka and the Maldives and many more countries with minimal due diligence, as investments in China have become unproductive. China is now thus exporting its unproductive investment abroad (Asia Maritime Transparency Initiative, 2020).

China in Europe

A very important project in Europe is to provide a railway link from the port of Piraeus in Greece to Eastern Europe. China, through its China Ocean Shipping Company, bought a 67% stake in the port's Pier I from the Piraeus Port Authority SA in January 2016.

Montenegro's debt problem is enormous. The World Bank estimates that public debt (including guarantees) as a share of GDP might climb to 83% in 2018 in the absence of fiscal adjustment. The source of the problem is one very large infrastructure project, a motorway linking the port of Bar with Serbia that would integrate the Montenegro in transport network with those of other Balkan countries. The Montenegro authorities concluded an agreement with China Exim Bank in 2014 for the latter to finance 85% of the estimated $1 billion cost for the first phase of the project. The estimated cost has since risen to $1.1 billion or over 25% of GDP. The road is being built in three phases, and the IMF believes the non-concessional terms would likely result in debt default (Horn et al., 2019).

The US has worried about China's intentions. Developing the economies of South and Central Asia is a long-standing US goal that intensified after the start of the US-led war in Afghanistan and President Barack Obama's pivot to Asia, but the American efforts are at their minimum for development projects. Several countries in Central and Eastern Europe have accepted BRI financing, and Western European states such as Italy, Luxembourg, and Portugal have signed provisional agreements to cooperate on BRI projects. There are fear that the BRI could make partner countries vassal states.

Origin of the Coronavirus: China's Unrestricted Warfare

Coronavirus created all over the world a fear of death. How this virus was originated. The standard explanation from the Chinese was that in the wet market of Wuhan as there are Bat meat and Pangolean meat, virus was originated there and gradually spread all over Wuhan and other areas of China and then all over the world. However, serious doubts are now raised in the non-Chinese world. The reason is Bat was not sold in the wet market of Wuhan. There are active research going on in the Institute of Virology in Wuhan on various deadly virus, under the control of the Chinese military. Questions are raised whether accidentally virus was released from that Institute or it was deliberate (Huang et al., 2020; Doremalen, 2020; Huang et al., 2020; Lucey & Kent, 2020; Metzl, 2021; Shi Zhang Li, 2015; Shi Zhang Li et al., 2005, 2013, 2015; Van Doremalen, 2020; Wu et al., 2020).

According to NTD News, a web magazine, since last December 2019 China imported masks and other personal protection materials worth millions of Dollars from all over the world through the overseas Chinese creating worldwide shortage, although China itself is the biggest producer of these items. Since November 2019, China knows about coronavirus, when one Chinese died in early November 2019 in Wuhan. The first foreign victim was in December 2019 in Thailand, which receive millions of Chinese sex tourists every year. Prof Lieber of Harvard University Biology department was arrested for receiving $1.2 million to support the Institute of Virology in Wuhan, the center of coronavirus. Thus, a conspiracy angle cannot be ignored.

According to Epoch Times, a web magazine (youtube.com/watch?v GDD7dtDaymM&t 316s) China has created this virus as a part of its strategic plan to create chaos in the world, which will serve its purpose of defeating the US on a world scale. Wuhan is the largest city in Central China. Institute of virology is controlled by the Chinese army. Chinese President Xi also came from the Chinese army. Thus, it is important to know to what direction their research is going.

On December3, 2019, an unknown pneumonia virus was detected in the wet market of Wuhan, which sells all kinds of wild animals including snakes, and domestic cats, dogs for food. One person was infected and died. It was told that the virus came from bat, but that market does not sell any bats. That market is closed down on January 26, 2020. Chinese government still insisted that the source of this new virus was that wet market.

In the British journal called Lancet, on February 24, 2020, a Chinese scientist Dr. Chaolin Huang et al. (2020), who is the Deputy Director of a specialized hospital in Wuhan for the victims of this new virus, published an article, which is the result of research by his team conducted for the period between December 1, 2019 and January 1, 2020. He and his team claimed that the virus obtained from the victims is unrelated to the wet market in 14 out of 41 cases, and there was no bats in the wet market at all (Webster, 2013).

Prof Judy Mikovits of the Institute of Antiviral Mechanism, of the Utah State University, US, where she was the Director, explained this new virus is 100% mutation of SARS virus, which created fear in 2002–2003 worldwide (Epoch Times). There is a Spike Protein, which can unlock the natural protection of human cells, but Spike Protein cannot naturally invade human cells, unless it was enhanced to do that artificially. Thus, this new virus must be manufactured. A group of Dutch scientists with Dr. Van Doremalen (2020) published their finding in March 13, 2020, in the New England Journal of Medicine, that HCOV-19 (which is also called SARS-COV2) is similar to SARS-COV 1. That supports the earlier finding of a group of Indian scientists with the lead scientist, Prasant Pradhan, and 8 other scientists of School of Biology of the IIT Delhi, that the unique insertion in the 2019-nCOV of spike protein of HIV-1 gp 120 and HIV-1 Gag, which give this virus ability to destroy body's natural immunity (Pradhan et al., 2020).

In 3 January, National Health Commission of China gave the order to the Wuhan Institute of Virology that all their documents and samples collected by Shi Zhang Li and her team should be destroyed. Who is this Shi Zhang Li?

She had studied up to Masters level in the Institute of Virology in Wuhan. Then she did her PhD in the University of Montpellier in France. France had collaborated with China on many scientific areas including China's nuclear explosion in 1964 when China has no nuclear reactor but France supplied the materials to China. France helped to create the Institute of Virology in Wuhan.

In 2002–2003, Shi Zhang Li discovered the SARS virus and in 2010, she and her team found out that Spike protein can help the coronavirus to move from one specie to another by adding a component from the HIV virus. That was published in China in Chinese language.

On October 2013, in the British journal Nature, Shi Zhang Li and her team published an article that a new virus, which causes Pneumonia, can be extracted from bats (2013). On November 2015, in the British journal Nature Medicine, she and her team published another article showing a synthetic virus which can go from one specie to another and she did an experiment on monkeys (Shi Zhang Li, 2015). This is the origin of the coronavirus.

That caused concern in the scientific community. Prof Simon Wain Hobson of the Institut Pasteur of Paris expressed his fear explicitly on this type of research of Shi Zhang Li. As a result, French government curtailed all collaboration with the Institute of Virology of Wuhan. President Obama stopped financing research on genetic manipulations.

Shi Zhang Li et al. (2015) and her team added a new component HIV-gp41 to this synthetic virus, which she has published in the Nature Medicine in 2015, which removes the protection of the human cells and help the passage of the Spike protein in the human cells, which makes this new virus deadly. The argument of the Institute of Virology of Wuhan on 24 January was that 2019-nCOV virus is identical to the virus BAT Cov Ra TG 13, which came from bats. Institute of Virology of Wuhan patented that virus (Anderson et al., 2020; Shi Zhang Li et al., 2015, 2005; Zhu et al., 2020).

The Director of Wuhan P4 Lab in Wuhan, Wang Yan Yi is now suspected of releasing that new virus either deliberately or accidentally. French government initially supported that P4 lab in Wuhan whose director was Yuan Zhiming and former Vice President of that P4 Lab was Jiang Mianheng, who is the son of the former Chinese President Jiang Zemin who in 1989, at the time of the visit of Gorbachev to China, killed 8000 students demanding democracy, in the Tiananmen Square in Peking.

Shi Zhang Li is now disappeared; she had created the 2019-nCov virus, which is now infamous as coronavirus by adding a component of HIV virus to the SARS virus thus making it deadly (Shi Zhang Li, https://www.nature.com/articles/nm.3985/). Jiang Zhicheng grandson of that killer ex-president of China Jiang Zemin got the exclusive right to manufacture and sell an antidote of coronavirus named Remdisivir from his pharmaceutical company in China.

The question is why on earth the Chinese researcher rather than doing research on how to cure people will put their energy on how to kill massive number of people with this invisible weapon of a virus. Behavior of the Chinese government caused suspicion. Why did it ask the overseas Chinese to buy up masks, gloves, and other personal protective items from most countries in December 2019 and send these back to China, causing worldwide shortages of these items which China itself produces and exports. Is that mean China knew about the possible pandemic, which would be caused by coronavirus in advance? Why does China not export Remdisivir, the possible cure for the pneumonia caused by the coronavirus? Why both Peking and Shanghai, both not far from Wuhan, have so few people affected by coronavirus, when the major victims are from Italy, the US, and Spain, which are thousands of miles from Wuhan? Why did, in last November and December 2019, millions of Chinese tourists go out of China to these countries? Why did some beautiful Chinese girls go to Italy in January 2020 and ask Italians to hug them? Are these all just coincidental?

Two senior officers of the People's Liberation Army of China, Qiao Liang and Wang Xiangsui (1999), wrote a book named Unrestricted Warfare or Warfare beyond Bounds in 1999, about how to defeat a technologically superior enemy through a variety of means, all banned by the international law, which China does not care (https://www.c4i.org/

unrestricted. pdf; 1999). These means can put the enemy in a condition that no direct military action would be needed. It is known as Fourth-Generation Warfare, first proposed by a team of American military strategists led by William Lind (2015), who suggested that there should not be any difference between combatants and civilians. This is totally unacceptable in India according to Kautilya in his Arthashastra, but the Western countries and China do not care about any ethics in war (Basu & Miroshnik, 2021). That is the reason Prithviraj Chouhan was captured by Mohammed Ghouri, who was defeated before by Chouhan but according to the ethics of war in India was released with honor (Talbot, 2015).

Thus, releasing a deadly virus can serve the purpose of China in another way. Most companies and airlines are in serious financial problem with their share prices are going down and they will be bankrupt soon. China can take advantage of this by buying up most of these companies in distress. India government took a preemptive action against these types of Chinese attacks on companies in India under financial stress but other countries are yet to take any action. Rothschild at the time of the battle of Trafalgar spread a rumor in London that Napoleon won the battle. As a result, share prices in London stock market collapsed and Rothschild purchased them all. China may do the same in very near future. Lives of a million people are too insignificant for that strategy of a war without any ethics.

References

ABC News. (2018, November 19). *Tonga gets five years' grace on Chinese loan as pacific nation joins belt and road initiative.* https://www.abc.net.au/news/2018-11-19/china-defers-tongas-loan-payments-as-nation-signs-up-to-bri/10509140.

ABC News. (2019, August 7). *Papua new guinea asks China for help with $11.8b national debt.* https://www.abc.net.au/news/2019-08-07/png-to-ask-china-for-help-refinancing-national-debt/11391186.

Andersen, K. G., Rambaut, A., & Lipkin, W. I. (2020). The proximal origin of SARS-CoV-2. *Nature Medicine, 26*(4), 45052.

Asia Maritime Transparency Initiative. (2020). Chinese investment in the Maldives: Appraising the string of pearls. *Asia maritime transparency initiative.* https://amti.csis.org/chinese-investment-in-the-maldives-appraising-the-string-of-pearls/.

Bandiera, L., & Tsiropoulos, V. (2019). *A framework to assess debt sustainability and fiscal risks under the belt and road initiative.* Policy Research Working

Paper No WPS 8891. Washington, DC: World Bank Group. http://documents.worldbank.org/curated/en/723671560782662349/pdf/A-Framework-to-Assess-Debt-Sustainability-and-Fiscal-Risks-under-the-Belt-and-Road-Initiative.pdf.

Basu, D., & Miroshnik, V. (2021). *Ethics, morality and business*. Palgrave-Macmillan-Springer.

Brazys, S., & Vadlamannati, K. (2018, May). *Aid curse with Chinese characteristics? Chinese development flows and economic reforms*. AidData Working Paper 52. https://www.aiddata.org/publications/aid-curse-with-chinese-characteristics-chinese-development-flows-and-economic-reforms.

Cerutti, E., & Zhou, H. (2018, February 9). *The Chinese banking system: Much more than a domestic giant*. VoxEU.org. https://voxeu.org/article/chinese-banking-system.

Chatham House—International Affairs. (2020). *Debunking the myth of 'Debt-trap diplomacy'*. https://www.chathamhouse.org/2020/08/debunking-myth-debt-trap-diplomacy.

Chin, G., & Gallagher, K. (2019). Coordinated credit spaces: The globalization of Chinese development finance. *Development and Change, 50*(1), 245–274.

CSIS.org. (2020). *It is a (Debt) trap! managing China-IMF cooperation across the belt and road*. https://www.csis.org/npfp/its-debt-trap-managing-china-imf-cooperation-across-belt-and-road.

Dezenski, E. (2020). *Below the belt and road: Corruption and illicit dealings in China's global infrastructure*. Foundation for Defense of Democracies.

Dhar, B. (2018). *India's comprehensive economic partnership agreements with ASEAN, Japan and Korea*. Third World Network.

Dhar, B. (2019a). India's withdrawal from the regional comprehensive economic partnership. *Economic and Political Weekly, 54*(45), 59–65.

Dhar, B. (2019b). Chinese cheer for Indian exports. *Hindu Business Line*.

Dhar, B. (2020). Political economy of India's trade liberalisation. In J. Plagemann, S. Destradi & A. Narlikar (Eds.), *India rising: A multilayered analysis of ideas, interests, and institutions*. Oxford University Press.

Dhar, B., & Reji, K. J. (2019). India's information technology industry: A tale of two halves. In K.-C. Liu & Uday S. Racherla (Eds.), *Innovation, economic development, and intellectual property in India and China: Comparing six economic sectors*. Springer Open.

Dijkstra, G. (2018). *Aid and good governance: Examining aggregate unintended effects of aid, evaluation and program planning, 68*, 225–232. https://www.sciencedirect.com/science/article/pii/S0149718917302975.

Doremalen, N. (2020). Aerosol and surface stability of SARS-COV-2 as compared with SARS-COV-1. *New England Journal of Medicine, 16*(April) (382), 1564–1567.

Dornan, M., & Brant, P. (2014). Chinese assistance in the Pacific: Agency effectiveness and the role of Pacific island governments. *Asia Pacific and Policy Studies, 1*(2), 349–363.

Duncan, R. (2016). Sources of growth spurts in Pacific island economies. *Asia and Pacific Policy Studies, 3*(2), 351–365.

Dziedzic, S. (2018, November 27). What's in the secret documents signed by China and vanuatu at APEC? *ABC News*. https://www.abc.net.au/news/2018-11-27/the-secret-documents-china-and-vanuatu-signed-at-apec/10557438?pfmredir=sm.

Dziedzic, S. (2019, March 13). China's 'payday loans' attacked, new US diplomat to Australia. *ABC News*. https://www.abc.net.au/news/2019-03-13/china-accused-payday-loans-pacific-us-ambassador-australia/10896280.

Export Finance Australia. (2018, October). PNG—Sovereign bond issue bodes well; but FX shortages remain. *World Risk Developments*. https://www.exportfinance.gov.au/resources-news/news-events/world-risk-developments/2018/world-risk-developments-october-2018/.

Ezell, S., & Atkinson, R. (2015). *False promises: The yawning gap between China's WTO commitments and practices*. Information Technology & Innovation Foundation.

FT.com. (2020). *China'S belt and road projects drive overseas debt fears*. https://www.ft.com/content/e7a08b54-9554-11e8-b747-fb1e803ee64e.

Gibson, J., & Nero, K. (2007). *Are Pacific Island economies growth failures? Geo-political assessments and perspectives*. http://citeseerx.ist.psu.edu/viewdoc/download?doi=10.1.1.465.3391&rep=rep1&type=pdf.

Glosserman, B. (2019). *Peak Japan: The end of great ambitions*. Washington, DC: Georgetown University Press.

Graue, C., & Dziedzic, S. (2018, January 10). Federal minister Concetta Fierravanti-wells accuses China of funding 'roads that go nowhere' in Pacific. *ABC News*. https://www.abc.net.au/news/2018-01-10/australia-hits-out-at-chinese-aid-to-pacific/9316732.

Guhathakurta, S. (1994). Electronics policy and the television manufacturing industry: Lessons from India's liberalization efforts. *Economic Development and Cultural Change, 42*(4), 845–868.

Hillman, J. (2018, March). *Game of loans: How China bought hambantota, CSIS Briefs*. https://www.csis.org/analysis/game-loans-how-china-bought-hambantota.

Horn, S., Reinhart, C., & Trebesch, C. (2019, July). *China's overseas lending*, NBER Working Paper No 26050. https://www.nber.org/papers/w26050.

Hu, B., Zeng, L.-P., Yang, X.-L., Ge, X.-Y., Zhang, W., Li, B., Xie, J.-Z., Shen, X.-R., Zhang, Y.-Z., Wang, N., Luo, D.-S., Zheng, X.-S.,Wang, M.-N., Daszak, P., Wang, L. F., & Cui, J. (2017). Discovery of a rich gene pool of bat SARS-related coronaviruses provides new insights into the origin of SARS coronavirus. *PLoS Pathog, 13*(11), e1006698. https://doi.org/10.1371/journal.ppat.1006698.

Hurley, J., Morris, S., & Portelance, G. (2018). *Examining the debt implications of the belt and road initiative from a policy perspective*, CGD Policy Paper, Center for Global Development. Washington, DC. https://www.cgdev.org/sites/default/files/examining-debt-implications-belt-and-road-initiative-policy-perspective.pdf.

Huang, C., Wang, Y., & Li, X. (2020, January 30). Clinical features of patients infected with 2019 novel coronavirus in Wuhan, China. *Lancet, 395*(10223), 497–506

Khosla, S. S. (2020, July 17). How India helped China to steal its industry and jobs. *Times of India*.

Knowledge@Wharton. (2020). *China'S belt and road initiative: Why the price is too high*. https://knowledge.wharton.upenn.edu/article/chinas-belt-and-road-initiative-why-the-price-is-too-high/.

Kundu, B., Pradhan, P., Pandey, A., Mishra, A., Gupta, P., Kumar, P., Tripati, P., Menon, M., Gomes, J., & Vivekanandan, P. (2020, January 20). *Uncanny similarity of unique inserts in the 2019-nCov spike protein to HIV-1 gp120 and Gag*, bioRxiv. https://doi.org/10.1101,2020.01.30.927871

Lind, W. (2015). *Victoria: A novel of 4th generation war*. Castalia House.

Lucey, D., & Kent, K. (2020). With evidence against the origin of COVID-19 being the seafood market in December, a call to share and discuss all data at the 73rd World Health Assembly in May, Science Speaks. https://sciencespeaksblig.org/2020/01/25/wuhan-coronavirus-2019-ncov-qa-6-an-evidence-based-hypothesis/.

Metzl, J. (2021, April 8). New probe into coronavirus origins. *South China Morning Post*.

O'Dowd, S. (2018, August 21). Power plays in the Pacific. *East Asia Forum*. https://www.eastasiaforum.org/2018/08/21/power-plays-in-the-pacific/.

Oxfam Report on WTO. (2019). *Eight Broken Promises*. file:///G:/WTO%205%20OXFAM%20report.pdf.

Pradhan, P., Pandey, A., Mishra, A., Gupta, P., Tripathi, P., Menon, M., Gomes, J., Vivekanandan, P., & Kundu, B. (2020). *Uncanny similarity of unique inserts in the 2019-nCoV spike protein to HIV-1 gp120 and Gag*. https://doi.org/10.1101/2020.01.30.927871.

Pradhan, P., Pandey, A., Mishra, A., Gupta, P., Tripathi, P., Menon, M., Gomes, J., Vivekanandan, P., & Kundu, B. (2020). *Uncanny similarity of unique inserts in the 2019-nCoV spike protein to HIV-1 gp120 and Gag*. https://doi.org/10.1101/2020.01.30.927871.

Qiao Liang & Wang Xiangsui. (1999). *Unrestricted Warfare*. PLA Literature and Arts Publishing House.

Rai, J. (2020, April 23). Here's a snapshot of key Chinese investors in Indian startups. *VCCircle*.

Rao, K. S. C., & Dhar, B. (2018). *India's recent inward foreign direct investment: An assessment*. Institute for Studies in Industrial Development.

Riordan, P. (2018, January 10). Coalition attack on China over pacific aid. *The Australian*. https://www.theaustralian.com.au/nation/foreign-affairs/coalition-attack-on-china-over-pacific-aid/news-story/29eb518cae5b114272a664aa56a67166.

Shi Zhang Li. (2015, December 30). Isolation and characterization of a novel bat coronavirus closely related to the direct progenitor of severe acute respiratory syndrome coronavirus. *Journal of Virology, 90*(6), 3253–3256.

Shi Zhang Li. https://www.nature.com/articles/nm.3985/.

Shi Zhang Li, Li, W., Shi, Z., & Yu, M. (2005). Bats are natural reservoirs of SARS-like coronaviruses. *Science, 310*(5748), 67679. https://doi.org/10.1126/science.1118391.

Shi Zhang Li, Ge, X. Y., Li, J. L., & Yang, X. L. (2013). Isolation and characterization of a bat SARS-like coronavirus that uses the ACE2 receptor. *Nature, 503*(7477), 53538. https://doi.org/10.1038/nature12711.

Shi Zhang Li, Menachery, V. D., Yount, B., et al. (2015, November 9). A SARS like cluster of circulating bat coronaviruses shows potential for human emergence. *Nature Medicine, 21*, 1508–1513.

Smith, N. (2020). How to rebalance China's unbalanced growth model. *Atlas Institute for International Affairs*. https://www.internationalaffairshouse.org/how-to-rebalance-chinas-unbalanced-growth-model/.

Talbot, C. (2015). *The last hindu emperor*. Cambridge University Press.

Van Doremalen, N. (2020). Aerosal and surface of SAR-COV 2 as compared with SARS-COV-1. *New England Journal of Medicine, 382*(16), 1564–1567.

Webster, T. (2013). Paper compliance: How China implements WTO decisions. *Michigan Journal of International Law, 35*(3), 534–535.

Whiting, N., Zhou, C., & Feng, K. (2019, September 19). What does it take for China to take Taiwan's Pacific allies, apparently, $730 million. *ABC News*. https://www.abc.net.au/news/2019-09-20/kiribati-to-switch-diplomatic-ties-from-taiwan-to-china/11532192.

Wroe, D. (2018, April 9). China eyes Vanuatu military base in plan with global ramifications. *The Sydney Morning Herald*. https://www.smh.com.au/politics/federal/china-eyes-vanuatu-military-base-in-plan-with-global-ramifications-20180409-p4z8j9.html.

Wu, F., Zhao, S., & Yu, B. (2020). A new coronavirus associated with human respiratory disease in China. *Nature, 579*(7798), 265–269.

Zhengli Li Shi, Menachery, V. D., Yount, B., & Baric, R. (2015). A SARS like cluster of circulating bat coronavirus shows potential for human emergence. *Nature Medicine, 21*, 1508–1513.

Zhu, N., Zhang, D., & Wang, W. (2020). A novel coronavirus from patients with pneumonia in China in 2019. *New England Journal of Medicine, 382*(8), 72733. https://doi.org/10.1056/NEJMoa2001017.a

Sources of Data

ADB, Pacific Economic Monitor. (2018, December). https://www.adb.org/sites/default/files/publication/471196/pem-december-2018.pdf.

ADB. (2017). *Meeting Asia's infrastructure needs*. Asian Development Bank. https://www.adb.org/sites/default/files/publication/227496/special-report-infrastructure.pdf.

AidData. *What's included in China's official finance?* https://www.aiddata.org/china-official-finance.

Government of India. (2006). *The national strategy for manufacturing, national manufacturing competitiveness council*.

Government of India. (2011). *National manufacturing policy*. Press Note 2 (2011 Series), Ministry of Commerce and Industry.

Government of India, Ministry of Petroleum and Chemicals. (1975). *Report of the committee on drugs and pharmaceutical industry*. Hathi Committee Report.

Government of India, Committee on Public Undertakings. (1969). *Forty-sixth report: Indian drugs and pharmaceuticals limited*. Fourth Lok Sabha. New Delhi: Lok Sabha Secretariat.

Government of India, Committee on Public Undertakings. (1976). *Eightieth report on hindustan antibiotics limited. Fifth Lok Sabha*. New Delhi: Lok Sabha Secretariat.

IMF Debt Limits Policy. https://www.imf.org/external/np/spr/2015/conc/index.htm.

OECD. *Official development assistance—Definition and coverage*. https://www.oecd.org/dac/stats/officialdevelopmentassistancedefinitionandcoverage.htm.

World Bank. (2018). *IBRD financial products: Lending rates and fees*. https://treasury.worldbank.org/en/about/unit/treasury/ibrd-financial-products/lending-rates-and-fees#1.

World Bank, IDA Lending Terms. http://ida.worldbank.org/financing/ida-lending-terms.

World Bank, Non-Concessional Borrowing Policy. http://ida.worldbank.org/debt/non-concessional-borrowing.

World Risk Report. (2018). (Berlin: Bündnis Entwicklung Hilft and Ruhr University Bochum—Institute for International Law of Peace and Armed Conflict, 2018), 40. https://reliefweb.int/sites/reliefweb.int/files/resources/WorldRiskReport-2018.pdf.

WTO. (1996, December 13). *Ministerial declaration on trade in information technology products*. WT/MIN(96)/16. Singapore. https://data.worldbank.org/.

WTO. (2017, October 2). Schedules of tariff concessions to the general agreement on tariffs and trade 1994—Certification of modifications: Schedule XII—India. WT/LET/181.

CHAPTER 5

American Empire and Its Expansion

American Empire and Its Consequence

American empire of Britain was started in fifteenth century and subsequently when Britain defeated both France and Spain to expand its American empire. The profit came from the sugar and cotton plantations and slave trade. This chapter explains how the American empire gave Britain these profits and after the independence of the American empire, how the US continued with the colonization process in Latin America through various multinational companies, and how the profits from these empires contributed to the development of American capitalism. When Spain and Portugal partitioned the world by signing the Treaty of Tordesillas on June 7, 1494, they declared a manifest destiny of European supremacy. Even the critics of colonization policies—starting with Bartolomé de las Casas (1474–1566) to the Marxist-Leninist criticism of the twentieth century—accepted this process of civilization. European settlers were varied, they were including adventurers, soldiers, farmers, and tradesmen, and even a few from the European upper classes. They included the Dutch, Swedes and Finns, the English Quakers, English Puritans, Germans, and the Scots. These groups melted together to form the US which became an independent nation in 1776. The British expelled the French and the Spanish. These colonies developed legalized systems of slavery with the slaves imported from Africa. Wars were recurrent between the French and the British, between the Original

© The Author(s), under exclusive license to Springer Nature Switzerland AG 2021
D. Basu and V. Miroshnik, *The Economic and Political Dangers of Globalization*, https://doi.org/10.1007/978-3-030-79895-6_5

native Indians and the British, and between the British and the Spanish (Andrews, 1914).

Paul Kennedy described, "From the time the first settlers arrived in Virginia from England and started moving westward, this was an imperial nation, a conquering nation" (Kennedy, 1987). Detailing George Washington's description of the early US as an "infant empire," Benjamin Franklin's writing that "the Prince that acquires new Territory removes the Natives to give his own people Room ... may be properly called [Father] of [his] Nation," and Thomas Jefferson's statement that the United States "must be viewed as the nest from which all America, North & South is to be peopled."

Noam Chomsky said that "the United States is the one country that exists, as far as I know, and ever has, that was founded as an empire explicitly" (Chomsky, 2016). It was the ideology of Manifest Destiny. It was realized with the Mexican–American War of 1846, when a vast part of Mexico was annexed. President James Monroe used his famous doctrine for the western hemisphere in 1823, it had some aggressive implications for American policy. Roosevelt claimed that he rejected imperialism, but he embraced the near-identical doctrine of expansionism even to the Far East, collaboration between US and British military activities in the Pacific were nothing but imperialism. American intervention in both Latin America and Hawaii resulted in various American investments, thus these were both political and economic investments (Lenin, 1917; Marx, 1863; Beeman, 2006; Elwell-Sutton, 1955; Smith & Adams, 2011).

President Wilson had definite imperialistic plan to open international markets to surplus US production, while he said categorically, that "Concessions obtained by financiers must be safeguarded by ministers of state, even if the sovereignty of unwilling nations be outraged in the process... the doors of the nations which are closed must be battered down."

President Wilson launched seven armed interventions on economical motives. In a 1933 speech he said: *"I was a racketeer, a gangster for capitalism. I suspected I was just part of a racket at the time. Now I am sure of it...I helped make Mexico, especially Tampico, safe for American oil interests in 1914. I helped make Haiti and Cuba a decent place for the National City Bank boys to collect revenues in. I helped in he rapingof half a dozen Central American republics for the benefits of Wall Street ... Looking back on it, I feel that I could have given Al Capone a few hints. The best he could do was to operate his racket in three districts. I operated on three continents. World War II as a "grand opportunity" for the US to emerge as "the premier power in the world*" (Wilson, 1902/2008). Trade and markets now considered to be the economic pillars of global power. The 1944 arrangement to create an international currency system but also created two central banking institutions, the International Monetary Fund and the World Bank, to supervise the global economy, they represent both American and European power.

According to the Pro-Empire British historian Niall Ferguson, the US is an empire and this is a good thing: "*What is not allowed is to say that the United States is an empire and that this might not be wholly bad*" (Ferguson, 2004). Ferguson has drawn parallels between the British Empire and the imperial role of the US in the late twentieth and early twenty-first centuries, though he describes, "*the United States' political and social structures as more like those of the Roman Empire than of the British.*" Ferguson argues that "*all of these empires have had both positive and negative aspects, but that the positive aspects of the U.S. Empire will, if it learns from history and its mistakes, greatly outweigh its negative aspects*" (Ferguson, 2004).

The Goals of Colonialists

The colonialists from Europe had highly developed military knowledge. They had the ability to build ocean-worthy ships. Initially, matters concerning the colonies were dealt with primarily by the Privy Council of England and its committees. Mercantilism was the basic policy imposed by Britain on its colonies from the 1660s, which meant that the government supported the merchants in order to increase both public and private wealth. The government promoted London-based merchants and kept out others by through trade barriers, regulations, and subsidies to domestic industries in order to maximize exports from the realm and minimize imports (Gasiorowski, 1991; Gruson, 1954; Fieldhouse, 1961).

The goal of mercantilism was to earn maximum trade surpluses. The government earns through duties and taxes. The government created its massive navies which protected and expanded the British colonies. The British Navy captured New Amsterdam which was renamed as New York in 1664. The colonies were markets for British industry. The British Britain found a market for their goods in the British colonies of North America, increasing her exports to that region by 360% between 1740 and 1770 (Smith & Adams, 2011) (Table 5.1).

Table 5.1 Slaves imported to American colonies and later states

- 1620–1700....21,000
- 1701–1760... 189,000
- 1761–1770.... 63,000
- 1771–1790.... 56,000
- 1791–1800.... 79,000
- 1801–1810... 124,000
- 1810–1865.... 51,000
- Total 597,000

Source Williams (1944)

The economy was based on slave labor imported from Africa and of other British countries. About 5% of the 12 million slaves brought from Africa. Others are from other countries of Latin America or Asia. Their numbers became 4 million by the 1860 Census. In his Theories of Surplus Value, Marx compared in passing the two types of colonization: "Two different aspects must be distinguished here. Firstly: There are the colonies proper, such as in the US, Australia, etc. The mass of the farming colonists, although they bring with them a larger or smaller amount of capital from the motherland, were not capitalists, nor do they carry on capitalist production. They are more or less peasants who work themselves and whose main object, in the first place, is to produce their own livelihood, their means of subsistence. Their main product therefore does not become a commodity and is not intended for trade. They sell or exchange the excess of their products over their own consumption for imported manufactured commodities" (Marx, 1867).

"The other, smaller section of the colonists who settle near the sea, navigable rivers, etc., form trading towns. There is no question of capitalist production here either." "In the second type of colonies— plantations— where commercial speculations figure from the start and production is intended for the world market, the capitalist mode of production exists, although only in a formal sense, since the slavery precludes free wage labor, which is the basis of capitalist production. The business, in which slaves are used, was conducted by capitalists. The method of production, which they introduce had not arisen out of slavery but is grafted on to it." In this case, the same person was capitalist and landowner. The elemental existence of the land confronting capital and labor did not offer any resistance to capital investments; hence, there was no competition between capitals. Neither did a class of farmers as distinct from property owners developed here. "*So long as these conditions endure, nothing will stand in the way of cost-price regulating market-value*" (Marx, 1863). What is important is that this capitalist production originated from the beginning of colonization an indigenous capitalist class, independent from the traders and bureaucracy: the bourgeois landowners. Latin American history has not yet been studied from this overall characterization: the existence from the beginning of an indigenous bourgeoisie linked to regional production.

The main concern of the conquerors and colonizers are the gold and silver mines for the world market, the desperate search of Eldorado, and not land to cultivate with feudal relations. This only proves the capitalist character of the conquest and colonization. "*The Spanish, Portuguese, English, French and Dutch colonization in America was essentially capitalist. Its objectives were capitalist and not feudal: organizing production and discoveries to make prodigious profits and to place goods on the world market. They did not inaugurate a system of capitalist production because in America there was not an army of workers in the free market. This is how the colonizers to exploit America as capitalist, were forced to resort to non-capitalist relations of production: slavery or semi slavery of the-indigenous peoples. The three pillars on which the colonization of America was settled were: production and discovery with capitalist aims; semi-slave or slave relationships; feudal forms and terminology (like in Mediterranean capitalism)*" (Luxemburg, 1951). The colonization has capitalist objectives, to gain profits, but it is combined with non-capitalist relations of production. They created economic forms in the New World that had a combined character. They welded pre-capitalist relations to trade relations, subordinating them to the demands and movements of merchant capital (Lenin, 1917).

England is small and contains relatively few natural resources. During Great Britain's mercantilist period, the prevailing economic wisdom suggested that the empire's many colonies could supply raw materials and resources to the mother country and subsequently be used as export markets for the finished products. The resulting favorable balance of trade was thought to increase national wealth.

Great Britain was not alone in this line of thinking. The French, Spanish, and Portuguese competed with the British for colonies; it was thought, no great nation could exist and be self-sufficient without colonial resources. Mercantilism, did however, lead to the adoption of enormous trade restrictions, which stunted the growth and freedom of colonial business. In the 1660s, for example, England passed the Navigation Acts, a series of laws designed to make American colonies more dependent on manufactured products from Great Britain. British authorities further enumerated a set of protected goods that could only be sold to British merchants, including sugar, tobacco, cotton, indigo, furs, and iron (Hilferding, 1981; Hobson, 1965).

Slave Trade

The British government also demanded trade in gold and silver bullion, ever seeking a positive balance of trade. The colonies often had insufficient bullion left over to circulate in their own markets, so they took to issuing paper currency instead. Mismanagement of printed currency resulted in periods of inflation. Additionally, Great Britain was in a near-constant state of war. Taxation was needed to prop up the army and navy. The combination of taxes and inflation caused great colonial discontent.

By 1830, one million Americans, most of them enslaved, grew cotton. Raw cotton was the most important export of the US, at the center of America's financial flows and emerging modern business practices, and at the core of its first modern manufacturing industry.

The humble fiber, transformed into yarn and cloth, stood at the center of the emergence of the industrial capitalism that is so familiar to us today. Our modern world originates in the cotton factories, cotton ports, and cotton plantations of the eighteenth and nineteenth centuries. The US was just one nexus in a much larger story that connected artisans in India, European manufacturers, and, in the Americas, African slaves and land-grabbing settlers. It was those connections, over often vast distances that created an empire of cotton—and with it modern capitalism (Williams, 1944).

We come to understand that the ability of European merchants to secure ever-greater quantities of cotton cloth from South Asia in the seventeenth and eighteenth centuries was crucial to the trans-Atlantic slave trade, as cloth came to be the core commodity exchanged for slaves on the western coast of Africa.

As machine production of cotton textiles expanded in Britain and continental Europe, traditional sources of raw cotton—especially cultivators in the Ottoman Empire as well as in Africa and India—proved insufficient. With European merchants unable to encourage the monocultural production of cotton in these regions and to transform peasant agriculture, they began to draw on slave-grown cotton, at first from the West Indies and Brazil, and by the 1790s especially in the US (Beeman, 2006).

As a result, Europe's ability to industrialize rested at first entirely on the control of expropriated lands and enslaved labor in the Americas. It was able to escape the constraints on its own resources—no cotton, after all, was grown in Europe—because of its increasing and often violent domination of global trade networks, along with the control of huge territories in the Americas. For the first few years of modern industry, the only significant quantities of raw cotton entering European markets were produced by slaves. By 1800, Liverpool became the most important port for both cotton and the slaves that producing these. We cannot know if the cotton industry was the only possible way into the modern industrial world, but we do know that it was the path to global capitalism. Europe and North America could have grown rich without slavery, but industrial capitalism and the Great Divergence in fact emerged from the violent caldron of slavery, colonialism, and the expropriation of land. In the first 300 years of the expansion of capitalism, particularly the moment after 1780 when it entered into its decisive industrial phase, it was not the small farmers of the rough New England countryside who established the US' economic position. It was the labor of African slaves in the American south (Parisot, 2019; Smith & Adams, 2011).

During its heyday, in fact, slavery was seen as essential to the economy of the Western world. No wonder the British journal The Economist worried in September 1861, when Union General John C. Frémont emancipated slaves in Missouri that such a "fearful measure" might spread to other slaveholding states.

After the Civil War, a new kind of capitalism arose, in the US and elsewhere. Yet that new capitalism—characterized first and foremost by states with unprecedented bureaucratic, infrastructural, and military capacities, and by wage labor—had been enabled by the profits, institutions, networks, technologies, and innovations that emerged from slavery, colonialism, and land expropriation.

The commercialization of northern agriculture, in turn, created the domestic market for both consumer and producer goods that supported a very consequential boom in industrial production during the two decades before the Civil War. In the southern states, plantations therefore represented a very weak market for capital-goods manufacturers.

Determined to become economically self-sufficient, meanwhile, slave-owners also bought only negligible quantities of foodstuffs from commercial farmers in the northern Midwest. Meanwhile, plantation slavery's economic requirements were pushing it relentlessly westward. Slave-based agriculture's inability to increase efficiency technologically left it able to do so only by physically expanding onto new (and especially more fertile) lands. That expansionist drive, if allowed to succeed, would have blocked the necessary expansion of commercial agriculture and capitalist industry (Beer, 1907).

Cotton Textiles

Cotton textile manufacturing was an industry built on low-wage labor; presumably, this industry offered opportunities in areas where farmers were unsuccessful. Yet, similar to the other manufactures which enlarged their market areas to the entire East before 1820, cotton textile production emerged in prosperous agricultural areas. That is not surprising, because this industry required substantial capital, technical skills, and, initially, nearby markets. These requirements were met in rich farming areas, which also could draw on wealthy merchants in large cities who contributed capital and provided sale outlets beyond nearby markets as output grew. The production processes in cotton textile manufacturing, however, diverged from the approaches to making shoes and small metal and wooden products. From the start, production processes included textile machinery, which initially consisted of spinning machines to make yarn, and later (after 1815), weaving machines and other mechanical equipment were added. Highly skilled mechanics were required to build the machines and to maintain them. The greater capital requirements for cotton mills, compared to shoes and small goods' manufactures in Connecticut, meant that merchant wholesalers and wealthy retailers, professionals, mill owners, and others, were important underwriters of the factories.

Starting in the 1790s, New England, and, especially, Rhode Island, housed the leaders in early cotton textile manufacturing. Providence merchants funded some of the first successful cotton spinning mills, and they drew on the talents of Samuel Slater, an immigrant British machinist. He trained many of the first important textile mechanics, and investors in various parts of Rhode Island, Connecticut, Massachusetts, New Hampshire, and New York hired them to build mills. Between 1815 and

1820, power-loom weaving began to be commercially feasible, and this effort was led by firms in Rhode Island and, especially, in Massachusetts. Boston merchants, starting with the Boston Manufacturing Company at Waltham, devised a business plan which targeted large-scale, integrated cotton textile manufacturing, with a marketing/sales arm housed in a separate firm. They enlarged their effort significantly after 1820, and much of the impetus to the growth of the cotton textile industry came from the success entrepreneurs had in lowering the cost of production.

The American Industrial Revolution

There were actually two Industrial Revolutions. The first occurred in Great Britain in the mid-seventeenth and early eighteenth centuries as that nation became an economic and colonial powerhouse. The Second Industrial Revolution occurred in the US beginning in the mid-1800s.

Railroads were of supreme importance to increased trade throughout the US; it was financed by Britain from its revenues from India. By the start of the Civil War, railroads already linked the most important Midwestern cities with the Atlantic coast, fueling the Midwest's industrial growth; these were financed by the British out of their revenues from India.

The industry was transformed in the Second Industrial Revolution by Henry Ford's pioneering use of the assembly line in the manufacturing process, which advanced on the development of another innovation, the automobile, first invented in 1885 by German Karl Benz. At the same time, public transit was exploding, with electric streetcars aboveground and the first US subway, in Boston, in 1897.

As the Second Industrial Revolution advanced, metallurgists would develop alloys making steel (another nineteenth-century innovation) even stronger, allowing for construction of the first skyscraper in 1885 in Chicago. The invention of the telegraph in 1844, the telephone in 1876, and the radio in 1895 would all have profound impacts on how the nation communicated, further enhancing its growth and expansion (Morgenthau, 1948).

In his 1879 letter to Danielson, Marx claims that railway companies had been the first historical example of joint-stock companies and the starting point of all other forms, starting with banking companies (Marx, 1879). Their formation took place with or without state support: Only in England was it possible without it, thanks also to the reinvestment of huge colonial profits, both from the US and India. In other countries, like the US, this process was supported by the Federal state with subventions and land concessions. Railway companies thus became the mainland proprietors, leading to a fusion between industrial capital and ground rent. Railway construction gave an impetus never before suspected to the concentration of capital, and also to the accelerated and immensely enlarged cosmopolitan activity of loanable capital, thus embracing the whole world in a network of financial swindling and mutual indebtedness, the capitalist form of "international brotherhood."

In his letter, Marx examines the cosmopolitan activities of the credit system and the opposite consequences of railways and international loans for leading industrial countries and 'agricultural' countries, in Austria and Italy above all, where the railways were a new source of state indebtedness and 'grinding of the masses.' In another letter to Danielson of February 19, 1881, he also considers the relation between railways and the public debt system in a colonial country such as India, which contributed a lot for the development of railroad in the US (Marx, 1879).

When the founding fathers of the US organized their 'democratic' Constitutional Convention in Philadelphia in 1787, the idea of the US was created as an imperial idea. The ideology of 'Manifest Destiny,' born in the 1840s, was simply the result of the basic organization and goal of the American state: to conquer western space, eliminate native peoples, and spread whiteness across the territory.

Latin American Empire of the US

The Banana Wars were a series of conflicts and military interventions in Latin America and the Caribbean caused or influenced by the US to protect its commercial interests. Panama, Honduras, Nicaragua, Mexico, Haiti, and the Dominican Republic were all venues of conflicts. The United Fruit Company and the Standard Fruit Company had significant commercial stakes and influence in Latin America and were behind many of the conflicts. The Banana Wars, also known as the "American-Caribbean Wars," were a series of occupations, police actions, and interventions involving the US in Central America and the Caribbean. This period of conflict started with the Spanish-American War in 1898 and the subsequent Treaty of Paris, which gave the US control of Cuba and Puerto Rico. Thereafter, the US conducted military interventions in Cuba, Panama, Honduras, Nicaragua, Mexico, Haiti, and the Dominican

Republic. The series of conflicts ended with the withdrawal of troops from Haiti in 1934 under President Franklin D. Roosevelt. Reasons for these conflicts were varied but were largely economic in nature. The conflict was called the "Banana Wars" because of the connections between US interventions and the preservation of American commercial interests in the region (Great White Fleet, 1928).

The United Fruit Company was known for their cruelty in the workplace and the racist social order they perpetuated. Though Chiquita and Fyffes are more subtle in their autocratic tendencies, they continue many of the same practices of political and social manipulation as their parent company once did (Council on Hemispheric Affairs). When the United Fruit Company invaded Guatemala, they bought out many of the local farmers to acquire land for their plantations. This did not leave room for the peasants, who relied on farming as the sole source of their income. Arbenz created an agrarian reform that took land from the company and gave it back to the poor farmers that needed it (Gleijeses). United Fruit was outraged by this reform. They immediately launched a propaganda campaign led by Edward Bernays to convince the US government and its people that Arbenz was a communist dictator (Smith & Adams, 2011). In a 1953 article by the *New York Times*, Guatemala was describes as "*operating under increasingly severe Communist-inspired pressure to rid the country of United States companies*" (Gruson, 1954).

The CIA hired civilian militias from Honduras to come into Guatemala and start a war against Arbenz and his followers. United Fruit also convinced US President Eisenhower to threaten Arbenz because he and many other prominent American government officials had stock in United Fruit (Gleijeses, 1992). With these pressures, Arbenz feared for his life and submitted his resignation. However, this did not satisfy United Fruit. They wished to make an example of Guatemala, so their other host nations wouldn't dare oppose them. They had the CIA pay off the Guatemalan military so they would let the Honduras militia win (Streeter). After the victory, the leader of the Honduras militia, Castillo Armas, was appointed as President of Guatemala and Armas was a puppet of the United Fruit Company for the rest of his term (Council on Hemispheric Affairs, www.Coha.org). He returned all of United Fruit's confiscated land and gave them preferential treatment in all Guatemalan ports and railways.

Other Latin American nations were influenced or dominated by American economic policies and/or commercial interests to the point of coercion. Theodore Roosevelt declared the Roosevelt Corollary to the Monroe Doctrine in 1904, asserting the right of the US to intervene to stabilize the economic affairs of states in the Caribbean and Central America if they were unable to pay their international debts. From 1909 to 1913, President William Howard Taft and his Secretary of State Philander C. Knox asserted a more "peaceful and economic" Dollar Diplomacy foreign policy, although that, too, was backed by force.

Although the US prided itself on being 'anti-colonial,' having broken away from British rule, US capitalism was nevertheless imperialistic from the very beginning. In 1845, for instance, Congress annexed 390,000 square miles of Mexican territory (the equivalent in area of the original 13 American colonies). Not surprisingly, Mexico declared war on the US, and the Mexican War of 1846–1848 followed. In his message to Congress in May 1846, President Polk asserted that the Mexican War was caused by the armed forces of Mexico having "invaded our territory and shed American blood on the American soil." In the 1890s, when the expansion of American imperialism continued, the US invaded Cuba and the Philippines, annexed Hawaii and other islands (Puerto Rico, etc.), and launched a military and commercial invasion of China to plunder the country. If they did not have formal colonial territories like Britain and France, the US nevertheless exerted de facto control of these conquered lands.

Colonialism, however, was replaced by economic neo-colonialism (Great White Fleet). Direct control by the Western powers, each through their own colonial administration, was replaced by the collective exploitation of the neo-colonial world by the advanced capitalist countries. This was reinforced by the military power of the Western powers, especially the power of US imperialism. The US emerged from the Second World War as by far the strongest economic power. One of the overriding aims of US foreign policy was to create a favorable world environment for the US corporations. In 1945, the US Treasury Secretary, Morgenthau, said that the US required a world system "in which international trade and international investment can be carried on by businessmen on business principles" (Morgenthau, 1945). This meant primarily US businessmen according to US business principles. The new world economic order—the World Bank, the IMF, GATT, the OECD, etc.—was dominated by the US. The dollar became the basic currency of world trade.

International investment and trade was dominated by the giant US companies, the multinational corporations, which spun a web of exploitation across the globe. By 1980, the top 200 multinational corporations accounted for approximately 29% of the aggregate domestic product of the capitalist world. About 90 of these companies were based in the US (with about 20 each in West Germany, the UK, and Japan; and in France). At the height of the post-war economic upswing, US multinationals and their affiliates accounted for between 20 and 25% of all world exports. They particularly dominated the world market in raw materials, minerals, and, of course, oil—all vital ingredients for the American economy. Through the exploitation of cheap labor and terms of trade which sold the underdeveloped countries short, the US corporations extracted super profits from the underdeveloped lands.

The world's financial system is also dominated by the big US banks. Much of the oil revenues accumulated by the oil producers after the 1974 price rise were deposited in private US banks, who 'recycled' it to neo-colonial countries—in some cases to finance arms purchases, in others to keep their economies afloat. This gave rise to the enormous burden of debt now placed on the poor and semi-developed countries. Far from helping these countries, the debt burden acts as a siphon, sucking out additional wealth from them. Owing to accumulated debt, neo-colonial countries as a whole are paying back to the advanced capitalist countries in excess of $50 billion a year more than they receive. The poor countries, or rather the poor in those countries, are being bled to death by the capitalist West.

The US has always been prepared to defend its economic interest with military power. Those it has defended in the name of 'democracy' have more often than not been dictators, viciously oppressive and corrupt, who would not have lasted five minutes without US backing. Those who have been crushed in the name of 'democracy' have invariably been movements or governments reflecting the struggle of the workers and peasants against exploitation by landlords and capitalists, and against the pillaging of their countries by foreign businesses. In short, US imperialism has always played a counter-revolutionary role on the world arena, ready to use its military power to intervene against any manifestation of social revolution.

In the nineteenth and early twentieth centuries, the US primarily acted as a self-appointed policeman in Latin America and the Caribbean. 'Banana republic' became political shorthand for the kind of corrupt and ruthless dictatorship propped up by the US to protect giant companies like United Fruit. Somoza, who ruled Nicaragua with an iron fist until his overthrow by the Sandinista movement in 1979, was a notorious example.

For the representatives of US imperialism, their police role is virtually a self-evident right. When US marines were previously sent to Nicaragua, in 1927, President Coolidge blandly explained: "We are not making war on Nicaragua any more than a policeman on the street is making war on passers-by." When the US emerged from the Second World War as one of the two nuclear superpowers, presidents such as Truman, Eisenhower, Nixon, and Reagan all asserted their right to act as global policemen. The TCC is "the dominant, or hegemonic, fraction of capital on a world scale" (Ferguson, 2004). Interventions in Chile, Venezuela, Brazil, Guyana, Columbia, Paraguay, Uruguay, and Argentina showed the demonstration of American power on Latin America (Grandin, 2006; Hopkins, 2018).

It manages global production chains and incorporates multiple class agents and formerly national groupings into a new power bloc whose material interests and class unity are located in transnational processes. The TCC is the most dynamic class force in the world economy and the competitive logic it triggers forces local and national capitalists to become more globally integrated as well. The result has been the formation of a new transnational power bloc, which integrates multiple levels of capital and gets organized through global patterns of production and accumulation instead of through national ones.

For Robinson (2004), this new power bloc has established a transnational state apparatus (TNS), which includes "*transformed and externally integrated national states, together with the supranational economic and political forums*," such as the International Monetary Fund, the World Bank, the World Trade Organization, and the United Nations. The TNS institutionalizes "*the new class relation between global capital and global labor*," and "*forge[s] together a new global capitalist historic bloc*" (Ferguson, 2004).

Multinational corporations are inextricably tied to the financial and political-military power of the particular states in which they are based, without which they could not exist for a moment, and on which their ability to engage effectively in international competition depends. In the case of the top hundred nonfinancial corporations in the world, three quarters have their home in just six countries: US, UK, France, Germany, Japan, and Switzerland.

Imperialism today is more aggressive and boundless in its objectives than ever. In the present period of declining US hegemony, as well as economic and ecological decline, the dollar-oil-Pentagon regime, backed by the entire triad of the US/Canada, China, Europe, and Japan, is exerting all of its military and financial power to gain geopolitical and geo-economic advantages. The goal is to subordinate still further those countries at the bottom of the world hierarchy, while putting obstacles in the way of emerging economies, and overthrowing all states that violate the rules of the dominant order.

Under these circumstances, global value/supply chains, along with energy, resources, and finance, the escalating US–China conflict is nothing short of a major crisis for global capitalism. With negotiations having all but collapsed there seems to be no "exit ramp" from the trade war that began in July 2018. This crisis points to a prolonged and increasingly rancorous struggle with potentially serious global effects economically, politically, and even militarily.

The executive order signed by Trump that bans US companies from supplying Chinese telecom giant Huawei Technologies is nothing less than a state-led campaign by the US to drive the company out of business and prevent Huawei, which has close links to the Chinese state, from achieving global dominance over 5G (fifth generation) wireless technology, the rollout of which is imminent. Trump's decision puts Huawei on what is informally called a "kill list." Currently Huawei, the global leader in 5G networks, sources half its microchips from US companies. Already, Hikvision and Dahua, Chinese companies making surveillance systems and facial recognition technology, have been named as the next possible targets.

The root of the conflict is a clash of imperial powers on a quest for global hegemony. In fact, the current struggle suggests that state capitalist policies, with governments intervening to steer economic developments and "control" the market, could become more common globally, coexisting with more deregulation and privatizations. The 70-nation BRI (Belt and Road Initiative) is an example of imperialism "with Chinese characteristics," launched by Xi's regime as a way to soak up China's chronic industrial overcapacity and provide new profitable outlets for its banking system when much of the Chinese economy is gorged on debt.

However, American capitalism was an extension of the British Empire. Later it became a separate nation with special relationship with the UK, thus acquiring the characteristics of the British Empire. Imperialism came first, capitalism and international capitalism in the US developed much later. Thus, Lenin was not correct in this matter.

American Empire

A national drive for territorial acquisition across the continent was popularized in the nineteenth century as the ideology of Manifest Destiny. President James Monroe presented his famous doctrine for the western hemisphere in 1823, it had some aggressive implications for American policy. The Indian Wars was escalated against the indigenous population began in the British era, but expanded to dominate North America. This was an explicitly colonial process in light of arguments that Native American nations were sovereign entities prior to annexation. The purpose was to acquire resources and land; the same process is going on today to maximize the profit of the "military–industrial complex."

The September 11, 2001 attack on America was payback for US imperialism, which created Al-Queada, Muzzaheedin, and Taliban and provided with weapons and training, which they had now turn against the US and the non-Muslim world. When Muslim Bosnians rose up against the efforts of the Serb to maintain the unity of the country in the early 1990s, they received support from many of the same Islamic extremists who also backed the mujahedeen in Afghanistan (Hopkins, 2018).

The Clinton Administration supported these Muslim extremists with the help of Pakistan and Turkey in the Balkans. Bush, Obama, and Trump went further. They invaded one country after another, starting with Iraq, then Libya, then Syria, repeating the history of the Western imperialism.

Afghanistan, Sudan, Libya, Egypt, Arabia, Mesopotamia (Iraq), Palestine, Persia, the Northwest Frontier (Pakistan)—these are all places where, in the nineteenth century, Western armies had to quell the resulting disorder or resistance against imperialism. The abolition of the Soviet Union gave the freedom to the Western countries to take off their masks and to bring back the nineteenth century in twenty-first century. Taliban brought nothing but grief to the people in Afghanistan but Trump gave them back the power on Afghanistan.

American actions have nothing to do to promote democracy or freedom. The first Bush Administration stood by as Saddam crushed the Shiite and Kurdish rebellions in Iraq after acting to help an undemocratic Amir of Kuwait against Iraq in the first Gulf war. The real purpose was to help the Western oil companies. The second Gulf war was based on a false fear that Iraq was trying to weapons of mass destruction, but the real purpose was to steal the oil fields of Iraq for the Western oil companies. War against Libya and Syria had the same purpose (Boot, 2002). This is old style imperialism of the nineteenth century to expand and to protect economic interest of the Western companies (Ritter, 2002).

The first stage of the American empire began with the Mexican–American War, but began to flourish at the conclusion of the Civil War. All the states east of the Mississippi River had been brought by force back under the rule of the federal government, a national taxation system had been established to provide revenues to the government. In the process, the vast majority of Native Americans were killed off in the US. By the time Woodrow Wilson assumed the presidency, the first stage had expanded to include Cuba, Guam, Puerto Rico, and the Philippines. Imperial footholds had been established in South America and East Asia. The 'military/industrial complex' became the dominant force in domestic and global commerce, conflict and social structure since 1945.

The American empire stretched throughout Europe to the borders of the Soviet Union. Strongholds of this stage were expanded to Africa, Japan, Israel, and Middle East. American corporations created a victorious war machine financed by profits of its multinational companies. Wars were fought in Korea, Vietnam, Laos, Cambodia, Angola, the Sinai Peninsula, and elsewhere. Profits from contracts for the development and deployment of weaponry became profitable on an epic scale. The military/industrial complex came to own whole swaths of the American political spectrum on both sides of the aisle, and attached itself as umbilical cord to the petroleum industry as a matter of basic expediency as one cannot fight wars without an abundance of oil and gasoline. Now, permanent war and rule by fear are accepted without question; the dominance of the military/industrial/petroleum combine is unquestioned (Hopkins, 2018; Immerwahr, 2019; Weiner, 2007).

In recent years, the US has used similar strategies against Venezuela, another oil-producing country. The Trump Administration was determined to depose Venezuela's elected President Nicolás Maduro. The US placed sanctions on Venezuela's oil exports, which provide 90% of the nation's revenue, confiscated oil assets of Venezuela, and asked Britain to do the same, while also insisting Venezuela should allow it to deliver humanitarian aid to the country.

In Venezuela, we can see a replay of the US invasion of Mexico in 1846. A key pillar of US post-Second World War hegemony was the domination by US companies of the 'world' oil resources concentrated in the Middle East. Oil is a strategic commodity that everybody needs and is crucial to military power. The reconstruction of Western Europe, crucial to the expansion and sustaining of capitalism, depended on cheap Middle East oil supplies. Oil is also essential to the US version of energy-intensive capitalism: the spread of the motorcar, suburbs, chemical-intensive agriculture, and cheap food were all dependent on cheap oil. General Wesley Clark, the NATO commander in charge of the destruction of Yugoslavia said in March 2007 that the US had the plan to invade seven countries in five years and it is because of oil. If there is no oil the Middle East will be like Africa, nobody would bother (Kinzer, 2006; Wilford, 2013).

Containing any threats from either the Soviet Union or local nationalism to the cheap energy needed by the capitalist world economy, which Middle East oil provided was one of the functions of hegemony. That made US military power indispensable. Moreover, the alliance of US oil companies and the US government with Saudi Arabia was pivotal to the oil price stability and global economic prosperity.

However, the particular way the US has exercised its 'oil protectorate' over the Middle East regularly has stimulated backlashes and periodic regional conflicts that actually put global energy security at risk. These challenges have been invariably stimulated either by a coercive intervention to sustain Western control of oil or by a linkage between oil and Western backing of Israel.

Nationalist challenges to Western control of Middle East oil began with Muhammed Mussadeq's nationalization of the Iranian oil industry; indigenous reaction to the subsequent CIA-sponsored coup to overthrow him would take decades to mature but it ultimately stimulated the Islamic revolution. Other major challenges to Western control of the oil market would come from the Arab world, where Arab nationalism saw a combination of Western imperialism and Zionism as the main threat and Arab nationalist control of Arab oil as the main key to challenging these forces (Heiss, 1997; Rearden, 2012).

The US managed, however, to turn the oil crisis to its advantage by striking a close alliance with Saudi Arabia by which it provided security in return for the Saudis' use of their position as 'swing producer' to moderate oil prices. Given the privileged position of the dollar as the international reserve currency in which oil is sold, the new wealth of the oil producers was disproportionately 'recycled' through US banks and via arms purchases and investments in the US.

US hegemony is based on the dollar as much as it's military and, since the 1970s, oil hegemony reinforced US dollar hegemony, because all countries needed dollars to buy oil and needed access to the American market to get them. That dollar allowed the US to levy a tax on the world's economy to finance massive US military spending and imperial overreach and to impose economic measures that hurt its competitors (Dreyfuss, 2005; Weiner, 2007).

After the oil price boom, the competitive position of Europe and Japan declined as the price of energy increased, ushering in the stagflation of the 1970s. This was followed by British Prime Minister Margaret Thatcher's attack on the European welfare state. The more limited damage of the boom to the US was very disproportionately distributed—there the consumers suffered, Texas oil barons got higher oil prices, and power shifted to the military/oil industries concentrated. In 1974, the US paid out \$1.7 billion for Saudi oil but \$8.5 billion were recycled from Saudi Arabia back to the US. In the longer term, the US–Saudi alliance by the early 1980s had secured the stabilization of oil prices followed by a precipitous price decline that kept energy-intensive US capitalism competitive. However, that has created the conflict between Iraq and Kuwait, and Iraq invaded Kuwait and Saudi Arabia to teach a lesson for being a pro-American (Hopkins, 2018).

The subsequent US war on Iraq was intended to avoid a potent challenge to US oil hegemony. If Iraq had retained Kuwaiti oil fields and remained in a position to intimidate Saudi Arabia, thereby acquiring 'control' of over 40% of world oil reserves, it might have had the power to shape the oil market in ways inimical to US interests. While the conservative Gulf rulers, by virtue of their security dependence on the US and their Western investments, had a shared interest with the West in ensuring stable access to oil at moderate prices, Iraq had no such stake. Iraq was, of course, in dire need of revenues and had to sell its oil at prices consumers would pay. Saddam's threat to make the terms of oil sales conditional on a favorable Western policy in the Arab–Israeli conflict caught US politicians between two powerful contradictory domestic demands—for cheap gasoline and the advancement of Israel's interests (Gendzier, 1999).

In the end, the war actually enabled Washington to reinforce its hegemony on the oil market. The US used the war to demonstrate its continuing indispensability to protecting the world capitalist control of oil against challenges while, in making it's Gulf clients, above all Saudi Arabia, more dependent on the US for their security. The war boosted America's relative economic standing for, while Japanese and European capitalism had become more energy efficient. US capitalism, protected by the special benefits of hegemony, had built American competitiveness on low oil prices. The war ensured prices would stay low and that Gulf petrodollars would be disproportionately recycled through US—not European or Japanese—banks and arms manufacturers. In addition, the US actually managed to make its imperial policing profitable by inducing its economic competitors (Germany, Japan) and clients (Saudi Arabia, Kuwait) to pay for the war (Elwell-Sutton, 1955).

US Imperialism and Libya

Prior to the intervention of NATO, there were no sectarian murders of Christians in Libya and Islamist militias tied to Al Qaeda were small groups with no broader influence. These forces were armed and promoted when, in 2011, the Obama Administration and its allies in Europe, led by French President Nicolas Sarkozy, and British Prime Minister Tony Blair invaded Libya (Basu & Miroshnik, 2012; Hopkins, 2018; Immerwahr, 2019).

The imperialist powers funneled massive amounts of money and weaponry to Islamist militias and Al Qaeda operatives, providing them with air support through a mass bombing campaign that killed tens of thousands of Libyans. The declared purpose was to establish democracy but the result was a chaos and disintegration of Libya.

A syndicate of western imperialist powers got hold of Libya's oil wealth and turn its territory into a neo-colonial base of operations for further interventions throughout the Middle East and North Africa. Syria became the major victim. Libya after the murder of Gaddafi became a training ground for CIA-backed Islamist forces preparing to fight the Syrian government of President Bashar al-Assad. Western media described the conflict that led to Gaddafi's ouster simply as a "civil war," without even mentioning NATO's six-month bombing of Libya in 2011 (Immerwahr, 2019). Gaddafi ruled for 42 years, leading Libya to a significant advance in social, political, and economic matters with standard of living comparable to that of Saudi Arabia.

After the Second World War, Libya was ceded to France and the UK, and both countries linked it administratively to their colonies in Algeria and Tunisia. In 1951, it became a nominally independent country but it was in backwardness in education, health, housing, social security, among others. In 1969, Colonel Muammar al-Gaddafi removed the king with the aim to share the benefits and wealth to all Libyans. Ambitious social programs in education, health, housing, public works and subsidies for electricity and basic foodstuffs led to a substantial improvement in the living conditions of Libyans, from being one of the poorest countries in Africa in 1969 to being the continent's leader in it's the U.N. Human Development Index in 2011. Libya had a literacy rate of 88.4%, a life expectancy of 74.5 years, gender equality, free housing, and free medical service among several other positive entitlements for the citizens. It used to provide jobs for 40,000 other Africans. In 2011, Libya had the highest GDP per capita and life expectancy on the African continent. Fewer people lived there in Libya below the poverty line than in Holland. Hugo Chavez and Maduro of Venezuela tried to emulate Gaddafi to uplift his people in Venezuela but could not because of American hostility (Kinzer, 2006; Wilford, 2013).

The uprisings in Benghazi by the Islamic terrorists sent there by France were enough for the U.N. Security Council and NATO to intervene on behalf of the 'Responsibility to Protect' (Resolution 1973) and launched a bombing campaign between March and October 2011 which had the result of the assassination of Gaddafi and the destruction of Libya. The Western-backed counter-revolution of 2011 has resulted in Libya becoming a failed state and its economy is in shambles. In 2011, the West's objective was clearly gain control of Libya's natural resources, mainly oil. Libya sits on a resource more valuable than oil, the Nubian Sandstone Aquifer, which is the world's largest underground source of freshwater (Hopkins, 2018; Immerwahr, 2019).

France's global mega-water corporations, like Suez, Ondeo, and Saur, control more than 45% of the planet's water market, which is already a $400 billion global industry. For France, the 2011 revolution in Libya was about gaining control of and privatizing Libya's astounding water resources.

The regime change revolution in Libya was a major instance of imperialist hydrological warfare. Now that Libya's water profits are flowing to the West, unsurprisingly, western parts of Libya are running out of drinkable water. Due to corporate greed and neglect, two-thirds of the nation's key water conduits are no longer functioning. From oil to water, and from arms to natural gas, the 2011 revolution in Libya has given billions of dollars for the West and only wrought misery and endless civil war for Libyans (Toh, 2017; Wilford, 2013).

American Empire in South East Asia

For Eisenhower and the Dulles brothers in the 1950s, Vietnam was just another small and impoverished country that could do nothing to against the US. After the Second World War, all Imperialist countries came back to Asia to reclaim their empires while Japanese gave them limited independence. French came back to Vietnam, Dutch came back to Indonesia, and the British came back to India, Burma, and Malaysia. War has never ended in Asia. French were defeated in the hands of the Vietnamese in 1954. UN came in and about to organize an election to be supervised by India, Canada, and Poland on behalf of the UN. However, just the day before the election in 1955 the US organized a coup and Ngo Ding Deim, a catholic became the Dictator in a Buddhist country. Kennedy organized another coup in 1963. By August that year the President of the US, Lyndon B. Johnson, ordered the first bombing of North Vietnam. More bombs were dropped over Vietnam in this campaign alone than the total dropped during the entire Second World War. Two million Vietnamese and more than 50,000 American soldiers would die in dis war. Chemical weapons would defoliate 10% of the country's surface. All these for just to stop the Soviet Union to expand its influence in South East Asia, as Vietnam had practically no natural resources (Hopkins, 2018; Immerwahr, 2019; Toh, 2017).

Iran and US

In 1908, oil was struck in Iran, but the ownership was to the British-owned Burmah Oil Company, renamed as the Anglo-Persian Oil Company (APOC), whereby Persia received 16% of "net profits." In 1921, a coup organized by the British brought a general, Reza Khan, into the government, first as the prime minister, and then by 1925 Reza Khan was crowned Reza Shah Pahlavi. In 1941, after the Nazi invasion of the USSR, the British and Commonwealth of Nations forces and the Red Army invaded Iran. The reason was to secure Iran's oil fields. Reza Shah's son, Mohammad Reza Pahlavi, became the Shah of Iran (Gasiorowski, 1987, 1991).

In late 1951, Iran's Parliament approved the oil nationalization agreement. Many Iranians felt that for the first time in centuries, they were taking control of the affairs of their country. Iranian parliament and people demanded more favorable concessionary arrangements, which Britain vigorously opposed.

By September 1951, the British had virtually ceased Abadan oil field production, forbidden British export to Iran of key British commodities (including sugar and steel), and had frozen Iran's hard currency accounts in British banks.

The US and British intelligence agencies organized a coup to oust Iran's democratically elected Prime Minister, Mohammad Mosaddegh in 1953 when Iran had sought to nationalize Iran's oil industry, which was under the Anglo-Iranian Oil Company (AIOC), a British corporation (now part of BP). Fearing a Communist takeover in Iran, UK Prime Minister Winston Churchill and the Eisenhower Administration decided to overthrow Iran's government and to put Prince Reza Pahlavi in power.

Just before the coup, by 1953, economic tensions caused by the British embargo and political turmoil began to take a major toll on Mosaddegh's popularity and political power. The people were increasingly blaming him for the economic and political crisis. Political violence was becoming widespread in the form of street clashes between rival political groups.

The US did the same for Venezuela in recent years. After the coup, five American petroleum companies, along with Royal Dutch Shell, and the Compagnie Française des Pétroles, were to extract Iran's petroleum. The overthrow of Iran's elected government in 1953 ensured Western control of Iran's petroleum resources and prevented the Soviet Union from competing for Iranian oil (Abrahamian, 1982; Heiss, 1997; Kinzer, 2003). In 1956, the US had organized a coup in Pakistan, located next to Iran, to put a military dictator Ayub Khan in power, replacing a democratic government of Iskandar Mirza. Pakistan was created by the British in 1947 to stop the Soviet Union to come to the Middle East.

US and Syria

Syria was invaded by the Arabic-speaking French Foreign Legion in 2011 in the pretext of Arab spring, the popular mass-movement starting in Tunisia. From Libya, where these French Foreign Legion members were went to Syria with Turkey providing base to them. Initially, they were added by Al-Queada, Al-Nusra, and ISIS to occupy both Syria and Iraq. US army came in with the excuse to protect the Kurds who were then fighting against those Turkish-backed invaders. The real purpose was to occupy the oil fields of Syria. Another purpose of the US involvement was to construct a pipeline through Syria and Turkey to supply oil and gas from Saudi Arabia and the Gulf Arab states to Europe. That could destroy Russian export of energy to Europe (Basu & Miroshnik, 2012; Toh, 2017; Wilford, 2013).

The invasion of Syria started in 2011, after the destruction of Libya, when Syria was a prosperous stable country with no apparent economic problems. Just like in the Ukraine and Georgia, and also in Egypt and Tunisia, some very violent crowds were hired by some strange shadowy agency, financed by a group of countries in the Arabian Gulf and Turkey. The purpose was to change the regime first by creating mass demonstrations and then concerted international denouncements by mainly the Western media, followed by some violence and ultimately a change of the regime by force.

The same pattern was used in country after country with two major exceptions, Libya and Syria. In both cases initial mass demonstrations were followed by armed insurrections supported by foreign powers. In Libya, the foreign powers were France, the US, the UK, and NATO, with some involvement from Saudi Arabia, Qatar, UAE, and Turkey. However, in Syria the armed groups came directly from Saudi Arabia, Qatar, UAE, Libya, Turkey, and France to change the regime.

The Libyan regime collapsed quickly because of the direct attacks from NATO. In Syria, NATO was not able to take part because of the opposition raised by Russia and China in the UN Security Council. In the meantime, the invading forces were not doing very well and were under serious attack by the government forces. The invading forces were crying out for Western military support. Thus, they had to find an excuse, which was created by a chemical attack on August 21, 2013, on the civilians in the suburb of Damascus, which was blamed on the Syrian government. The fact is that whether or not there were any chemical weapons in Syria, the US, France, Saudi Arabia, Qatar, and UAE would have invaded Syria anyway (www.wsws.org/en/articles/2012/.../syri-a22.htm). Economics and oil are the real issues.

Oil and Syria

Syria has an estimated reserve of petroleum worth about 2.5 billion barrels. This is higher than the reserves of all other Arab countries except Iraq. Syria is also fortunate to have a very large reserve of natural gas. Thus, it has every potential to have large-scale chemical industries. Since

1964 Syrian oil and natural gas fields have been in the public sector of Syria. Foreign companies, except the Russians, are not allowed to enter that sector. Until the disturbances started, Syria used to earn at least $4 billion every year from its export of petroleum (www.eia.gov/country/cab.cfm?fips=SY).

In Iraq, most important petroleum fields have already been taken over by the US–French–UK oil companies. Iraq has lost control of its oil resources. The same is planned for the Syrian oil fields. That was the reason foreign invaders have targeted these oil fields to deprive Syria of its export earnings. In future when the occupation of Syria is complete Western oil companies will take over these oil fields after getting rid of the Russians, who discovered and developed these fields for Syria (Mostafa, 1994).

There is more to it. The foreign forces are guided by Turkey, Saudi Arabia, and Qatar because of their plan to set up a long pipeline, controlled by US and other Western oil companies, to export natural gas to Europe. Syria is an impediment to that plan. Thus, the Syrian war is the war of the natural gas pipeline. During the invasion of Iraq in 2003, the pipeline of Kirkuk–Banias connecting Iraq to Syria was destroyed by the US forces. However, recently an alternative pipeline between Ain Zalah and Suweidiva was opened to connect Iraq to Syria. Plans are there to set up more pipelines for both petroleum and natural gas. The purpose of these proposed pipelines is to export both petroleum and natural gas from Iraq directly to the European market.

However, another development is possibly more important (www.oxfordenergy.org/wpcms/wp-content/.../NG-78.pdf).

In 2011, Syria, Iraq, and Iran had made an arrangement to construct a pipeline to export Iranian natural gas to Europe via Iraq and Syria first and then to Lebanon and ultimately to Greece through a submarine pipeline. This proposed pipeline would be 6000 miles long, with a capacity of 100–120 million cubic feet of natural gas every day. The estimated cost would be at least $10 billion. In 2013, Syria, Iran, and Iraq had finalized the agreement to share the cost. Western oil companies are against this plan (www.al-monitor.com). They will surely destroy the proposed pipeline, if the foreign forces can occupy Syria. This is the reason for the war.

The first target of the foreign invaders was the city of Homs in Syria, near the Turkish border. Homs is the place where the existing gas pipeline from Egypt ends. This pipeline was established by the Western oil companies to export natural gas from Egypt, Saudi Arabia, Qatar, and UAE. The plan was to extend the pipeline from Homs to Turkey to export natural gas from the Arab countries in the Persian Gulf area to Europe (www.glo balresearch.ca/iran-white…agreement/5359718).

As a result, Syria has invited the wrath of the Arab states of the Gulf. These countries have sent terrorists trained by the Taliban in Pakistan and the Arab-speaking soldiers of the French Foreign Legion, a lot of them from Libya, to destroy Syria and the planned pipeline from Iran to Lebanon. Al-Qaeda and the Taliban also have joined in. This is the reason US Secretary of States John Kerry of the Democratic Party and then President Trump of the Republican Party wanted to hand over Afghanistan to the Taliban, created by Pakistan, as the price (www.dawn.com/news/105 0763). Newly elected Democratic Party President Biden has no objection, as that would make sure that the Russians couldn't have any influence on Afghanistan.

Afghanistan

Afghanistan was destroyed by the US-supported Pakistani mujahideen in 1992 for the same reason (http://www.counterpunch.org/brzezinski.html). The plan was to build a gas pipeline from Turkmenistan to Pakistan via Afghanistan to avoid the existing route via Russia. The socialist government of Afghanistan would not have allowed it given its close relationship with the Soviet Union. Thus, it had to go in 1992. However, there was a dispute in 1995 between the mujahideen government of Afghanistan and UNICAL, the US energy company constructing the pipeline. Thus, the Taliban was formed out of the ranks of the Pakistani army, who took over Afghanistan replacing the Mujahideen. However, Iran and Russia created a new armed group called the Northern Alliance to fight the Taliban. As a result, the proposed pipeline was never finished.

The Rationale

The reason why the US and its Western allies are so interested in the oil and gas resources of the Middle East lies in the economics of US dollar. Since 1972 the US dollar has not been backed by gold but instead it is just a paper currency, which the US can print at will. The US government can exchange the dollar for any commodities or services anywhere in the world using that paper currency. No other country has that facility to print its own money to pay for imports. The value of the dollar depends on its control over the international trade of the world. Petroleum and natural gas dominate world trade considering its share of the value of the total world trade. Petroleum and natural gas are traded, except for a few countries, in terms of the US dollar only. This system provides and protects the value of the US dollar; otherwise, it will have no value at all. Thus, it is extremely important for the Federal Reserve Board (FRB) to protect the US dollar by controlling the oil and gas resources of the world in advance.

The question is which private companies control the FRB, if not the US government. They are: Rothschild Bank of London, Warburg Bank of Hamburg, Rothschild Bank of Berlin, Lazard Brothers of Paris, Kuhn Loeb Bank of New York, Israel Moses Seif Banks of Italy, Goldman, Sachs of New York, Warburg Bank of Amsterdam, and Chase Manhattan Bank of New York. There are other banks and individuals who also have significant shares of the FRB. They are: First National Bank, National Bank of Commerce, James Stillman National City Bank, Hanover National Bank, Chase National Bank, J. P. Morgan (Equitable Life/Mutual Life), William Rockefeller, Paul Warburg, and 13 other individuals. These banks and individuals also control all major Western oil and gas companies. For example, Bank of America, JP Morgan Chase, Citigroup, and Wells Fargo own the four major oil companies, Exxon Mobil, Royal Dutch/Shell, BP, and Chevron Texaco (www.globalresearch.ca/the-federal-reservecarte l.../25080).

The interests of the FRB and the Western oil companies thus coincide. Those, who own FRB, are the same people who own the Western oil & gas companies. FRB, a private company, has the exclusive right to print US dollar, which they lend, since 1913, to the US government and earns huge amount of money doing nothing.

Oil is not just by far the most important commodity traded internationally; it is the lifeblood of all modern industrialized economies. Until recently, all OPEC countries agreed to sell their oil for dollars only. So long as this remains the case, the Euro was unlikely to become the major reserve currency. The countries, that have refused to accept the US dollar for payments for their exports of oil and natural gas, were Saddam Hussein's Iraq, Colonel Gaddafi's Libya, Venezuela, Syria, Iran, the old Soviet Union, and now Putin's Russia. Iraq and Libya were invaded and the Western oil companies have taken over their oil fields. There is an economic sabotage against Venezuela to kill the economy. Syria is on the verge of total destruction. Iran is the next target. Western countries are using the so-called Islamic terrorists to destabilize these rebel oil-producing countries with the ultimate aim of destabilizing Russia, which the US still considers its prime enemy. This is the very reason Russia is supporting Syria when invasion of Syria was planned long in advance.

From 2015 onwards, Russia came to support Syria. As a result, ISIS and other Islamic groups retreated. Then US allowed Turkey to occupy a whole province of Syria and areas in Kurdistan. The Kurds now are with the Syrian government. US still is occupying the oil fields of Syria. The country of Syria is now destroyed. At least 12 million out of 22 million people became refugees, with at least 570,000 were killed.

In 1963, the Arab socialist Baath Party came to power and implemented socialist policies. Per capita income of Syria before the war in 2010 was US$4058, a middle-income country. However, economic sanction instigated by the Western countries devastated the economy even before the actual war started in 2011 (Hopkins, 2018; Wilford, 2013).

Iraq, Libya, Syria, and Venezuela are the examples of how successful and stable countries can be destroyed because of the American and Western aim to control the oil market. Who is the next? Algeria perhaps.

US and Latin America

The Cold War had key consequences in Latin America, considered by the US to be the leader of the Western Bloc. Fighting communism became the argument justifying the aggressive US presence in Latin America. In April 1948, the Organization of American States was established. Member states pledged to fight communism on the American continent. Throughout the 1960s and 1970s, the US supported a number of coups against democratically elected leaders. By 1976, South America was covered by military dictatorships called juntas (Hopkins, 2018).

Operation, which overthrew the democratically elected President of Guatemala, Jacobo Árbenz Guzmán, in 1954, was to be one of the first in a long series of US interventions in Latin America during the Cold War. In the same period, the US suspended economic relations and/or broke off diplomatic relations with several dictatorships between 1961 and 1963, including Argentina, the Dominican Republic, Ecuador, Guatemala, Honduras, and Peru. In March 1964, the US approved a military coup in Brazil, overthrowing left-wing President João Goulart. The next year, the US, under Operation Power Pack, dispatched troops to the Dominican Republic to stop a possible left-wing takeover. In 1973, the US organized a coup in Chile against a democratically elected government of Salvador Allende. By 1976, South America was covered by similar military dictatorships, called *juntas*. In Paraguay, Alfredo Stroessner had been in power since 1954; in Brazil, Goulart was overthrown in 1964, as mentioned; in Bolivia, General Hugo Banzer overthrew leftist General Juan José Torres in 1971; in Uruguay, considered the "Switzerland of South America," Juan María Bordaberry seized power in the 1973 coup (Hopkins, 2018; Immerwahr, 2019).

US and Bolivia

Bolivia had socialism from 2006, then in South America's most impoverished nation, socialism was destroyed by a US-backed coup that led to the resignation of President Evo Morales in 2019. While Morales, Vice President García Linera, and others have fled the country for asylum in Mexico in 2019. US President Donald Trump celebrated the overthrow of Morales as a "significant moment for democracy in the Western Hemisphere," warning that Venezuela and Nicaragua are next (Hopkins, 2018; Immerwahr, 2019).

This reflects the fundamental continuity in Washington's imperialist policy in Latin America under Democrats and Republicans alike, from the abortive 2002 coup against Hugo Chavez in Venezuela by George W. Bush to the 2009 US-backed overthrow of President Manuel Zelaya in Honduras by Barack Obama, to the ouster of Morales by Trump in 2019. This is driven both by the desire of US transnationals to lay claim on Latin America's resources and markets—not least Bolivia's vast energy and mineral reserves, including 70% of the world's lithium—and by the strategic confrontation between US imperialism and China, whose trade with the region rose to $306 billion last year.

Morales's government came to power with huge popularity in 2006 like Hugo Chavez in 1998 in Venezuela. Like Chavez, Morales declared himself an adherent of the "Bolivarian Revolution" and socialism. The leader of the coca growers' union and the first Bolivian president from the country's long-oppressed indigenous population, Morales won broad popular support. In the end, the bourgeois army, which Morales never disbanded, proved loyal to its roots in the fascist-military dictatorships of Generals Hugo Banzer and Luis García Meza and the national security state doctrine of the Pentagon's School of the Americas (Hopkins, 2018; Immerwahr, 2019).

Morales went in with a mandate to shatter the neoliberal policies of austerity and privatization that had shaped Bolivian society for the past two decades. From 1985 until Morales's election in 2005, Bolivia was under the yoke of one version or another of the Washington consensus. Morales passed a law seizing tens of thousands of square miles of land deemed unproductive or illegally held and redistributed it to landless peasants. He placed the natural gas, oil, telecommunications, and electricity industries under state control. He continually raised the minimum wage, which has tripled since he entered office.

Morales also dramatically increased social spending. He invested in building roads, schools, and hospitals, an expansion of infrastructure that was particularly transformative in the countryside. He established modest but deeply popular cash transfer programs: a universal noncontributory pension system for Bolivians over the age of 60; assistance to households with elementary school-aged children who can demonstrate their children are attending school; and funds for pregnant women or mothers with children under the age of two without health insurance.

During the Morales era, Bolivia has seen per capita income increase threefold and has rapidly transitioned from a low-income country to a lower-middle-income country. Inflation and the exchange rate have remained exceptionally stable. At the same time, Bolivia levels of inequality went from well above the Latin American average to well below it. Bolivia's movement toward socialism had defied right-wing predictions of food shortages, labor camps, and the collapse of private life. Instead, it has stepped in the direction of European social democracy and illustrated how a developing economy can modernize and grow swiftly without subjecting itself to austerity.

In Venezuela, the regime is presiding over one of the greatest economic catastrophes the Western Hemisphere has seen in recent history. Bolivia, though, has endured because of three distinguishing qualities. Venezuela's economy has relied entirely on one resource oil and the US put an embargo and sanctions that no country could dare to buy oil from it. In addition, both the US and the UK confiscated all assets of Venezuela in American and British banks. With the collapse of the oil price since 2014 Venezuela is in serious crisis. It has survived because of assistance from Russia and China, who are buying oil from Venezuela, defying American prohibition.

Morales, by contrast, had focused on the long term. Bolivia's main money makers are natural gas and mineral exports like zinc, but Morales had tried to diversify the economy by investing in agriculture and industrialization. He invested in health, education, and aid for the poor, but began with a fairly minimalist welfare state to ensure sustainability.

Bolivia's gradualist economic outlook was presided over by Morales's long-standing finance minister, Luis Arce. Another quality that helped Bolivian socialism was Morales's emphasis on racial inclusiveness—a feature that has both widened participation in the economy, and also inspired more buy-in from Bolivia's majority-indigenous population. Morales had wielded symbolic power as Bolivia's first indigenous president, but also used the letter of the law to create a society that embraces and defends its multicultural diversity. The constitution he passed in 2009, which changed the country's official title from "The Republic of Bolivia" to "The Plurinational State of Bolivia," officially recognized 36 indigenous languages. Laws were passed banning racial discrimination and requiring children to learn local indigenous languages. There was a rise in the number of lawmakers who identify as indigenous.

The end of the commodity boom affected Bolivia's economically and undermined the basis for Evo Morales' class conciliations policy. Since 2006, Bolivia's government has reaped the benefits of natural gas exports. After the neoliberal regime collapsed in 2003, Evo's election in 2005 led to what Evo's government called the "nationalization" of gas. More accurately, the government renegotiated contracts with foreign gas companies, yielding a much higher percentage of royalty payments, or rents, to the government.

The Shape of a Socialist Boom

By 2017, Bolivia was 42% richer than when Morales took office. For the average Bolivian, the results were even better—the country's Gini coefficient, a measure of income inequality, fell by more than 19% since Morales took office. Poverty has declined by 25% since he was elected. He had to pay the price for that as the US does not like a country trying to uplift her people, sooner or later it would be destroyed like Libya and Syria and Iraq (Anderson, 2020; Krauss & Daniel, 2019). He had to go in 2019, in a coup supported by President Trump and extreme violence returned particularly against the native indigenous population.

References

Abrahamian, E. (1982). *Iran between two revolutions*. Princeton: Princeton University Press.

Anderson, J. L. (2020, March 16). The fall of Evo Morales. *New Yorker*.

Andrews, C. M. (1914). Colonial commerce. *American Historical Review, 20*(1), 43–63.

Basu, D., & Miroshnik, V. (2012). *Structural revolution in international business*. Basingstoke: Palgrave Macmillan.

Beeman, R. (2006). *The varieties of political experience in eighteenth-century America*. University of Pennsylvania Press.

Beer, G. L. (1907). British colonial policy, 1754–1765. *Political Science Quarterly, 22*, 1–48.

Boot, M. (2002). *The savage wars of peace: Small wars and the rise of American power*. New York: Basic Books.

Chomsky, N. (2016). *Who rules the world*. London: Penguin.

Dreyfuss, R. (2005). *Devil's game: How the United States helped unleash fundamentalist Islam*. New York: Henry Holt.

Elwell-Sutton, L. P. (1955). *Persian oil: A study in power politics*. London: Lawrence and Wishart.

Ferguson, N. (2004). *Colossus: The rise and fall of the American empire*. London: Penguin.

Fieldhouse, D. K. (1961). Imperialism: An historiographical revision. *The Economic History Review, 14*(2), 187–209.

Gasiorowski, M. J. (1987). The 1953 coup d'état in Iran. *International Journal of Middle East Studies, 10*(3), 261–286.

Gasiorowski, M. J. (1991). *U.S. foreign policy and the Shah: Building a client state in Iran*. Ithaca: Cornell University Press.

Gendzier, I. (1999). *Notes from the minefield: United States intervention in Lebanon and the Middle East, 1945–1958*. Boulder: Westview Press.

Gleijeses, P. (1992). *Shattered hopes: The Guatemalan revolution and the United States*. New Jersey: Princeton University Press.

Grandin, G. (2006). *Empires workshop: Latin America and the roots of US imperialism*. New York: Henry Holt.

Great White Fleet, United Fruit Company. (1928). http://www.ediblegeography.com/spaces-ofbanana-control/.

Gruson, S. (1954, May 23). Guatemala hints UN case on arms. *New York Times*.

Heiss, M. A. (1997). *Empire and nationhood: The United States, Great Britain, and Iranian oil, 1950–1954*. New York: Columbia University Press.

Hilferding, R. (1981). *Finance capital*. London: Routledge.

Hobson, J. A. (1965). *Imperialism: A study*. The University of Michigan Press.

Hopkins, A. G. (2018). *American empire: A global history*. Princeton, NJ: Princeton University Press.

Immerwahr, D. (2019). *How to hide an empire: A history of the greater United States*. New York: Picador.
Kennedy, P. (1987). *The rise and fall of the great powers*. London: Penguin.
Kinzer, S. (2003). *All the Shah's men: An American coup and the roots of Middle East terror*. London: Wiley.
Kinzer, S. (2006). *Overthrow: America's century of regime change from Hawaii to Iraq*. New York: Henry Holt.
Krauss, C., & Daniel, V. (2019, November 11). Evo Morales urges resistance to new Bolivian Government. *New York Times*.
Lenin, V. I. (1917). *Imperialism, the highest stage of capitalism*. https://www.marxists.org/archive/lenin/works/1916/imp-hsc/.
Luxemburg, R. (1951). *The accumulation of capital*. New York: Monthly Review Press.
Marx, K. (1863). *Theories of surplus value*. www.marxists.org/archive/marx/works/1863/theoriessurplus-value/ch12.htm.
Marx, K. (1867). *Capital* (vol. 1). New York, NY: Cosimo.
Marx, K. (1879). *Letters to Danielson, Selected Correspondences by Marx and Engels, 1975*. Moscow: Progress Publishers.
Morgenthau, H. (1945). *Germany is our Problem*. New York: Harper & brothers.
Morgenthau, H. (1948). *Politics among nations*. New York: McGraw-Hill.
Mostafa, E. (1994). *Oil, power and principal: Iran's oil nationalization and it's aftermath*. Syracuse: Syracuse University Press.
Parisot, J. (2019). *How America became capitalist: Imperial expansion and the conquest of the west*. London: Pluto Press.
Rearden, M. (2012). *Council of war: A history of the joint chiefs of staffs*. Washington, DC: NDU press.
Ritter, S. (2002). *War on Iraq*. New York: Context Books.
Robinson, W. (2004). *A theory of global capitalism: Production, class, and the state in a transnational world*. Baltimore: Johns Hopkins University Press.
Smith, T. J., & Adams, A. E. (2011). *After the coup: An ethnographic reframing of Guatemala 1954*. Champaign: University of Illinois Press.
Toh, H. S. (2017). *Is China an empire*. Singapore: World Scientific.
Weiner, T. (2007). *Legacy of ashes: The history of the CIA*. New York: Doubleday.
Wilford, H. (2013). *America's great game: The CIA's secret Arabizes and the making of the modern Middle East*. New York: Basic Books.
Williams, E. (1944). *Capitalism and slavery*. Chapel Hill: University of North Carolina Press.
Wilson, W. (1902/2008). *A history of the American people*. New York: Cosimo Publications.

CHAPTER 6

American Collaboration and Resistance to China

China and the USA: Effects of China's Entry to the WTO

China entered the WTO in 2001. Conservatives all over the world supported that expecting that they can control China and China will be a democratic country. However, the results are totally opposite. The reports of Scott and his associates of the Economic Policy Institute explained the effects of massive trade deficits of the US with respect to China and its contribution on the unemployment situation in the US (Scott, 2017; Scott & Wething, 2012; Kimball & Scott, 2014).

Because imports from China have increased while exports to China have not increased much less, the US is both losing jobs in manufacturing (in particular electronics and high tech, apparel, textiles, and a range of heavier durable goods industries) and missing opportunities to add jobs in manufacturing productions (in export-oriented industries such as transportation equipment, agricultural products, computer and electronic parts, chemicals, machinery, and food and beverages) (Scott, 2017a; Scott & Glass, 2016; Bivens, 2008a, 2008b, 2013).

The growth of the US trade deficit with China between 2001 and 2017 was responsible for the loss of 3.4 million US jobs, including 1.3 million jobs lost since 2008 (the first full year of the Great Recession, which technically began at the end of 2007). Nearly three-fourths (74.4%) of the jobs lost between 2001 and 2017 were in manufacturing (2.5 million

© The Author(s), under exclusive license to Springer Nature Switzerland AG 2021

D. Basu and V. Miroshnik, *The Economic and Political Dangers of Globalization*, https://doi.org/10.1007/978-3-030-79895-6_6

manufacturing jobs lost). The trade deficit in the computer and electronic parts industry grew the most: 1,209,000 jobs were lost in that industry, accounting for 36.0% of the 2001–2017 total jobs lost. Surging imports of steel, aluminum, and other capital-intensive products threaten hundreds of thousands of jobs in key industries such as primary metals, machinery, and fabricated metal products as well (Scott, 2017b).

> Global trade in advanced technology products, often discussed as a source of comparative advantage for the US, is instead dominated by China. In 2017, the US had a $135.4 billion trade deficit in advanced technology products with China, and this deficit was responsible for 36.1% of the total US–China goods trade deficit that year. In contrast, the US had a $24.5 billion trade surplus in advanced technology products with the rest of the world in 2017. Between 2001 and 2011 alone, growing trade deficits with China reduced the incomes of directly impacted workers by $37 billion per year, and in 2011 alone, growing competition with imports from China and other low wage-countries reduced the wages of all US non–college graduates by a total of $180 billion (Nölke et al., 2019).

China has aggressively sought to obtain technology from American companies and undermine American innovation and creativity. The cost of China's intellectual property theft costs United States innovators billions of dollars a year, and China accounts for 87% of counterfeit goods seized coming into the US. China's counterfeit fashion goods undermine seriously famous brand names of Italy and France.

United States Trade Representative's (USTR) Sect. 301 investigation identified four of China's aggressive technology policies that put 44 million American technology jobs at risk. The examples are: forced technology transfer; requirements of licensing at less than economic value; Chinese state-directed acquisition of sensitive United States technology for strategic purposes; and outright cyber theft. China uses foreign ownership restrictions, administrative review, and licensing processes to force or pressure technology transfers from American companies. China requires foreign companies that access their *New Energy Vehicles* market to transfer core technologies and disclose development and manufacturing technology (Bivens, 2013; Nölke et al., 2019).

The Conflict Over Chinese Steel Exports

The Dispute Settlement Body (DSB) confirmed violations of the WTO's anti-dumping and anti-subsidy rules on the part of Chinese producers and the Chinese government. Chinese industrial policy suggests a rejection of not only the ways in which existing WTO rules are applied, but also the validity of the underlying idea that fair competition is primarily based on market principles.

China joined with the status of a so-called *Non-Market Economy* (NME). This status lowered the threshold for determining illegitimate state support and hence will allow the application of anti-dumping and anti-subsidy measures against Chinese steel exports. China's accession protocol mandated the expiration of its NME status on 11 December 2016 (Article 15); however, any country, which still consider China as a NME country, can impose measures to control Chinese exports as India did recently.

Chinese trade officials dispute the existence of illegal subsidization and defend the continuation of state support in the steel sector and elsewhere in the economy as WTO compatible (Ministry of Commerce of China, MOFCOM, 2016a). They denounce the decision of trading partners in India, Europe, and the Americas to allow anti-dumping proceedings against imports from China. However, India, Europe, and the USA argue that domestic prices in China are artificially low because of widespread subsidies and preferential treatment.

From the 1980s onwards, the Chinese steel industry served as an important object of state intervention (Ten Brink, 2019). Assistance came in the form of direct monetary supports and low-interest loans from banks or the supply of goods and services like water, electricity, land, transportation, and other production factors at nominal prices from other state-affiliated units. China does not respect the relevant WTO rules on anti-dumping and anti-subsidies, since doing so would make the steel industry unviable. 'Belt and Road Initiative' was created to support the steel industry in a substantial way.

Chinese Subsidies in Agriculture

Agriculture was the core issue in the Doha Development Round, and there are many conflicting issues. Traditionally, developing countries have put pressure on Western nations to liberalize their agricultural sector and to revise existing rules on agricultural subsidies accordingly. China introduced its own subsidy schemes (Hopewell, 2019). Chinese subsidies, including seed subsidies, direct payments, and agricultural input subsidies, increased from RMB 14.5 billion in 2004 to RMB 167.5 billion in 2014. In response, the US objected to the WTO against China in September 2016 claiming that in 2015 Chinese subsidies were nearly US$ 100 billion above WTO-permissible levels (USTR, 2016a).

The conflict over agricultural subsidies potentially undermine fair competition among trading partners. However, when the General Agreement on Tariffs and Trade (GATT), the WTO's predecessor, was created in 1947, the US, Australia, Canada, and their European partners put in place a protectionist regime that was according to their domestic requirement and included the provision of subsidies to protect their small-scale farmers.

The level of domestic support that China is allowed in its WTO treaty allows for subsidies of up to 8.5% of the value of production for China's farmers (International Food Policy Research Institute, 2008, p. vii). This level of subsidies falls in between the suggested subsidies for developed country members (5%) and developing country members (10%). Chinese policy-makers claim, China should be granted subsidy levels higher than the current threshold, because the existing rules on subsidies are biased toward developed countries. China is not entitled to use the special agriculture safeguard to protect domestic producers. Legitimacy of domestic support measures should correspond to the country's stage of economic development. This differs from subsidies to large farms and agribusinesses provided in the US and EU and should thus be considered a legitimate exemption (MOFCOM, 2016b). The US and other developed countries argued that China being 'the world's second largest economy' (USTR, 2016b), China cannot claim 'developing country' status.

Chinese policy-makers have relied on agricultural subsidies to achieve social goals, a practice that is common in Western nations as well. China remains a net food importer and its competitiveness remains rather low regarding most agricultural products. The agricultural support is seen as necessary for employment, poverty alleviation, and development. Arable land is scarce in China and farms are often in hilly, mountainous areas, which is reflected in the small average size of farms.

Liberalization is risky given the fear of unemployment in rural areas. In fact, large parts of China's population continue to depend on subsistence farming. Agriculture remains highly protected in Western nations (Scott,

2017a). In contrast to the highly commercialized forms of agricultural production in the EU and US, the setup of the Chinese agricultural sector requires different requirements regarding subsidies.

China's IT Sector: Selective Support for the WTO's Liberal Trade Order

The IT industry includes both companies involved in the production of IT-related goods, such as semiconductors, computer hardware, or communications equipment, and those providing consulting and IT services. Chinese policy-makers advanced an argument similar to the one they used with respect to agriculture: China is a developing country. Chinese IT industry has long been dominated by foreign (East Asian and Western) companies and is thus characterized by a profound integration into global production and supply chains. Export-oriented domestic firms already benefitted significantly from the original ITA agreement, which China joined in 2003. In 2004, China turned into the world's largest exporter of ITA products. The prospects for China to benefit from the extended ITA agreement are very high, and consequently, the state has a strong interest in liberalization. More than 60% of IT products are produced by export-oriented enterprises in zones that attract foreign R&D centers. The overall success of export-oriented firms, in turn, led Chinese officials to prefer tariff cuts (USTR, 2018).

The US has objected to Chinese regulation, 2017 Cyber Security Law, as incompatible with WTO commitments. It is difficult for foreign firms to enter the Chinese e-commerce market. In addition, the CCP retains direct influence over key firms. China bends existing WTO rules to justify alleged cases of rule-breaking and is questioning the validity of the prevailing liberal compromise. China does not support the WTO's liberal trade order but wants to use WTO for its benefit (Hopewell, 2019; Narlikar, 2019; Nölke et al., 2019; Stephen & Parízek, 2019; Bishop & Muzaka, 2019; Wu, 2016).

The US Trade Deficit with China Since China Entered the WTO

Table 6.1 displays changes in the US–China goods trade deficit and job displacement from 2001 to 2017. As the table shows, imports from China

Table 6.1 US–China goods trade and job displacement, 2001–2017

	2001	*2008*	*2017*
US goods trade with China ($billions, nominal)			
US total exports	$19.2	$71.5	$130.4
US general imports	$102.3	$337.8	$505.6
US trade balance	−$83.0	−$266.3	−$375.2
US trade-related jobs supported and displaced (thousands of jobs)			
US total exports—jobs supported	179.2	564.2	959.1
US general imports—jobs displaced	1,170.7	3,616.9	5,311.3
US trade deficit—net jobs displaced	991.5	3,052.7	4,352.2

Source US Census Bureau, US International Trade Commission (2018), Bureau of Labor Statistics

increased dramatically in this period, rising from $102.3 billion in 2001 to $505.6 billion in 2017. US exports to China rose at a rapid rate from 2001 to 2017, but from $19.2 billion in 2001 to $130.4 billion in 2017. As a result, China's exports to the US in 2017 ("U.S. general imports") were nearly four times greater than US exports to China (USITC, 2018).

Overall, the US goods trade deficit with China grew from $83.0 billion in 2001 to $375.2 billion in 2017, an increase of $292.2 billion. Since China entered the WTO in 2001, the US trade deficit with China has increased annually by $18.3 billion, or 9.9%, on average. The data reveal that the cumulative US trade deficit with China over the 2002–2017 era was $4.2 trillion (USITC, 2018).

Between 2008 and 2017, the US goods trade deficit with China increased $108.9 billion. This 40.9% increase occurred despite the Great Recession-induced collapse in world trade between 2008 and 2009 and the 23.4% decline in the US trade deficit with the rest of the world between 2008 and 2017. As a result, China's share of the overall US goods trade deficit increased from 32.2% in 2008 to 46.5% in 2017 (USITC, 2018; U.S. Census Bureau, 2018c).

China and the US Job Losses

Each $1 billion in exports to another country from the US supports some American jobs. However, each $1 billion in imports from another country leads to job loss—by eliminating existing jobs and preventing new job creation—as imports displace goods that otherwise would have been made in the US by domestic workers. The net employment effect of trade depends on the changes in the trade balance. An improving trade balance can support job creation, but a growing trade deficit usually results in growing net US job displacement.

The employment impacts of the growing US trade deficit with China are estimated by the Economic Policy Institute, using an input–output model that estimates the direct and indirect labor requirements of producing output in a given domestic industry. The model includes 205 US industries, 76 of which are in the manufacturing sector (Scott, 2017a, 2017b; Scott & Glass, 2016). The Economic Policy Institute has examined the job impacts of trade in recent years by subtracting the job opportunities lost to imports from those gained through exports through a model which estimates the amount of labor (number of jobs) required to produce a given volume of exports and the labor displaced when a given volume of imports is substituted for domestic output. The difference between these two numbers is essentially the jobs displaced by the growing trade deficit, holding all else equal (Scott, 2017a).

As shown in the bottom panel of Table 6.1, US exports to China in 2001 supported 179,200 jobs, but US imports displaced production that would have supported 1,170,700 jobs. Therefore, the $83.0 billion trade deficit in 2001 displaced 991,500 jobs in that year. Net job displacement rose to 3,052,700 jobs in 2008 and 4,352,200 jobs in 2017. As a result, since China's entry into the WTO in 2001 and through 2017, the increase in the US–China trade deficit eliminated or displaced 3,360,600 US jobs. Also shown in Table 6.1, the US trade deficit with China increased by $108.9 billion (or 40.9%) between 2008 and 2017. During that period, the number of jobs displaced increased by 1,299,400 (or 42.6%). For comparative purposes, the growth of the US–China trade deficit between 2001 and 2017 represents a direct loss of 1.5% of US GDP in 2017. Total jobs lost or displaced between 2008 and 2017 alone amounted to 1,299,400, either by the elimination of existing jobs or by the prevention of new job creation through the displacement of domestic production by imports (Scott, 2017a, 2017b; Scott & Glass, 2016) (Table 6.2).

The growth in manufactured goods imports explained virtually all (99.4%) of total growth in imports from China between 2001 and 2017 and included a wide array of products. Computer and electronic parts were responsible for 39.7% of the growth in imports in this period, including computer equipment ($50.4 billion, or 12.5% of the overall growth in imports) and communications, audio, and video equipment

Table 6.2 US jobs displaced by the growing goods trade deficit with China since 2001 (in thousands of jobs)

Year	*Jobs displaced (thousands)*
2001	0.0
2002	225.5
2003	459.3
2004	872.3
2005	1,334.9
2006	1,686.8
2007	1,998.0
2008	2,061.2
2009	1,713.6
2010	2,339.2
2011	2,645.0
2012	2,785.8
2013	2,823.8
2014	2,990.0
2015	3,191.6
2016	2,999.6
2017	3,360.6

Source US Census Bureau, US International Trade Commission (2018), Bureau of Labor Statistics Employment Projections Program (2017a, 2017b), Economic Policy Institute

($81.3 billion, or 20.2%). Other major importing sectors included electrical equipment ($34.2 billion, or 8.5%), machinery ($30.5 billion, or 7.6%), apparel ($20.7 billion, or 5.1%), and miscellaneous manufactured commodities ($29.3 billion or 7.3% [Scott, 2017a, 2017b; Scott & Glass, 2016]).

Other hard-hit industries include apparel (169,000 jobs displaced, equal to 5.0% of the total), electrical equipment, appliances, and components (145,300 jobs, or 4.3%), fabricated metal products (144,100 jobs or 4.3%), furniture and related products (135,200 jobs or 4.0%), miscellaneous manufactured commodities (126,600 jobs or 3.8%), textile mills and textile product mills (119,100 jobs or 3.5%), plastics and rubber products (78,700 jobs or 2.3%), and motor vehicles and motor vehicle parts (44,700 jobs or 1.3%). In addition, surging imports of steel, aluminum, and other capital-intensive products threaten hundreds of thousands of jobs in key metal-using industries such as primary metals, machinery, and fabricated metal products (Scott, 2017a, 2017b; Scott & Glass, 2016).

Between December 2001 and December 2017, 3.2 million US manufacturing jobs were lost. The growth of the US trade deficit with China was responsible for the displacement of 2.5 million manufacturing jobs in this period, or about 78.1% of manufacturing jobs lost (USTR, 2016b, 2018, 2019).

Thus, manufacturing job loss due to the growing trade deficit with China accounts for roughly four out of five US manufacturing jobs lost or displaced in this period. Even if macroeconomic policy is adjusted to offset the negative impact of the growing trade deficit with China on total employment, the structure of production and employment in the United States has been negatively affected (Scott, 2017a, 2017b; Scott & Glass, 2016).

The growing US goods trade deficit with China has displaced millions of jobs in the US and has contributed heavily to the crisis in US manufacturing employment, which has heightened over the last decade largely due to trade with China. Moreover, the US is piling up foreign debt, losing export capacity, and facing a more fragile macroeconomic environment (USTR, 2016b, 2018, 2019).

The growing US trade deficit with China has eliminated 3.4 million US jobs between 2001 and 2017, including 1.3 million jobs lost since 2008 (the first full year of the Great Recession). Nearly three-fourths of the jobs lost were in manufacturing. These losses were responsible for a substantial share of the 3.2 million US manufacturing jobs lost between December 2001 and December 2017. The growing trade deficit with China has reduced wages of those directly displaced by $37 billion through 2011 alone, and it is largely responsible for the loss of nearly $2,000 per worker per year, due to wage suppression, for all non-college-educated workers in the US (USTR, 2016b, 2018, 2019; Scott, 2017a, 2017b; Scott & Glass, 2016).

Currency Manipulation

A major cause of the rapidly growing US trade deficit with China is currency manipulation. Unlike other currencies, the Chinese Yuan does not fluctuate freely against the dollar. While the value of its currency should have increased as China exported more and more goods, it has instead remained artificially low, and China has aggressively acquired dollars to further depress the value of its own currency. China has tightly pegged its currency to the US dollar at a rate that encourages a large bilateral surplus with the US. China had to purchase $453 billion in US Treasury bills and other securities between December 2008 and December 2009, alone, to maintain this peg. China has acquired a total of $2.4 trillion in foreign exchange reserves as of December 2009. About 70% of these reserves are held in US dollars (Hopewell, 2019; Nölke et al., 2019).

This intervention makes the Yuan artificially cheap relative to the dollar, effectively subsidizing Chinese exports. The best estimates place this effective subsidy at roughly 40% of the US dollar, even after recent appreciation in the Yuan. Currency intervention also artificially raises the cost of US exports to China by a similar amount, making US goods less competitive in China (Davies, 2018). It is not new as China caused the Asian Financial Crisis in 1998 through a massive devaluation in 1994, but IMF-World Bank refused to blame China but blamed 'Crony Capitalism' in East Asian countries. IMF-World Bank in 1998 behaved like the WHO today, which also shielded China from any criticism regarding the spread of COVID-19.

Other policies by the Chinese government also encourage exports. China extensively suppresses labor rights, which lowers production costs within China. An AFL-CIO study estimated that repression of labor rights by the Chinese government has lowered manufacturing wages of Chinese workers by 47–86.

China has provided massive direct subsidization of export production in many key industries. Finally, it maintains strict, non-tariff barriers to imports. As a result, China's exports to the United States of $337.5 billion in 2008 were more than five times greater than US exports to China, which totaled only $67.2 billion (Table 6.1). China's trade surplus was responsible for 68.5% of the US total non-oil trade deficit in 2008, making the China trade relationship this country's most imbalanced and a disasterous by far (Nölke et al., 2019; Stephen & Parízek, 2019).

US Security and China

In the US, the government has woken up to the national security implications of losing sensitive capabilities to China; the Committee on Foreign Investment in the United States (CFIUS) now plays a very active role in screening potential takeovers on national security grounds.

The EU has no CFIUS, only a largely toothless screening mechanism. Some countries are stricter: Earlier this month, the German government introduced a new bill that allows regulators to scrutinize investments that are likely to affect the country's security. (Previous German legislation requires government approval for all investments over 10% that pose a direct threat to national security.) The UK government screens acquisitions in the military, dual-use, computing hardware, and quantum technology sectors (Nölke et al., 2019; Stephen & Parízek, 2019).

Canyon Bridge, a Cayman Islands-based outfit that is majority-owned by China Reform, bought Imagination in 2017, but the UK government could not intervene. When China Reform attempted to put four directors on Imagination's board and thus seize control of the company, British members of Parliament rebelled. China Reform's majority stake in Imagination is part of a major Chinese acquisition spree in Europe and North America over the past few years (Stephen & Parízek, 2019).

In 2019, for example, Chinese entities invested 11.7 billion euros (nearly $13 billion) in European Union countries, the vast majority of it in mergers and acquisitions and only a minimal share going to forming new companies. In 2018, Chinese entities invested some $25 billion in the US (Nölke et al., 2019; Stephen & Parízek, 2019).

Dependency of American Businesses on China

Here we have data up to 2017–2018. Contrary to the popular perception, Apple (AAPL) generates only about 17% of its revenue from China. Boeing (BA), Caterpillar (CAT), General Motors (GM), Starbucks (SBUX), Nike (NKE), and Ford (F) are some other US companies with a strong presence in the country. But none of them get more than 25% of their revenue from China (ten Brink, 2019).

Topping the list is Wynn Resorts (WYNN), which operates three casinos in Macau. It also has two casinos in Las Vegas and another in Everett, Massachusetts. Wynn Resorts' Macau casinos account for 75.2% of its revenue. According to Tijori Finance, the Macau operations generate about 77.1% of its operating profits (USTR, 2018).

Semiconductor giant Qualcomm (QCOM) is close behind with 66.6% revenue exposure. A large chunk of Qualcomm's shipments go to factories that assemble smartphones and other products. China is home to some of the world's largest smartphone vendors including Xiaomi, OnePlus, Oppo, Vivo, Lenovo, and others, most of which use Qualcomm chips in their products.

Micron Technology (MU) occupies the third spot with 57.1% revenue exposure to China. By comparison, the US accounts for merely 11.9% of its revenue. It is one of the world's leading makers of computer data storage solutions such as USB flash drives and NAND flash memory.

Qualcomm is not the only semiconductor company in the top ten. Qorvo (QRVO) has 52% revenue exposure to China. It makes radio frequency systems that are used in wireless and broadband communications. Qorvo was created following the merger of TriQuint Semiconductor and RF Micro Devices (Li, 2019; USTR, 2018).

Broadcom gets close to 50% of its revenue from China, according to Tijori Finance. Broadcom is involved in designing, developing, and marketing semiconductor and infrastructure software products. Dallas-based technology giant Texas Instruments (TXN) is a leading manufacturer of semiconductors and a wide range of integrated circuits. It sells its products directly to electronics manufacturers, most of whom are concentrated in China. About 44.3% of Texas Instruments' revenue comes from China alone. Oxford, Massachusetts-based IPG Photonics (IPGP) is a leading maker of fiber lasers. It doesn't have a manufacturing facility in China, but the dragon is a huge market for the company. IPG Photonics has 43.1% revenue exposure to China.

AMD is another chipmaker heavily exposed to the country. About 39% of its revenue comes from China. The Santa Clara-based company manufactures motherboard chipsets, graphics processors, and microprocessors for both consumer and enterprise markets (USTR, 2018).

Veeco Instruments (VECO) makes processing systems that are used to build semiconductors, photonics, and display technologies. Its revenue exposure to China is 35.8%. Maxim Integrated Products (MXIM) rounds up the top ten with 35.7% revenue exposure. It designs and manufactures analog and mixed-signal integrated circuits. Intel gets 26.5% of its revenue from China while Nvidia relies on the country for 23.9% of its revenue (Rasmussen, 2017; USTR, 2018).

Wall Street is the main financier of China. Companies from China and Hong Kong have raised $6.6 billion through Initial Public Offerings (IPO) in the US financial market through Wall Street Banks in 2021 which is eightfold increase from the same period in 2020. The largest IPO is the $1.6 billion listing of e-cigarette maker RLX Technology Inc., followed by the $947 million offerings of the software company Tuya Inc. This is despite the warning given by the US Securities and Exchange Commission that it will do financial audits of Chinese companies, which

China opposes. Non-compliance could result in a delisting from the New York Stock Exchange or NASDAQ. Even then, Chinese companies raised about $15 billion through IPOs in the US financial market in 2020. Ali-Baba the e-commerce giant raised in 2014 $25 billion in 2014.

Didi Chuxing has filed application for US IPO of $100 billion in 2021. Uber like trucking start-up Full Truck Alliance is trying on an IPO of $2 billion in 2021. Many Chinese companies do their listings in both New York and Hong Kong. Thus, Chinese financial strength is the result of the collaboration from the Wall Street Banks. It was not a surprise that they supported CNN, MSNBC, and New York Times to go against Trump.

Human Rights

Apple CEO Tim Cook published a note in 2020 on racism in the US and launched a $100 million initiative to promote racial equality, following in the steps of Amazon, and Facebook (https://blog.Aboutamazon.com/policy/; www.apple.com/speaking-up-on-racism/).

The reports from the western Chinese region of Xinjiang have described alarming, widespread, and worsening violations of the human rights of its predominantly Muslim, ethnically Turkic inhabitants, primarily the region's approximately 11 million ethnic Uighurs. These include stifling surveillance measures on Xinjiang streets and in Uighur homes, and the arbitrary detention of perhaps over one million Uighurs in hastily built camps for the purpose of "transformation through education" (WWW.Washingtonpost.com/world/asia-pacific/2018/05/16/).

Unconvinced, on August 28, 2019, a bipartisan group of American lawmakers pushed the US State Department to levy sanctions against responsible Chinese policy-makers under the Magnitsky Act; the State Department has not yet done so, but has stated that it is "deeply troubled." A list of companies of the USA include the Fortune 500 companies (the highest-revenue US-based corporations) which are collaborating with the Chinese on operations, investments, or partnerships in Xinjiang (tssps://manage.the diplomat.com/wp-content/2018/08/).

Trump and China

President Trump ordered American businesses to leave China and suggested in a tweet that he has the authority to do so. American business is deeply intertwined with China, and untangling it would be messy and potentially destructive for the global economy. American tariffs and growing tensions between Washington and Beijing are forcing many companies to rethink their reliance on China. The country's convenience and its vast and growing consumer market, however, make it difficult for many businesses to abandon it entirely (www.nytimes.com/2019/08/23/business/China-tariffs-trump.Html?).

Trade and international law experts were considering reviewing the International Emergency Economic Powers Act of 1977. The general conclusion was that the president may, in fact, have the authority to carry out many threats against companies doing business with China. However, Trump could not win. Biden will never do anything to disturb China.

Link of China to the Global Economy?

While President Trump wanted to distance American industry from China, the country is essential to global commerce. China already makes a quarter of the world's manufactured goods. China's growing consumer class accounts for a huge proportion of global sales of many products.

Factories began to leave China, as both countries imposed higher tariffs on each other's products during Trump regime. However, the process is slow and difficult. Relations between China and the US may improve during the Biden regime. Companies that have moved their supply chains could find themselves at a competitive disadvantage compared to those that have stayed in China.

Low-wage, low-skill industries like shoe manufacturing, toy-making, and apparel production have already shifted toward Southeast Asia or places like India or Bangladesh, because blue-collar wages in China have soared eightfold in dollar terms over the past 15 years.

Other sectors, notably electronics, are finding it more difficult to cut ties. China dominates production of a vast array of components, with multiple companies bidding aggressively to supply practically anything a company might want. Even Vietnam, despite its proximity to China and the strong presence of electronics giants like Samsung, does not yet have a well-developed supply chain for electronics (www.nytimes.com/2019/07/30/technology/trump-trade-war-vietnam.html).

Would Companies Return to the United States?

Low unemployment has made it hard for companies to find factory workers in the United States. Workers in China commonly accept overnight shifts, allowing factories to run day and night, and often agree to live in factory dormitories for several years. American workers will not accept these kind of treatments. The US also cannot match China's ability to make the small parts that power the Chinese manufacturing machine. "When Apple tried to build a modest number of high-end computers in Austin, Texas, it had trouble finding a nearby supplier that could make the right kind of screws. It ended up relying on a small business that delivered 28,000 screws over 22 trips" (www.nytimes.com/2019/01/28/technology/iphones-apple-china-made.html).

A rapidly lengthening list of Western companies, among them Marriott and Daimler, and Coach and Versace, have apologized in the past two years for products or online offerings that could be given the impression that Taiwan or Tibet was not part of China.

American companies doing business in China are taking a lot of risks. Some US businesses have received encouragements from China. PayPal (PYPL), for example, got a license to provide digital payments last month. In 2020 that BlackRock (BLK) has talked to Chinese tech firm Tencent (TCEHY) about a possible tie-up. JPMorgan Chase (JPM) won an auction in August 2020 that it will manage its asset management business in China. Tesla (TSLA) spent 2020 building a massive factory in Shanghai, for electric cars. Corporate America is " very much interested" in China and was opposed to Trump.

The US government banned on doing business with some Chinese firms, like Huawei. However, that decision in May 2020 to blacklist the tech company created difficulties for its American suppliers, like Intel (INTC) and Micron (MICR).

WTO accession promoted the US corporate investment in China. It went up and up in the first decade of the twenty-first century. For example, in 2012 Hospital Corp. of America, a company made walking boots, air-casts, slings, and other low-end medical equipment. After China joined the WTO this firm moved production mostly from the southeastern part of the US to the province of Guangdong in southeastern China. The same experience was shared by many other companies of the US. By 2015, the share of China's exports to the US that came from foreign-owned companies was at least 60%.

This Chinese development strategy actually dates back to the early 1980s (Nölke et al., 2019). Its evolution over four decades is now reaching its zenith. The current China 'Manufacturing 2025' policies, for example, target ten specific industries including new advanced information technology, automated machine tools and robotics, aerospace and aeronautical equipment, maritime equipment and high-tech shipping, modern rail-transport equipment, new-energy vehicles and equipment, power equipment, agricultural equipment, new materials, and biopharmacy and advanced medical products. In areas such as new electric vehicles and battery technology, semiconductors, solar panels/modules, and wind power, interventions have been extensive, ongoing and highly prominent (Autor et al., 2012; Autor & Hanson, 2014).

However, some companies are objecting. Honeywell in 2015 said that it was tried with China's demands for technology transfer. Executives at CISCO and Microsoft said the same. The complaints about companies like Huawei stealing intellectual property also increased. Ongoing trade negotiations in early 2019, for example, centered on Chinese state subsidies, government-directed credit (via the state-controlled banking system), and public procurement, as well as forced technology transfer. In short, China appears to be using domestic legal, regulatory, and government interventions to favor its domestic firms. Policy-makers, moreover, appear strongly committed to this type state-controlled capitalism (Bernstein, 2016; Rogin, 2020).

In the European Union, like the US, sentiment has also swung strongly against Chinese interventions. Greater reciprocity from China (i.e., market access, fewer institutional and regulatory blocks on foreign MNEs) has become a key issue, as has a strategic response from Europe. Recent EU attempts led by France and Germany, for example, to create a European champion in train-making (and engage with China using similar strategic approaches) have been launched. In early 2019 efforts were made by France and Germany to merge the train manufacturing operations of Alstom (France) and Siemens (Germany). This was a direct response to Chinese industrial support for CRRC (the biggest train maker in the world). The merger was blocked, however, by the EU's very own competition commission; thus there are enemies within (Joyce, 2020; Pierce, & Schott, 2016; ten Brink, 2019).

The Chinese legislative system, moreover, lacks transparency and favors domestic firms, particularly in some high-tech-related industries such as renewable energies and robotics (Gao, 2019). Many current geopolitical conflicts between China and US/EU are related to such asymmetrical industrial policies (Shi, 2010).

Biden Family and China

When Biden visited China as the Vice President of the US government of the Obama Administration, his son Hunter Biden had long meetings with some major companies and the representatives of the central bank of China. The result was that Chinese central bank invested $1.5 billion in a company of Hunter Bidden. That was the beginning. Hunter Biden visited China 6 times when his father was the vice president of the US. When Xi visited the US in 2012, Yung Sun Group, close the Communist Party of China, invested $1.2 billion in companies owned by Hunter Biden. A Taiwanese businessman Michael Leen has acted as the middleman between Hunter Biden and the Chinese government (Areddy & Duehren, 2020).

CEFC is a major energy company of China in the private sector with close connection with the Communist Party, which is the norm in China. It is owned by a Ye Jing Ming, who gave $4.8 million to Hunter Biden for legal consultancy so that Hunter Biden can recommend any legal firm or individual lawyer for China, in which Kamala Harris and her husband's law firm DLA Piper is a major beneficiary. Hunter Biden became co-owner of that energy company CEFC with $10 million per year as compensation. Hudson West is another Chinese company of Patrick Ho, an American Chinese company involved in transferring nuclear and other scientific secret to China. Hunter Biden used to get $1 million every year as retainer from that company. Ho was convicted in the USA in 2016. Rosemont Seneca is an American company with close link with China to manufacture military equipment with the stolen American technology. Hunter Biden and the son of John Kerry, the former Secretary of State for Obama Administration, made a deal of $18 billion to help that company (Areddy & Duehren, 2020).

John Kerry, along with Hillary Clinton, was responsible for the destruction of Libya and Syria and the creation of the ISIS, the Islamic terrorist organization, which has nearly occupied both Iraq and Syria at one time before Russia destroyed the ISIS. John Kerry also organized the coup in Ukraine to remove an elected government of Yanukovych in 2014 by giving $5 billion to different terrorists in Ukraine. The US after the coup removed 40 tons of gold from the central bank of Ukraine and the Ukrainian government in collaboration with Bank of China invested in an investment fund controlled by Hunter Biden. Also, Hunter Biden is in the board of Ukrainian energy company Borisma Joe Biden knew about the involvement of his son with China, according to an American-Ukrainian associate of Hunter Biden, Bobulinski and in fact Joe Biden helped his son in that matter as the former Vice President of the US (Sonne & Grimaldi, 2014; Wright, 2020).

China and the Democratic Party

The national committee of Democratic Party is involved closely with China. Fox TV on 24 August 2020 declared that China financed the election campaign of Hillary Clinton in 2015–2016. Kamala Harris and her husband earned millions of Dollars from China by legal support to the state-owned Chinese companies through their legal firm.

Hillary Clinton created a movement supported by the leading members of the Democratic Party including former President Obama and Nancy Pelosi, against Russia and wasted three years of time and enormous amount of money through the useless investigation of Justice Mueller, who could not prove any Russian involvement in the US election of Trump. Susan Rice, the former National Security Adviser to Obama, declared both Trump and General Flynn, the National Security Adviser to Trump in the transitional government in 2016, as Russian agents (Clinton, 2000; Sonne & Grimaldi, 2014).

That Russia-campaign of the Democratic Party was designed to divert attention from China, according to American journalist Sebastian Gorka in the Fox TV on 18 March 2016. Biden declared China only as a competitor not an enemy of the US. Bill Clinton promoted China as the strategic partner. Obama had no objection against China joining the World Trade Organization as a free enterprise economy, which is totally false, as nothing can happen in China without the support of the Government of China. Kamala Harris supported in her interview in the Fox TV on September 5, 2020, the Black Lives Matter (BLM) movement. BLM created riots, looting, and chaos in cities after cities to support a known criminal George Floyd, killed by the police. That BLM movement was financed by China through some extremist organization like Freedom Road and Liberation Road (Gonzalez, 2020).

General Spalding of the Hoover Institute, Stanford University, declared that coronavirus was created by China to create chaos in the US election.

Nobel Prize winner French scientist who discovered the HIV virus, Luc Montagnier, said that coronavirus was created in the laboratory, it was not natural that HIV virus and Malaria virus can be mixed naturally. China has created it the Wuhan Laboratory by Shi Ziangli Li and her associates, who published their achievement in the scientific journal Nature in 2015. Li Meng Yan from the Hong Kong School of Public Health knew about that. She had escaped to Britain but her mother was arrested by China (Zhengli Li et al., 2015).

China knew that postal ballots would be used because of the coronavirus and that would give tremendous opportunity to rig the election for Joe Biden. Most of the hardware and software used to count the votes are from China. Large number of ballot papers, which supported Trump, were discarded. Thousands of dead people voted in the election. Ballots were stamped outside the polling stations. Ballots arrived long after the polling date were accepted so long as these are for Joe Biden.

Dr. Shiva Ayyadurai of MIT, along with Phil Evans and Benny Smith, have analyzed the voting pattern and the Dominion System hardware, which was used along with Smartmatics-Sequoia software to calculate the votes in the recent election of the US. Most of the hardware and the software came from China. According to Ayyadurai, at least 69,000 votes in four counties in Michigan alone were switched from Trump to Biden by the software after the voting, during the counting. In 2014, Dominion System donated huge amounts to the Clinton Foundation. Just before the 2020 election, the Dominion System donated $106 million to the Governor of Georgia who employed Dominion System to count the votes in the Presidential Election in 2010. Both Dominion System and Smartmatics-Sequoia have close contact with the Chinese government and possible fronts for the Chinese government. Face Book's owner Mark Zuckerberg donated $350 million to the Center for Tech and Civil Life, a private organization, who in turn distributed that money to various election officers in the swing states to do the alleged rigging in the election (Comment's on Shiva's election system analysis, The Intellectual Wilderness, 2020, 20 November; Special Report on Dominion Voting Systems Technology, Contra Costa Herald, 12 December 2020).

Joe Biden and the Future of India

Joe Biden will be another Bill Clinton, who created the Taliban in 1995 and sent his national security assistant Robin Rafael to Kandahar to congratulate the Taliban in 1996 when they occupied Afghanistan. Clinton also pressurized Russia not to supply the engines of India's rockets and missiles and asked Russia to cut off all arm supplies to India. Clinton declared the entire Kashmir as a disputed area. At the same time, Clinton declared China as a strategic partner of the US. Joe Biden is supported by the leading Indians in the American politics and the corporate world, like Kamala Harris, Pramila Jayapal, and Sundar Pichai of Google, who are paradoxically anti-Indian. YouTube, owned by Google, is promoting a bunch of anti-Indian Bangladeshi Muslim journalists, who took asylum in the US, by putting up anti-Indian videos regularly (Ashbridge, 2021; Madan, 2021).

China's entry into the WTO was supposed to bring it into compliance with an enforceable, rules-based regime that would require that it open its markets to imports from the US and other nations. The US also negotiated a series of special safeguard measures designed to limit the disruptive effects of surging Chinese imports on domestic producers. However, the core of the agreement failed to include any protections to maintain or improve labor or environmental standards and, prior to 2007, the administration rejected all requests for special safeguards protection.

China's entry into the WTO has further tilted the international economic playing field against domestic workers and firms and in favor of multinational companies from the US and other countries as well as state- and privately owned exporters in China. This shift has increased the global "race to the bottom" in wages and environmental quality and closed thousands of US factories, decimating employment in a wide range of communities, states, and entire regions of the US. US national interests have suffered while US multinationals have enjoyed record profits on their foreign direct investments.

Appendices

Appendix 1

Semiconductors, for example, are reported to have received over $150 billion in Chinese government subsidies. According to the US President's Council of Advisors on Science and Technology, Chinese industrial policies in this sector pose real threats to semiconductor innovation and US national security. New battery technologies have similarly received great support, with large state-owned groups like CATL now emerging as one of the largest players on the world stage. Similarly, support (and overcapacity) in wind and solar-power sectors have been prominent to date.

Appendix 2

Here are the biggest US firms to be controlled, or are soon to be controlled, by Chinese companies.

1. **Starwood Hotels**

Deal size: $14.3 billion
Acquirer: Anbang Insurance
Date: March 14, 2016
The Chinese insurer bought the company that owns New York's Waldorf-Astoria. Anbang announced it was buying a number of hotels owned by Blackstone. Starwood would add 1,300 hotels around the world to Anbang's portfolio.

2. **Smithfield Foods**

Deal size: $7.1 billion
Acquirer: Shuanghui International
Date: May 29, 2013
Shuanghui, a private firm based in Henan, expanded its ability to supply a fast-growing market with premium-brand pork at higher prices. Shuanghui might use Smithfield as a channel to sell its products in the US.

3. **Ingram Micro**

Deal size: $6.3 billion
Acquirer: Tianjin Tianhai Investment Development Co.
Date: February 17, 2016

No. 62 on the Fortune 500, Ingram Micro was purchased by a Chinese firm that specializes in aviation and logistics.

4. **General Electric Appliance Business**

Deal size: $5.4 billion
Acquirer: Qingdao Haier Co.
Date: January 15, 2016
General Electric struck a new one with China-based Qingdao Haier.

5. **Terex Corp.**

Deal size: $5.4 billion
Acquirer: Zoomlion Heavy Industry Science
Date: January 26, 2016
The 83-year-old Connecticut-based company makes machinery for construction, agricultural, and industrial purposes.

6. **Legendary Entertainment Group**

Deal size: $3.5 billion
Acquirer: Dalian Wanda
Date: January 12, 2016
It is the largest China-Hollywood deal to date.

7. **Motorola Mobility**

Deal size: $3.1 billion
Acquirer: Lenovo
Date: January 12, 2014
Computer maker Lenovo consolidated its phone business with Motorola's. The new handsets will go by the brand "Moto." Lenovo has downsized Motorola's old business and implemented layoffs.

8. **AMC Entertainment Holdings**

Deal size: $2.6 billion

Acquirer: Dalian Wanda
Date: May 20, 2012
When Dalian bought AMC, it was the US's second-largest movie chain.

References

Areddy, J. T., & Duehtrn, A. (2020, December 22). Hunter Biden's family name aided deals with foreign tycoons. *Wall Street Journal*.

Ashbridge, E. (2021, March 17). US-India relations. *The Diplomat*.

Autor, D, & Hanson, G. (2014). *Labor market adjustment to international trade* (NBER Reporter, no. 2).

Autor, D. H., Dorn, D., & Hanson, G. (2012, May). *The China Syndrome: Local labor market effects of import competition in the United States* (Working Paper no. 18054). National Bureau of Economic Research.

Bernstein, J. (2016, October 31). Sometimes, your trade deficit is thrust upon you, post everything. *Washington Post* blog.

Bivens, J. (2008a). *Everybody wins, except for most of us: What economics teaches about globalization*. Economic Policy Institute.

Bivens, J. (2008b). *Trade, jobs, and wages: Are the public's worries about globalization justified?* (Issue Brief no. 244). Washington, DC: Economic Policy Institute.

Bivens, J. (2013). *Using standard models to benchmark the costs of globalization for American workers without a college degree* (Briefing Paper no. 354). Washington, DC: Economic Policy Institute.

Clinton, B. (2000). Expanding trade, protecting values: Why I'll fight to make China's trade status permanent. *New Democrat, 12*(1), 9–11.

Davies, C. (2018, March 10). It is up to China to save the global trading system. *Financial Times*. https://www.ft.com/content/6d85636e-22ca-11e8-8138-569c3d7ab0a7

Gao, H. (2019). *Data regulation with Chinese characteristics*. ,https://ssrn.com/abstract=3430284

Gonzalez, M. (2020, September 15). *This BLM Co-Founder and Pro-Communist China group are partnering up*. Washington, DC: The Heritage Foundation.

Hopewell, K. (2019). US-China conflict in global trade governance: The new politics of agricultural subsidies at the WTO. *Review of International Political Economy, 26*(2), 207–231.

Joyce, K. (2020, May 12). *Huffington Post*.

Kimball, W., & Scott, R. (2014, December). *China trade, outsourcing and jobs: Growing U.S. trade deficit with China cost 3.2 million jobs between 2001 and 2013, with job losses in every state* (Briefing Paper no. 385). Washington, DC: Economic Policy Institute.

Li, F. (2019). Why have all western internet firms (WIFS) failed in China? A phenomenon-based research. *Academy of Management Discoveries, 5*(1), 13–37.

Madan, T. (2021). *India and the Biden administration, Agenda 2021.* Brooking Institution.

Narlikar, A. (2019). Regional powers' rise and impact on international conflict and negotiation: China and India as global and regional players. *Global Policy, 10*(2), 22–28.

Nölke, A., ten Brink, T., May, C., & Claar, S. (2019). *State-permeated capitalism in large emerging economies.* Routledge.

Pierce, J., & Schott P. (2016). The surprisingly swift decline of U.S. manufacturing employment. *American Economic Review, 106*(7), 1632–1662.

Rasmussen, C. (2017). *Jobs supported by exports 2016: An update.* U.S. Department of Commerce. Washington, DC: International Trade Administration.

Rogin, J. (2020, April 30). *Washington Post.*

Sonne, P, & Grimaldi, J. V. (2014, May 13). Biden's son, Kerry family friend join Ukrainian gas producer's board. *Wall Street Journal.*

Scott, J. (2017). The future of agricultural trade governance in the World Trade Organization. *International Affairs, 93*(5), 1167–1184.

Scott, R. E. (2017a). *Growth in U.S.–China trade deficit between 2001 and 2015 cost 3.4 million jobs: Here's how to rebalance trade and rebuild American manufacturing.* Economic Policy Institute.

Scott, R. E. (2017b). *We still haven't recovered well-paying construction and manufacturing jobs.* Economic Policy Institute

Scott, R. E., & Glass, E. (2016). *Trans-Pacific partnership, currency manipulation, trade, and jobs: U.S. trade deficit with the TPP countries cost 2 million jobs in 2015, with job losses in every state* (Briefing Paper no. 420). Washington, DC: Economic Policy Institute.

Scott, R. E., & Wething, H. (2012). *Jobs in the U.S. auto parts industry are at risk due to subsidized and unfairly traded Chinese auto parts* (Briefing Paper no. 336). Washington, DC: Economic Policy Institute.

Shi, J. (2010). China's indigenous innovation and government procurement. *Bridges, 14*(3), 19–20.

Stephen, M. D., & Parízek, M. (2019). New powers and the distribution of preferences in global trade governance: From deadlock and drift to fragmentation. *New Political Economy, 24*(6), 735–758.

ten Brink, T. (2019). *China's capitalism.* University of Pennsylvania Press.

War on Want. (2014, April 17).

Wright, T. (2020, December 23). The risk of John Kerry following his own China policy. *The Atlantic.*

Wu, M. (2016). The "China, Inc." challenge to global trade governance. *Harvard International Law Journal, 57*(2), 261–324.

Zhengli Li, S., Menachery, V. D., Yount, B., & Baric, R. (2015). A SARS like cluster of circulating bat coronavirus shows potential for human emergence. *Nature Medicine, 21*, 1508–1513.

Sources of Data

Bureau of Economic Analysis (BEA). (2018). *Industry data: GDP-by-industry.*

Bureau of Labor Statistics (BLS). (2018a, August 28). *Displaced workers summary: Worker displacement: 2015–17* (news release).

Bureau of Labor Statistics (BLS). (2018b). *Employment, hours, and earnings from the current employment statistics survey (national): Manufacturing employment, seasonally adjusted.* https://data.bls.gov/cgi-bin/surveymost?ce.

Bureau of Labor Statistics (BLS). (2018c). *"Employment level" [Labor force statistics from the current population survey data series LNS12000000].*

Bureau of Labor Statistics, Employment Projections Program (BLS-EP). (2017a). Chain-Weighted (2009 Dollars) Real Domestic Employment Requirements Table for 2001. *In historical employment requirements tables, 1997–2016.*

Bureau of Labor Statistics, Employment Projections Program (BLS-EP). (2017b). *Domestic industry output chain weighted deflator, 2009=1000.*

Ernst & Young. (2017). *Debt in the steel sector.* http://www.ey.com/Publication/vwLUAssets/ey-debt-in-the-steel-sector-august-2016/$FILE/ey-debt-in-the-steel-sector-august-2016.pdf

International Food Policy Research Institute, China: Shadow WTO Agricultural Domestic Support Notifications (IFPRI Discussion Paper 793, 2008), Washington, DC.

International Monetary Fund (IMF). (2018). *World Economic Outlook Database.* April 2018 Edition. Data extracted September 2018.

MOFCOM. (2016a, August 4). *Statement of the head of the Trade Relief Investigations Department of the Ministry of Commerce on the EU's final anti-dumping measures on cold-rolled steel sheet products from China, 商务部贸易救济调查局负责人就欧盟对中国冷轧钢板产品实施最终反倾销措施发表谈话.* http://www.mofcom.gov.cn/article/ae/ag/201608/20160801372689.shtml

MOFCOM. (2016b, September 13). *Statement of the head of the Treaty and Law Department of the Ministry of Commerce on the U.S. suing China for agricultural support policies at the WTO, 商务部条约法律司负责人就美国在世贸组织起诉中国农业支持政策发表谈话.* http://www.mofcom.gov.cn/article/ae/ag/201609/20160901392733.shtml

MOFCOM. (2017, February). *Director of trade remedy and investigation bureau of MOFCOM Wang Hejun comments on US final ruling on anti-dumping and countervailing investigation against stainless steel plate imported from China*. http://english.mofcom.gov.cn/article/newsrelease/policyreleasing/201702/20170202513073.shtml

Ministry of Commerce People's Republic of China (MOFCOM). (2019). *MOFCOM department of Foreign investment administration comments on China's absorption of foreign investment in January-December 2018*. http://english.mofcom.gov.cn/article/newsrelease/policyreleasing/201901/20190102827255.shtml.

U.S. Census Bureau. (2018a). *Advanced technology product code descriptions* (web page). Accessed September 2018.

U.S. Census Bureau. (2018b). *ATP data—Imports and exports by ATP group*. Accessed September 2018.

U.S. Census Bureau. (2018c). *U.S. trade in goods and services—Balance of payments (BOP) basis, 1960–2017*. Foreign Trade: Historical Series. Published June 6, 2018.

U.S. Census Bureau. (2018d). *U.S. trade in goods by country*.

U.S. Census Bureau. (2018e). *Trade definitions*. Accessed October 18, 2018.

U.S.–China Business Council. (2014, December 12). *USCBC: EPI study on US jobs, trade deficit, and China currency is wrong*. U.S.–China Business Council.

U.S. International Trade Commission (USITC). (2014, August). *A note on U.S. trade statistics*.

U.S. International Trade Commission (USITC). (2018). *USITC interactive tariff and trade DataWeb*.

USTR. (2016a, September 13). *United States challenges excessive Chinese support for rice, wheat, and corn*. https://ustr.gov/about-us/policy-offices/press-office/press-releases/2016/september/united-states-challenges

USTR. (2016b, May 10). *The United States challenges China's non-compliance at the WTO on behalf of American farmers*. https://ustr.gov/about-us/policy-offices/press-office/press-releases/2016/may/us-challenges-china-non-compliance-at-WTO

USTR. (2018). *Findings of the investigation into China's acts, policies, and practices related to technology transfer, intellectual property and innovation under Section 301 of The Trade Act of 1974* (p. 10). Washington, DC. https://ustr.gov/sites/default/files/Section301

USTR. (2019, July 16). *Statement on WTO Appellate Report on China countervailing duties*. https://ustr.gov/about-us/policy-offices/press-office/press-releases/2019/july/statement-wto-appellate-report-china

CHAPTER 7

Global Slavery

People on Sale

Slavery used to exist from very ancient time, but although it was abolished formally in early nineteenth century, it existed in different names and in different forms. Indentured labors in the British Empire, slaves in Latin America, and Arab countries, including North Africa used to exist even in late nineteenth century and in early twentieth century. Today, the slaves are mainly children and women. Globalization by increasing the trade and production activities by the transnational companies provided incentives for slavery by increasing the demand for cheap laborers. Who can be the cheaper than a child labor?

There are 170 million child slaves in the world today, 5.5 million are in forced labor; this is accounting for almost 11 percent of all world children. The illegal profits made from the use of forced labor in the private economy worldwide amount to $150.2 billion per year. Two-thirds of the profits, amounting to an estimated $99 billion per year, are generated by commercial sexual exploitation exacted by fraud or force. More than one-third of the profits, $51.2 billion, are made from forced child labor exploitation including child sexual exploitation, child recruitment in armed conflict, and child drug trafficking (International Labour Organization, 2014 Report: The Economics of Forced Labour) (Fig. 7.1).

© The Author(s), under exclusive license to Springer Nature Switzerland AG 2021

D. Basu and V. Miroshnik, *The Economic and Political Dangers of Globalization*, https://doi.org/10.1007/978-3-030-79895-6_7

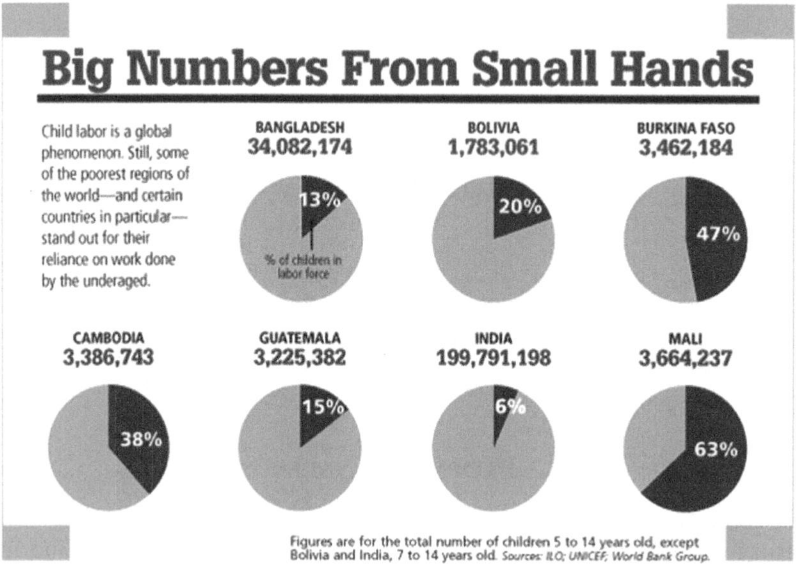

Fig. 7.1 Big numbers from small hands

Business Aspect of Human Trafficking

https://www.imf.org/external/pubs/ft/fandd/2018/09/human-trafficking-in-southeast-asia-caballero.htm.

170 millions of children are being smuggled, sexually abused, maimed, killed for their vital organs, recruited as soldiers or otherwise enslaved. By 2030, according to the UN, 69 million children under 5 years will die from mostly preventable causes, 167 million will live in poverty, 263 million are out of school, and 750 million women will have been married as children (Fig. 7.2).

The average age at which girls first become victims of prostitution in the US is 10 to 14. It is not only the girls on the streets who are affected; boys and transgender youth enter into prostitution between the ages of 10 and 13 on average (Estes and Weiner "The Commercial Sexual Exploitation of Children In the U. S., Canada and Mexico"). The US ranks 134th out of 160 countries by prevalence of population in modern

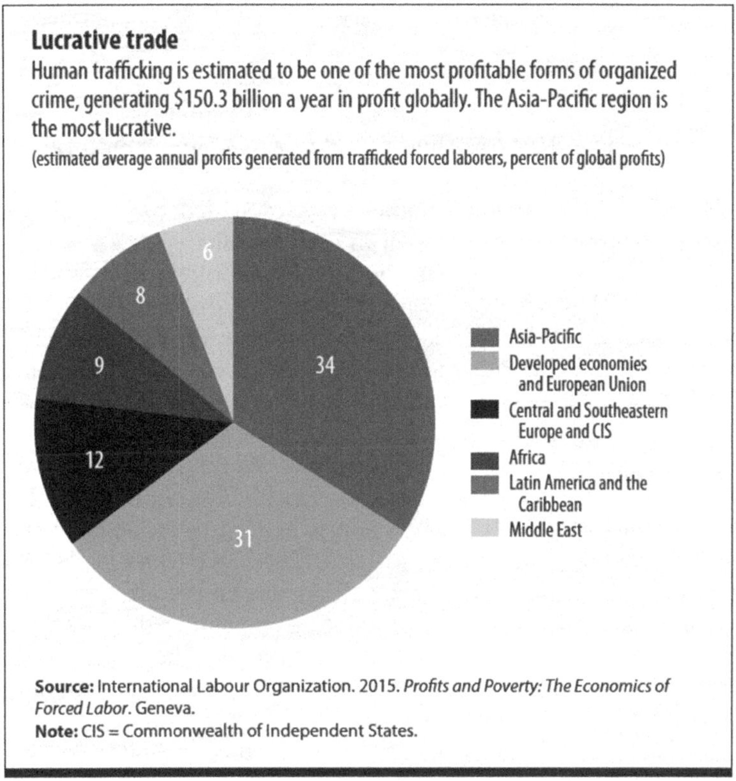

Fig. 7.2 Lucrative trade

slavery. There are an estimated 160,000 slaves in the US, according to The Global Slavery Index.

(http://www.ipsnews.net/2017/06/this-is-the-nation-of-170-million-enslaved-children).

Globally over 1.5 billion people live in countries that are affected by conflict, violence, and fragility. Meantime, around 600 million people are affected by disasters every year, a third of them are children. And a significant proportion (more that 5 millions children) of the 170 million children engaged in forced child labor live in areas affected by conflict and disaster. These are the facts. Up to you to reflect on the immediate future of humankind.

Conflicts and disasters have a devastating impact on people's lives, says United Nations.

"They kill, maim, injure, force people to flee their homes, destroy livelihoods, push people into poverty and starvation and trap people in situations where their basic human rights are violated." Of this total of 170 million children victims of modern slavery, about 100 million boys and 70 million girls. Human trafficking is estimated to generate more than 150,2 billion dollars every year in illegal profits.

Amid such a huge human tragedy, children are often the first to suffer as schools are destroyed and basic services are disrupted, the United Nations reported. "Many children are internally displaced or become refugees in other countries, and are particularly vulnerable to trafficking and child labour. Ultimately, millions of children are pushed into child labour by conflicts and disasters."

This why, on the occasion of the 2017 World Day Against Child Labour, marked June 12, the UN focuses on the impact of conflicts and disasters on child labor. "Urgent action is needed to tackle child labour in areas affected by conflict and disaster. If The SDGs (Sustainable Development Goals) aim to "eradicate forced labour, end modern slavery and human trafficking and secure the prohibition and elimination of the worst forms of child labour" is to be achieved by 2030." The UN stresses the need to intensify and accelerate action to end child labor, including in areas affected by conflict and disasters. "And we need to do it together."

Child labor and forced labor in conflicts and humanitarian settings was discussed at the IV Global Conference on Child Labour (Buenos Aires, 14–16 November 2017). For its part, the UN Children Fund (UNICEF) warns that child labor deprives children of their right to go to school, exposes them to violence, and reinforces intergenerational cycles of poverty.

> Yet, this serious violation of human rights is not inevitable. Child labour is preventable through integrated approaches that simultaneously address poverty and inequity, improve access to and quality of education and mobilize public support for respecting children's rights.

UNICEF also reminds that, worldwide, about 170 million children aged 5 to 17 are engaged in child labor, accounting for almost 11 percent of all world children.

The UN specialized agency reports, adding that the continued persistence of child labor poses a threat not only to the health and well-being of children, but also to national economies and the achievement of global development goals.

Child labor is defined as work for which the child is too young—i.e., work done below the required minimum age. The Convention on the Rights of the Child (CRC) recognizes every child's right, "to be protected from economic exploitation and from performing any work that is likely to be hazardous or to interfere with the child's education," or that is likely to harm the child's health or, "physical, mental, spiritual, moral or social development."

Other international instruments further define a child's right to be protected from the "worst forms of child labour," including recruitment in armed conflict, sexual exploitation, and drug trafficking. The lives and futures of millions of children are in jeopardy, UNICEF warns. "We have a choice: Invest in the most excluded children now or risk a more divided and unfair world."

> Every child has the right to a fair chance in life. But around the world, millions of children are trapped in an intergenerational cycle of disadvantage that endangers their futures – and the future of their societies.

(http://www.ipsnews.net/2016/08/one-humanity-millions-of-children-tortured-smuggled-abused-enslaved/).

"In places such as Iraq, Nigeria, Somalia, South Sudan, Syria and Yemen, children suffer through a living hell," the UN chief said as he opened the Security Council's debate on children and armed conflict on August 2, 2017.

Meanwhile, the future of humankind continues to be bleak, "unless the world focuses more on the plight of its most disadvantaged children," alerts a United Nations report.

> Denying hundreds of millions of children a fair chance in life does more than threaten their futures – by fuelling inter-generational cycles of disadvantage, it imperils the future of their societies," said UNICEF Executive Director, Anthony Lake, on the release of The State of the World's Children, the agency's annual flagship report. "We have a choice: Invest in these children now or allow our world to become still more unequal and divided.

The UNICEF report notes that significant progress has been made in saving children's lives, getting children into school, and lifting people out of poverty. This progress has been neither even nor fair, the report flags. "The poorest children are twice as likely to die before their fifth birthday and to be chronically malnourished than the richest."

Across much of South Asia and sub-Saharan Africa, children born to mothers with no education are almost three times more likely to die before they are five than those born to mothers with a secondary education, says UNICEF's report. "Girls from the poorest households are twice as likely to marry as children than girls from the wealthiest households."

Worst in Sub-Saharan Africa

Nowhere is the outlook grimmer than in sub-Saharan Africa, where at least 247 million children live in multidimensional poverty, deprived of what they need to survive and develop, and where nearly 60 percent of 20- to 24-year-olds from the poorest fifth of the population have had less than four years of schooling, the report warns.

At current trends, the report projects, by 2030, sub-Saharan Africa will account for nearly half of the 69 million children who will die before their fifth birthday from mostly preventable causes; more than half of the 60 million children of primary school age who will still be out of school; and 9 out of 10 children living in extreme poverty.

The UNICEF report goes on to warn that about 124 million children today do not go to primary- and lower-secondary school, and almost two in five who do finish primary school have not learned how to read, write, or do simple arithmetic.

Meanwhile, there is another lost generation—the youth. "Today, over 70 million youth are looking for jobs while nearly 160 million are working, yet living in poverty. These figures embody a massive waste of potential and a threat to social cohesion," on August 12 wrote Azita Berar Awad, Director of Employment Policy Department at the International Labour Organization (ILO).

More than half a billion children live in areas with extremely high flood occurrence, 160 million live in high drought severity areas. Of the 530 million children in the flood-prone zones, some 300 million live in countries where more than half the population lives in poverty—on less than \$3.10 a day.

"Youth unemployment and decent work deficits depreciate human capital and have a significant negative influence on health, happiness, anti-social behaviour, and socio-political stability. They impact the present and future well-being of our societies," she added.

Moreover, Berar stressed, conditions in youth labor markets are changing constantly and rapidly, so are the profiles and aspirations of young women and men who are entering the labor force every day.

> For most, expectations of decent work are not only about earning an income and making a livelihood. Youth see decent work as the cornerstone of their life project, the catalyst for their integration into society, and the pathway to their participation into the broader social and political arena.

https://inews.co.uk/news/uk/human-trafficking-uk-cases-rise-sexual-exploitation-modern-slavery-561742.

3000 Vietnamese child slaves in the UK

https://georgedowdell.org/2015/05/29/vietnamese-child-slaves-in-uk/.

Some 3,000 Vietnamese children are enslaved by criminal gangs in the UK to work in brutal conditions in the European country. "By our calculations there are around 3,000 Vietnamese children in the UK who are being used for profit by criminal gangs," said Philip Ishola, the former head of the UK's Counter Human Trafficking Bureau. Many of the trafficked children end up working on cannabis farms Vietnamese child slaves in the UK, while some are forced to work in nail bars, garment factories, brothels, and private homes.

"The police and the authorities are now aware that trafficked children are being forced to work in cannabis farms but this is really only the tip of the iceberg," Ishola wrote. According to the United Nations Office on Drugs and Crime, some 30 Vietnamese children are smuggled into the UK per month.

"Children are an increasingly valuable assets to criminal gangs because they are easy to get hold of, easily intimidated, and exploited, and easy to keep isolated and unaware of what is really happening around them," Ishola wrote. The report referred to a boy called Hien as one of the many kids enslaved in the UK. At the age of 5, he was smuggled to reside in a house in London, where he was beaten and exploited by a group of men. After his "uncle" abandoned him, Hien became homeless and slept in parks before being picked up by a Vietnamese couple, who later forced him to work in cannabis farms. "I was never paid any money for working there," he said. "I did not stay there for money but because I was afraid and I hoped the whole thing would end soon." Hien was arrested by the police and sent to young offenders' institution in Scotland on charges of cannabis cultivation. The boy was released after 10 months when he was identified as a victim of trafficking.

Smugglers use increasingly sophisticated methods, including the use of social media, to lure Vietnamese children.

"Vietnamese children are brought to the UK, taken in by Vietnamese adults and put to domestic work," said Swat Pandi, from the UK's National Society for the Prevention of Cruelty to Children (NSPCC).

"The child feels indebted to the adults for food and shelter and is told they need to return the favor by looking after cannabis plants. These children suffer high levels of neglect, emotional abuse and… are highly vulnerable to physical and sexual abuse," according to Pandi.

Traffickers have also expanded their working arena to Scotland and Northern Ireland, according to Daniel Silverstone, a criminologist at London Metropolitan University.

"A few years ago it was almost exclusively cannabis farms, but their business interests have now become much more diverse. So we're seeing an expansion into Scotland and Northern Ireland, the use of nail bars for forced labor and money laundering, and moves into drugs like crystal meth," said Silverstone.

To add insult to injury, a 2013 report by the Centre for Social Justice indicated that 60 percent of trafficked children who are taken out of trafficking and come under the care of a local authority go missing, nearly a third of them within a week of arrival.

Despite the UK government's promise to end modern slavery, and the ratification of first Modern Slavery Bill in March, Lynne Chitty, a charity director, said there has been no change in the number of Vietnamese children coming under her charity's services.

> It's very much business as usual," she stated, adding, "We still have a problem with immediate safeguarding and appropriate placements for trafficked children.

Us Sex Trafficking

The revelations about billionaire Jeffrey Epstein, who is accused of sex trafficking girls, paint a grim picture of sex trafficking in the US. The buying and selling of human beings is strong in America more than 150 years since the end of the Civil War. Sex trafficking, as the federal government defines it, is "the recruitment, harboring, transportation, provision or obtaining of a person for the purpose of a commercial sex act" by means of "force, fraud, or coercion." This is a form of modern-day slavery. Found in massage parlors, escort services, residential brothels, and street prostitution, some might be victims for weeks and others for years.

Sex trafficking tends to occur in motels and impoverished neighborhoods along the interstate highway system as well as in major urban centers. Some of the busiest corridors of the interstate include I-5 in the West, I-95 in the East and I-80, stretching from coast to coast.

The nonprofit organization Polaris operates the National Human Trafficking Hotline, which takes tips on sex and labor trafficking. Although the Polaris data are not from a random-sample survey, they shed light on types of sex trafficking in the US. In 2017, Polaris received more than 6,000 hotline tips about sex trafficking across America. Among these data, the top venues for sex trafficking included illicit massage parlors, hotels and motels, and residential brothels.

The National Association of Truck Stop Operators has collaborated with the US Department of Homeland Security's Blue Campaign. The National Association of Truck Stop Operators offers trainings to help truckers, truck stop owners and employees identify the signs of human trafficking, such as malnourishment, lack of eye contact, and disorientation.

Who Are the Victims?

Reliable data on the number of sex trafficking victims in the US are hard to come by.

In the US, studies show that most victims of sex trafficking are young women and girls. They are, on average, 15–17 years old. Risk factors for sex trafficking include a history of child abuse, substance abuse, poverty, involvement in child protective services, involvement in juvenile detention, and prior sexual exploitation. Runaway and homeless youth are especially at risk for sex trafficking. A study conducted in Philadelphia, Washington, D.C. and Phoenix found that 24% of homeless youth identified themselves as victims of sex trafficking. Among these sex trafficking victims, 33% identified as LGBTQ. A young person is more likely to meet her trafficker for the first time online rather than in person, due to the rise of social media.

Who Are the Traffickers

Traffickers include mom-and-pop operations, crime rings, gangs, and cartels. Sometimes, when a victim of sex trafficking has been groomed enough, she becomes "the bottom," helping her trafficker recruit other victims. Research shows that modern-day slaveholders have a complicated mindset, condescending and paternalistic, not necessarily one of pure evil. Slaveholders can think they are doing a favor to the enslaved, by taking care of them, giving them food and shelter, and even "protecting" them from a world in which they would otherwise be disposable.

How Much Money Does the Commercial Sex Economy Generate?

A 2014 study of sex trafficking in seven major U.S. cities found that revenues from underground commercial sex ranged from US$39.9 million in Denver to $290 million in Atlanta. Although many experts suspect that major sporting events, like the Super Bowl, might encourage the demand for commercial sex, preliminary research suggests the effect is negligible.

The breadth of sex trafficking in the US has prompted federal responses. The FBI has organized Operation Cross Country, a collaboration of dozens of field offices and hundreds of local law enforcement organizations. In October 2017, Operation Cross Country XI conducted a nationwide sting leading to the freeing of 84 minors and the arrest of 120 traffickers.

With better data collection methods and a stronger national coordinated effort, the US could eventually come closer to the day when modern slavery is no more.

UK Child Trafficking

There is no reliable figure on the number of trafficked children in the UK. The estimates of the UK government suggest that there are 13,000 people nationally who are victims in 2011 with 3000 children. Other estimates suggest that the total number of victims can be 136,000 and 4550 are children in 2019 (Home Office, 2020, National Referral Mechanism Statistics). Among the child victims, 52 percent are British, 9 percent are from Vietnam, 6 percent each from Eritrea, and Albanian, 5 percent are from Sudan. Other significant countries are Romania, Afghanistan, Nigeria, Iran, and Ethiopia.

https://www.ecpat.org.uk/Handlers/Download.ashx?IDMF=b92ea99a-6dd8-480c-9660-e6c0f0764acf.

https://theaseanpost.com/article/where-are-our-girls.

China

Trafficked Brides

In China, men outnumber women by 34 million. Compounded by the Confucian preference for a male descendent, the One-Child policy there gave rise to sex-selective abortions, female infanticide, and forced sterilization. This led to a gender disparity in births where 121 boys were born for every 100 girls in 2004. The Chinese Academy of Social Sciences estimates that by 2020 there will be up to 40 million more Chinese men of marrying age compared to Chinese women.

To fill in the gap, girls from neighboring countries are sold to Chinese men for them to marry and produce offspring. Vietnam and China share a long mountainous and porous border, which has made it easier for traffickers to kidnap girls and move them to China. Traffickers could be anyone—from people disguised as job recruiters and tourists to even the victim's own relatives in a desperate attempt to get money.

Michael Brosowski, founder of Hanoi-based charity, Blue Dragon Children's Foundation, which rescues Vietnamese trafficking victims, stated that "there's a lot of money in human trafficking. The people who sell girls can make tens of thousands of dollars on a sale" (https://theaseanpost.com/article/trafficked-brides-heading-china).

It was reported that in some rural areas of Vietnam, the disappearance of girls has become so prevalent that many villagers would assume that if a girl has been missing for more than a few days, she must already be on the other side of the border.

Out of the 6,000 victims identified by Vietnam's Department of General Police, only around 600 have returned to Vietnam.

It has also been reported that girls from Lao, Cambodia, and Myanmar have been sold off to China as brides or sex slaves in brothels. Tricked, lured, or kidnapped—their fate is unknown as they are never heard from again. When it comes to tracking missing girls, Asia is the deepest black hole.

How Many Children Are Victim to Child Trafficking?

Worldwide

- 170 million children are victims of forced labor
- 215 million children are engaged in child labor
- 115 million of those children are involved in hazardous work

Given the hidden nature of human trafficking, it is almost impossible to understand the full scope and scale of the issue. Among the most trusted sources for understanding, the global situation is the research by the International Labour Organization (ILO). According to its report on forced labor by the ILO: "There are 5.4 victims of modern slavery for every 1,000 people in the world."

Breakdown

Human trafficking and modern slavery do not discriminate; they affect men and women of all ages.

By Age

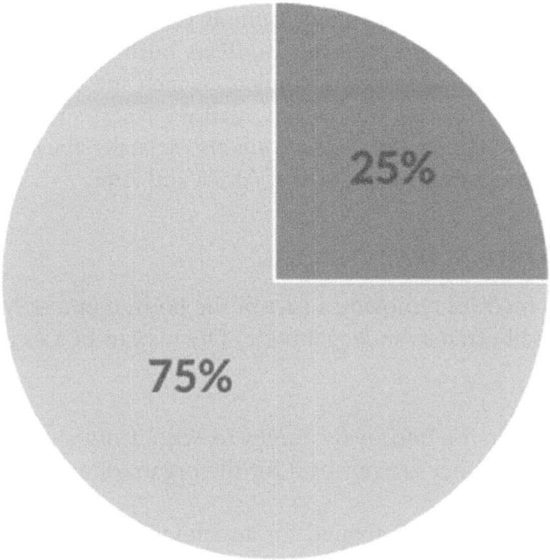

30.2 Million Victims (75%) Are Aged 15 or Older, with the Number of Children Under the Age of 15 Estimated at 10.1 Million (25%).

- 37% victims of trafficking in forced marriage were children.
- 21% victims of sexual exploitation were children.

By Industry

There are many forms of exploitation into which people can be trafficked and held in slavery.

These crimes are happening in every corner of the world and can include any person, regardless of age, socio-economic background, or location. As a result, each case can look very different. Below are some of the most commonly reported forms of human trafficking and modern slavery. Forced labor takes place in many different industries.

Child Soldiers

These are children and young people, ranging from as young as four up to 18, who are used for any military purpose. It affects both males and females. Children may be used for frontline combat—which means they are made to commit acts of violence—or within auxiliary roles, such as informants or kitchen hands. Often, the children are also sexually abused. This type of practice is most prevalent in parts of Africa and Asia.

Organ Harvesting

The trafficking in organs involves removing a part of the body, commonly the kidneys and liver, to sell often as an illegal trade. Organs can be taken in a number of ways:

- Trade—a victim formally or informally agrees to sell an organ, but are then cheated because they are not paid for the organ, or are paid less than the promised price
- Ailments—a vulnerable person is treated for an ailment, which may or may not exist, and the organs are removed without the victim's knowledge
- Extortion—a victim may be kidnapped from their family and organs removed without consent (Fig. 7.3)

https://trac.syr.edu/tracreports/crim/629/.

http://migrationdataportal.org/sites/default/files/2020-07/ctdc-age.png.

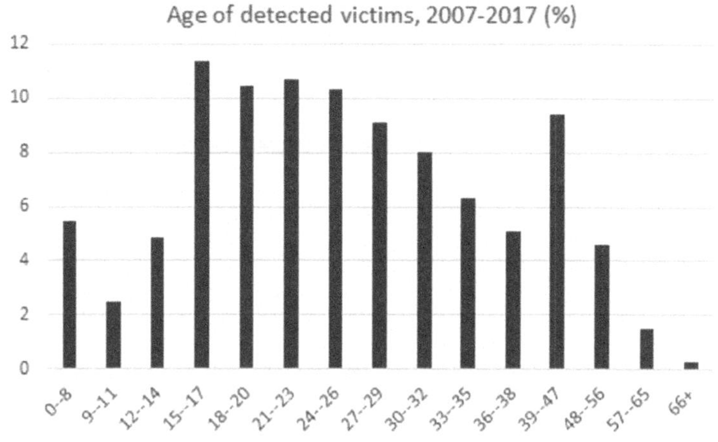

Source: The Counter Trafficking Data Collaborative (CTDC) (2019).

Note: The data in this chart are from the Counter Trafficking Data Collaborative (CTDC); the global data hub on human trafficking featuring the largest case level datasets on human trafficking from different organizations around the world. For more information, go to www.ctdatacollaborative.org.

Fig. 7.3 Age of detected victims, 2007–2017 (%)

Recent Trends

http://migrationdataportal.org/sites/default/files/2020-07/ctdc-age.png.

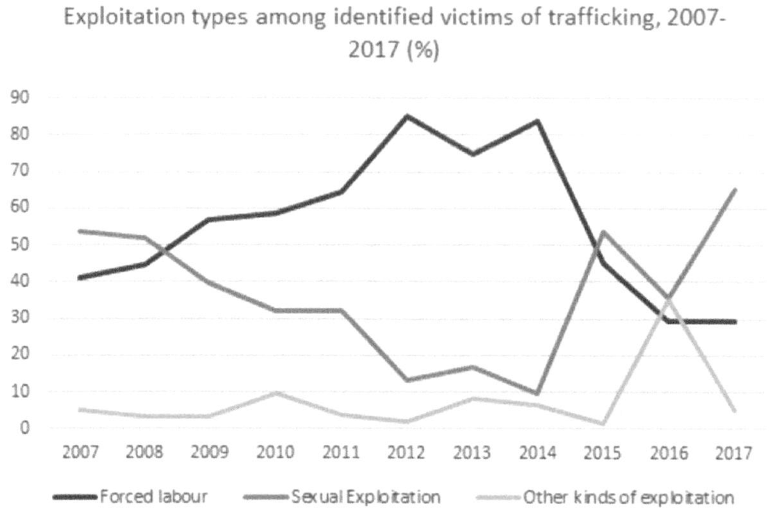

Source: The Counter Trafficking Data Collaborative (CTDC) (2019).

Note: The data in this chart are from the Counter Trafficking Data Collaborative (CTDC); the global data hub on human trafficking featuring the largest case level datasets on human trafficking from different organizations around the world. For more information, go to www.ctdatacollaborative.org.

Fig. 7.4 Exploitation types among identified victims of trafficking, 2007–2017 (%)

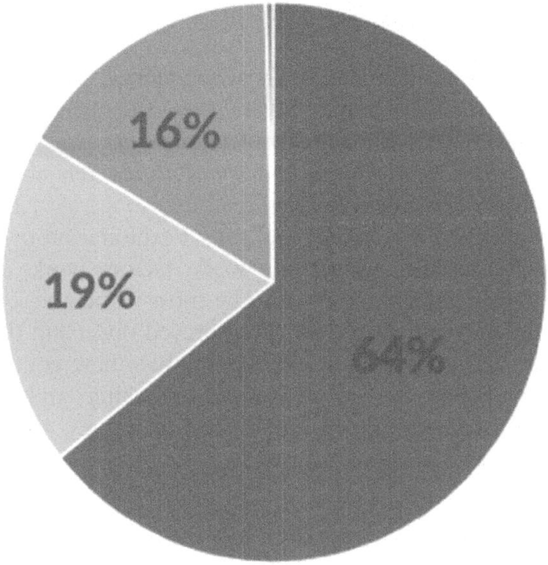

While every industry is susceptible, those highlighted in the report are broken down as follows:

- 16 million (64%) forced labor victims work in domestic work, construction, or agriculture.
- 4.8 million (19%) persons in forced sexual exploitation.
- 4 million (16%) persons in forced labor imposed by state authorities (Fig. 7.4).

Debt Bondage

Debt bondage affected half of all victims of forced labor imposed by private actors. Debt bondage is used as a method of control and prevents trafficking victims from escaping.

The Fight Against Child Trafficking

Child Trafficking is a Crime and Represents the Tragic End of Childhood. Child trafficking refers to the exploitation of girls and boys, primarily for forced labor and sexual exploitation. Children account for

27% of all the human trafficking victims worldwide, and two out of every three child victims are girls.

Sometimes sold by a family member or an acquaintance, sometimes lured by false promises of education and a "better" life—the reality is that these trafficked and exploited children are held in slave-like conditions without enough food, shelter, or clothing, and are often severely abused and cut off from all contact with their families.

Children are often trafficked for commercial sexual exploitation or for labor, such as domestic servitude, agricultural work, factory work, and mining, or they're forced to fight in conflicts. The most vulnerable children, particularly refugees and migrants, are often preyed upon and their hopes for an education, a better job, or a better life in a new country. Every country in the world is affected by human trafficking, and as a result, children are forced to drop out of school, risk their lives, and are deprived of what every child deserves—a future.

27% of Trafficking Victims Are Children

The majority of human trafficking victims are involved in forced labor. Labor trafficking involves the use of fraud, coercion, or force in order to get a victim to provide labor or services. More than two-thirds of trafficking victims fall into this category, including more than 10 million adults and nearly 4 million children.

The International Labor Organization reports that forced labor generated USD $150 billion in illegal profits per year. "Specifically, $51.8 billion USD in forced labor profits come from the Asia–Pacific region, including India" (IBLA 2019).

Children Are 4 Times More Likely to Be Trafficked for Labor Rather Than Sex

Children who are trafficked for labor purposes might be removed from their families and forced to perform domestic household services, or work in factories or agriculture.

Though millions of children are trafficked, there is a much larger number of children involved in child labor that is not considered trafficking. There are an estimated 168 million child laborers around the world, with around half of them participating in what is known as "hazardous work"—work that endangers the child's physical, emotional, or social well-being.

Often, girls around the world are forced to drop out of school or denied access to income-generating opportunities. The resulting social exclusion can trap girls in a cycle of extreme poverty, as well as increased vulnerability to trafficking and exploitation (Save the Children, 2020). This lack of education ultimately limits the lifetime earning potential for girls, thus perpetuating the cycle of poverty for their own children.

India

Labor trafficking affects every country in the world, especially the Asia–Pacific region, where 1 in every 250 people are victims. (IBLA, 2019). 7 in 10 victims of sexual exploitation in the world are trafficked in the Asia–Pacific. (IBLA, 2019).

Trafficker Tricks

India is heavily involved in sex trafficking as a source, destination, and transit country, despite legislation and increased efforts to combat trafficking. Often, traffickers will come to a village claiming to be recruiting employees for a large business or corporation.

They promise job training, excellent salaries, and the ability to move into higher positions over time. The young women they lure—generally with their parents' consent or coercion—leave the village with these traffickers and find that once they are in a big city they are sold to a brothel, or otherwise forced to engage in commercial sex work. If they resist, they risk being beaten, raped, or killed. Alone and in an unfamiliar place, there is nothing they can do.

A young man will visit a village saying he is looking for a wife and that he is willing to accept a girl without a marriage dowry. The thought of getting a daughter married without having to pay the typically exorbitant dowry is too tempting for impoverished families. The girl is given to the man thinking she will be married and taken care of, but instead she is whisked away and forced into the sex trade. Daily more than 700 children crossed the US border from Mexico without their parents.

Comments

In 2021, Biden rescinded Trump's declaration of a national emergency, suspended construction of Trump's border wall, and vowed to end governmental practices of rapid-fire deportations. However, it also raised the concern of law enforcement officials and residents about a return of caravans, chaos, and potential for violence. The abrupt shift in policy almost overnight changed conditions and migrant expectations along the border—renewing hope for hundreds of thousands of migrants from Mexico and Central America of a return to more porous borders and pathways to legal status. While agents are seeing an increase of families and unaccompanied children attempting to cross or being smuggled across the border, they also see more serious criminal activity. In February 2021 alone, agents in the Texas Rio Grande Sector have uncovered hundreds of pounds of drugs, such as cocaine, as well as arrested convicted sex offenders trying to reenter the US. In 2021, journalists have repeatedly asked the White House, Department of Homeland Security and Department of Health and Human Services for access to US facilities housing migrant children. Those requests have either been declined or ignored, with US officials often citing concerns over the COVID-19 pandemic and privacy interests of the children.

In the WTO meeting in Seattle in 1999, there was a demand that labor conditions and treatment should be in the WTO agenda, but it was ignored by the WTO by saying it should be the job of the ILO, which has no power to implement any punishment on any country (Monbiot, 1999; Smith, 2014; UNHDR, 1999).

> Working people have long and bitter experiences with capitalist institutions which claim to champion the interests of the masses. Following World War II the United Nations was established ostensibly to ensure world peace and promote democracy. Instead, it has chiefly functioned as an instrument of the US and other imperialist powers to justify one military intervention after another, from the Korean War, to Vietnam, to the virtual destruction of Iraq.
>
> An agreement to ban child labor and slavery signed by the WTO or any similar institution would be a dead letter. The operations of the global capitalist market, with transnational corporations and investors crisscrossing the globe to find the cheapest sources of labor, have created an economic demand for the exploitation of the most vulnerable segments of society.

The more these governments open up their countries to the exploitation of transnational corporations and global investors, and the dictates of the IMF and World Bank, the more conditions emerge for the proliferation of child labor and even worse forms of exploitation (White, 2000). We agree with these conclusions.

References

Estes and Weiner "The Commercial Sexual Exploitation of Children In the U. S., Canada and Mexico". (maggiemcneil.files. wordpress.com/2011/04/estes-weiner-2001.pdf).

https://www.worldschildren.org/child-trafficking-statistics/.

https://www.savethechildren.org/us/charity-stories/child-trafficking-awareness?cid=Paid_Search:Google_Grant:LP_Longtail:Nonbrand:052720&ds_e=GOOGLE&s_kwcid=AL!9048!3!379852267159!b!!g!!help%20end%20child%20trafficking&ds_c=gg+-+What+We+Do&ds_ag=gg+-+trafficking&ds_k=help+end+child+trafficking&gclsrc=aw.ds&&gclid=Cj0KCQiAhs79BRD0ARIsAC6XpaXWWwWi4zzq7S5-ez70nGE0xs5nKZnD8W-a4ovu3pQ81oJ7rr9x_M4aAn8QEALw_wcB&gclsrc=aw.ds.

https://www.stopthetraffik.org/about-human-trafficking/the-scale-of-human-trafficking/.

http://migrationdataportal.org/sites/default/files/2020-07/ctdc-age.png.

https://www.imf.org/external/pubs/ft/fandd/2018/09/human-trafficking-in-southeast-asia-caballero.htm.

https://theaseanpost.com/article/trafficked-brides-heading-china.

https://www.ilo.org/ipec/informationresources/wcms_221513/lang-en/index.htm.

https://trac.syr.edu/tracreports/crim/629/.

https://www.ecpat.org.uk/Handlers/Download.ashx?IDMF=b92ea99a-6dd8-480c-9660-e6c0f0764acf.

https://theaseanpost.com/article/where-are-our-girls.

https://inews.co.uk/news/uk/human-trafficking-uk-cases-rise-sexual-exploitation-modern-slavery-561742.

https://georgedowdell.org/2015/05/29/vietnamese-child-slaves-in-uk/.

http://www.ipsnews.net/2016/08/one-humanity-millions-of-children-tortured-smuggled-abused-enslaved/.

http://www.ipsnews.net/2017/06/this-is-the-nation-of-170-million-enslaved-children.

https://www.imf.org/external/pubs/ft/fandd/2018/09/human-trafficking-in-southeast-asia-caballero.htm.

https://www.dol.gov/agencies/ilab/our-work/child-forced-labor-trafficking.

International Bureau of Labor Affairs. (2019). International Labour Organization 2014 Report: The Economics of Forced Labour, Geneva: ILO.
Monbiot, G. (1999). *Still bent on World Conquest, The Guardian, December 16.*
Smith, N. (2014). *The dark side of Globalization, The Atlantic, January 6, 2014.* New York.
UNHDR. (1999). *Globalization with a human face.* New York: UNHDR.
White, J. (2000). Reply to the article by Dipak Basu on Child labor, World Socialist, 7 January.

CHAPTER 8

The Future

Nature of Capitalism

Capitalism is an economic organization that encourages individuals to engage in economic activities in different capacities in large scale to produce, distribute, and consume in collaboration with smaller-scale enterprises within the existing legal and institutional characteristics. The elements of production such as raw materials, machines, and labor are privately with no or restricted state interference.

Private motive is the biggest incentive behind the functioning of capitalist system. It induces the owners to produce more to maximize their gain. The prices are not controlled by any regulatory body or the government. If the prices are high, producers gain more profit, but at the same time consumers will buy less.

Competition is also a major characteristic of capitalism that influences the production, distribution, and consumption of goods. Individual buyers and sellers cannot influence the market decisions in theory; the tendency for the producers or sellers to monopolize the system can undermine that. That can make flexible prices rigid, which do not adapt themselves to the changes in demand and influence supply.

Imperialism, on the other hand, is a concept of expanding a country's power through colonization, use of military force or other means. Imperialism is of three types basically—political, economic, and cultural. Imperialism can be 'formal' which means complete control of another

© The Author(s), under exclusive license to Springer Nature Switzerland AG 2021

D. Basu and V. Miroshnik, *The Economic and Political Dangers of Globalization*, https://doi.org/10.1007/978-3-030-79895-6_8

country. It can be also through technological and economic superiority, forcing other countries to accept debts or trade agreements on unequal terms.

There is a close relationship between imperialism and capitalism in the sense that imperialism expands the profit of the capitalists to help by capturing the market and natural resources. Cultural imperialism is a part of the capitalists' design to explore new buyers of products manufactured by them through continuous advertisement to change the taste and culture of the targeted countries.

J. A. Hobson (1902) mentioned the objective of imperialism is to find out a profitable utilization of the capital, but he has not analyzed the source of this surplus capital. The profits of capitalists created over-savings, according to him, or it was sourced somewhere else. He could not identify the source of these over-savings; as a result, he put forward the argument that "strong organized industrial and financial interests that stand to gain from imperialism find ways to put this expense on the general public in the name of patriotism." According to Hobson, a redistribution of income in favor of the poor will provide full employment in the home market and the capitalists do not need to find out colonies to employ their excess savings.

According to Lenin (1917) in the "monopoly stage of capitalism," imperialism has the characteristics of concentration of production and capital into monopolies (large-scale firms), the merger of bank and industrial capital, and the division of territories of the world among the great capitalist powers, who also need raw materials for production from the colonies. However, unlike Hobson, Lenin could not find a solution in the redistribution of income because the lust of the capitalists would prohibit that and the worse condition of the masses will continue until there will be a revolution.

Joseph Schumpeter (1919) interpreted imperialism to be "the objectless disposition on the part of the state to unlimited forcible expansion." Schumpeter thought, nations and classes seek "expansion only for the sake of expanding and dominion only for the sake of ruling." He thought that imperialism is a remains of feudalism and with the advancement of capitalism the interest of the dominant classes will be diverted to the competition. Thus, the interest for war decreases as the "competitive system advances"; however, the world history proves him wrong.

Schumpeter could not explain the origin of capitalism or imperialism. "Nationalism as a theory of imperialism" has different other names, "power politics" (Cohen, 1973) and "mercantilism" (Brown, 1974). The theory of nationalism gave importance to imperialistic behavior as a reflection of a nation trying to maximize its honor and prestige, in the world, so the interests of political leaders and capitalist owners may coincide for colonial expansion, and ultimately economic interests determine the final result (Gilpin, 1981).

The Philosophy of Utilitarian

The philosophical basis of the 'Globalization' process is the philosophy of capitalism, i.e., the utilitarianism of Bentham (1780), James Mill (1817), John Stuart Mill (1863), and other writers. The idea is that maximization of self-interests is the virtue and the rational. Individuals, while their maximizing selfishly their own interests, maximize the combined social welfare of the society; the process was explained as the 'invisible hands of the market' by Adam Smith (1776). This virtue of self-interest is the motive force of capitalism and is the so-called 'Protestant ethics' (Weber, 1946). The idea of the modern-day economists who are the high priests of 'Globalization' is not any different from their eighteenth-century predecessors.

According to Bentham (1780) "*what is good is pleasure or happiness, … therefore one state of affairs is better than another if it involves a greater balance of pleasure over pain.*" John Stuart Mill (1863) said, "*Pleasure is the only thing desired; therefore pleasure is the only thing desirable.*" General happiness that results from these pursuits of pleasures is the effects but not intention. All human actions are based on self-preservation and self-interest. Selfishness is a virtue, which brings economic prosperity. In the pursuit of profit maximization, the producers allocate resources only to satisfy demands so as to use most efficient production system to minimize cost. Consumers are satisfied to receive high-quality goods at the lowest cost. Because economic growth depends on acquisitive actions, self-serving behavior is justified. To enhance economic growth, the state should intervene as little as possible restricting itself to the defense and judicial system leaving everything else to the spirit of free enterprise.

This doctrine of 'laissez-faire' was propagated by the originators of modern Western economists, David Ricardo and J. B. Say, and further decorated, using mathematical tools, by Jevons, Marshall, Knight, and Walras and very recently by Milton Friedman or Robert Lucas (Basu & Miroshnik, 2016). The argument remains the same although the society has changed and the 'perfect competition' as imagined by Adam Smith is not a reality in the days of monopolistic market of large multinational corporations. The idea is that the capitalism, leaving it to itself, can recover from any crisis and any public intervention can only make things worse. Thus, any public actions are nothing but distortions to the system, which must be minimized so that the multinational companies can pursue their self-interests freely so as to maximize the interest of the world economy.

The efficiency of the market is to satisfy demand, which can only be created by people who can afford to create demand. Those, who cannot, are rejected by the market. As prices are determined by the monopolistic multinational companies, the number of people rejected by the system cannot be determined by the policies of the national governments. For a country with poverty, the number of these rejected people can go on increasing, thus producing a growing army of the so-called 'underclass' who exist in large numbers even in the developed countries. Whether the doctrine of selfishness as a virtue can be acceptable to the humanistic culture, which is based on renunciation and selfless work, is debatable. The issue is the same for other cultures as well. The alternatives are the economics of Kautilya and Aristotle, both are based on humanistic culture.

Economics of Kautilya

Kautilya (about 350BC) was the Prime Minister of Chandra Gupta Maurya, the emperor of India, whose reign was from Afghanistan to Assam. Chandra Gupta Maurya defeated Seleucus I Nicator, the Commander of Alexander in charge of Babylon, and married his daughter. His recommendations are in the book he wrote called Artha Shashtra or Economics in Sanskrit (Artha Shashtra, 1992). Ethical philosophers formulate and formalize existing standards by proposing new standards, new norms, and patterns of conduct, which they recommend for observance by the people. According to Kautilya, the state had a moral purpose: To bring about order, and the king at all times has to be guided by dharma. (Kautilya was also known as Chanakya, which means 'Moralist' in Sanskrit.)

Kautilya attributed a lot of importance to 'dharma.' According to him, 'the ultimate source of all law is dharma.' He enticed in the name of 'dharma' to the sense of honor and duty and to human dignity, to moral responsibility, and to enlightened loyalty. It is quite understandable that the judge in the Arthashastra was called 'Dharmashta' or upholder of dharma.

He comments, "A King who administers justice in accordance with 'dharma,' evidence, customs, and written law will be able to conquer whole world."

Social welfare is the main focal point of Kautilya's economic notions. The state was required to help the poor and helpless and to be proactive in contributing to the welfare of its citizens. Kautilya gave more emphasis to human capital formation that is relevant in current times because development is not possible without human capital growth.

He explored ethically possible avenues to maximize the level of wealth in the public sector. He was aware of the limits placed on governments to raise revenue through taxation.

He confessed the taxation is the main source of revenue. The power of taxing of the state is boundless but taxation should not be excessive. He supported that tax base should be increased not the tax rate. He commented the excessive burden of tax on people. Kautilya stated that "King must collect taxes like honey bee, enough to sustain but not too much to destroy."

He highlights fairness, stability of tax structure, fiscal federalism, avoidance of heavy taxation, ensuring of tax compliance, and subsidies to encourage capital formation. He advocated limiting the taxation power of the state, having low rates of taxation, maintaining a gradual increase in taxation, and most importantly devising a tax structure that ensured compliance many postulates of Kautilya's philosophy of political economy are applicable to modern times. Preferably, the government should collect taxes and do welfare of people.

Kautilya recommended a mixed economy and argued for a very active role by the government. Kautilya's Arthashastra depicts a bureaucratic welfare state, in fact some kind of socialized monarchy, in which the bureaucrats administer the details of the economy for the common good.

Aristotelian Economics

Aristotle (384–322 B.C.), one of the most important thinker who has ever lived, advanced a body of thought with respect to the development of the components of a market economy. He explains that means or instruments of production are valuable because their end-products are useful to people. The more useful or desirable a good is, the higher the value of the means of production is. For Aristotle, the individual human action of using wealth is what constitutes the economic dimension. The purpose of economic action is to use things that are necessary for life (i.e., survival) and for the Good Life (i.e., flourishing). The Good Life is the moral life of virtue through which human beings attain happiness.

Aristotle explains that ontologically the operation of the economic dimension of reality is inextricably related to the moral and political spheres. The economic element is integrated into real action with other realms relating to the acting human person.

Nicomachean Ethics Aristotle states, the use value or utility of a good or service depends upon its being productive of an individual person's good. He explains that the use value of a given article can vary among individuals and that the demand for the item is a function of its use value. Aristotle observes that, as the quantity of the good possessed increases, the use value of that good will begin to decline at some threshold point. The exchange value and demand are affected by the circumstances of rarity or scarcity. He explains that money was introduced to satisfy the requirement that all items exchanged must be comparable in some way.

In the *Politics*, he says that the right to property is limited to what is sufficient to sustain the household and the *polis* life of the city. He explains that exchange between households requires mutual judgments of equal participants in the life of the *polis*. The life of the household is a sound and productive means to *polis* life if it produces only the necessary goods and services that provide a setting for the exercise and development of the potentialities required for *polis* life. He says that distributive justice is natural justice and involves balancing shares with worth. In turn, justice involves straightening out by removing unjust gain, restoring unjust losses, and other forms of retribution for loss and/or damages.

In the *Politics*, Aristotle advanced the synergistic idea of social aggregation with the aggregate benefits to people exceeding the objective total of the benefits to individuals *qua* individuals. Aristotle thought that money departs from its natural function as a medium of exchange when it becomes the beginning and end of exchange with no limit to the end it seeks. The ease of exchange permitted by the use of money makes it possible to engage in large production projects for exchange purposes instead of for direct household use. This can corrupt natural exchange for which money is a valuable instrument. Money, rather than serving simply to facilitate commodity exchange, can become the goal and end in itself.

The lack of effective natural restraints leads to the unlimited desire for wealth. There exist no natural conditions restricting a person's desire to acquire money wealth.

For Aristotle, retail trade is not a way of attaining true wealth because its goal is a quantity of money. He criticizes money-making as a way of gaining wealth. Aristotle says that the usurer is the most unnatural of all practitioners of the art of money-making. The lending of money at interest is condemned as the most unnatural mode of acquisition (Younkins, 2002).

The Idealistic Economic Policy

The Indian view of life is that the personal life of an individual is ultimately subject to the same universal law as of all nature. The fundamental principle is the 'theory of *Karma*,' which says that each action eventually causes a certain effect. Everything in nature, from abstract thought to practical action, is determined and directed by this law. Man sets himself the goal of freeing himself from the bondage of the nature. The meaning of a man's life according to the Indian culture "is the awareness of the soul to its bondage and its efforts to stand up and assert itself" (Romain Rolland, 1930).

According to the message of Krishna in 'Bhagawat Gita,' this freedom can only be achieved by *Karma Yoga* or selfless works and *Gnana Yoga* or pure knowledge (Bhagawat Gita, Ch 3, Verse 3, 1962). *Karma Yoga* recommends working for the sake of the work itself, not for the fruits of works. Work without pay, absence of attachment to the result, generally to the point of complete disregard for one's personal interest, complete selflessness is the *Karma Yoga*. This is essentially opposite to the 'utilitarianism,' which is the philosophy of the 'Globalization.'

Sri Aurobindo (1947) has explained it further. Principal contradiction of human life is that between the individual and society or aggregate. The essence of ideal law of human development demands that individual should harmonize his life with the life of the social aggregate. Individualism, the ideal of the Western culture propagated by the 'Globalization' process does not correspond to the ideal view of life according to this universal law of nature.

Following the basic philosophical premise that the universe is subject to the action of identical universal laws, Vedantic philosophy according to Vivekananda (Vivekananda, Vol. IV, 1946a) says, society develops cyclically. With each cycle, society rises to higher and still higher stages achieving more and more perfection. Vivekananda divided the whole of the Indian society into two classes, the rich (the upper class) and the poor (the lower class). The lower class, the *Sudras* or the workers are the people, the masses; the future is theirs. "The only hope of India was from the masses, for the upper classes were physically and morally dead" (Vivekananda, 1946b). World at present is being ruled by the merchant class. However, the supremacy of the merchant class is coming to an end. In future, ".... the supremacy of the workers must emerge. Under it, just distribution of material values will be achieved; equality of the rights of all members of society to ownership of property established and caste differences obliterated" (Vivekananda, Vol. IV, 1946a).

Vivekananda did not specify how this can be achieved. However, he has mentioned the nature of that ideal state in future. "If it is possible to form a state in which the knowledge of the priest-period, the culture of the military, the distributive spirit of the commercial and the ideal of equality of the last (period of the workers) can all be kept intact, minus their evils, it will be an ideal state" (Vivekananda, 1946b). The first three periods, according to Vivekananda, have already occurred for the world and now the time has come for the fourth (Vivekananda, 1946b).

In order to achieve this ideal state, according to Vivekananda, one must understand the causes of the downfall of the colonized world. The causes are, perversion of religion, tyranny toward the masses, absence of due education and instructions, underestimating the role of the women, and physical and spiritual weakness and inertia (Vivekananda, 1946b). Down the centuries, the rulers and the dominant castes neglected the interests and the lot of the simple people and that was one of the greatest social evils. Without support of the lower class, there should be no question of serious reforms. Highly developed production and material well-being, cannot by themselves, make men happy if their 'spiritual civilization' is low.

In capitalism, wealth is being concentrated in the hands of the few. The dominion of the capitalist class today is justified in the name of economic growth and production efficiency. The resultant deprivations are visible even in the developed countries. In the US, about 12 million people are homeless, one-third of the people cannot afford even primary health care, 17% of the children are living below the poverty line, about 23% of the people are functionally illiterate, and there is no security of either job or life. Albert Einstein has explained, "The United States is fortunate in producing all the important industrial products and foods in her own country, in sufficient quantities. The country also possesses almost all important raw materials. Because of her tenacious belief in "free enterprise" she cannot succeed in keeping the purchasing power of the people in balance with the productive capacity of the country. For these very same reasons there is a constant danger that unemployment will reach threatening dimensions" (Einstein, 1948).

Globalization and Imperialism

J. A. Hobson (1902) argued along similar lines of Marx by stating that the growth of imperialism was directly correlated with an expansion of capitalism as well... As he states, "Imperialism is the endeavor of the great controllers of industry to broaden the channel for the flow of their surplus wealth by seeking foreign markets and foreign investments to take off the goods and capital they cannot sell or use at home" (Hobson). According to Marx (1957), imperialism served as a means to extract a large amount of "raw materials" and resources in a relatively cheap manner—all at the expense (and exploitation) of the indigenous peoples of the world that came into contact with the imperial powers. Ironically, Marx viewed "the expansion of capitalist societies into the world as a necessary evil that would, ultimately, shift societies toward the path of communism." For Marx—who believed that society followed a series of progressing epochs—imperialism was simply the next (and unavoidable) step for capitalism's relentless expansion. Globalization is the integral part of capitalism.

Lenin's theory argues that financiers under the monopoly-capitalist system had discovered that "it was more profitable to employ surplus capital abroad than in domestic industry," thus, setting the stage for intense "overseas investment" through imperialist measures of colonization (Lenin, 1917). According to historian, D. K. Fieldhouse, Lenin firmly believed that only through complete colonization "could really comprehensive economic and political controls be imposed which would give investments their highest return" (Fieldhouse, 1967).

Davis (2000) points out that other empires used drought and famine to expand their power and influence over indigenous peoples during this time as well. In a brief discussion of the Portuguese, Germans, and Americans, Davis argues that "global drought was the green light for an imperialist land-rush" in which these empires would use drought and disease to suppress largely powerless people into submission. The extremely violent form of colonialism began to emerge in the late nineteenth century, resulting in the division of Africa from the 1880s, and the increasing conflicts between the major powers. Lenin (1917) said the new imperialism was fundamentally an economic phenomenon. This is particularly true if we try to explain the latest American, French, British, and Turkish policy toward the oil-producing countries of the Middle East, Iraq, Libya, Syria, and Venezuela.

According to Lenin (1917), an adequate definition of modern imperialism needs to embrace "five essential features" (Imperialism: The Latest Stage of Capitalism, Ch. VII):

1. The concentration of production and capital developed to such a high stage that it created monopolies.
2. The merging of bank capital with industrial capital and the creation of 'finance capital.'
3. The export of capital became extremely important.
4. The formation of international capitalistic monopolies which divide up the world among themselves.
5. The territorial division of the whole world among the greatest capitalist powers is nearly completed.

The integration of industrial and banking capital was certainly an important aspect of capitalism in the twentieth century and in recent years. More investment was still flowing into the US, Argentina, and Japan when Lenin was writing that Britain was taking finance capital out of India and investing abroad. Similarly, today the Wall Street banks are taking finance from all over the world and investing in China, not in the US.

Thus, wars between colonial powers were fundamental in one of capitalism's basic features: The tendency for capital to become more centralized and concentrated—larger and larger units of production controlled, because of mergers and acquisitions, by fewer and fewer capitalists.

By the end of the nineteenth century, this process was already well developed, allowing dominant capitalist firms to have monopoly or near monopoly status in particular sectors of their national economies. Thus, inequality and concentration of financial power is the essential character of capitalism.

Bukharin argued that there is a tendency for capital and the government to become more and more closely allied. The end-point of this process is for government and capital to merge together and form what he called "state capitalist trusts"; China is the modern equivalent of that (Bukharin, 1915). There is a simultaneous tendency for production, trade, and investment to come out of national boundaries and to expand on a global scale. Thus, competition for market and resources led to political and military rivalries between countries for territory, influence, and power. This is the foundation of modern imperialism and globalization. "*Acquisition, however, assumes the character of "national" (state) acquisition where the beneficiaries are huge state companies of the bourgeoisie of finance capital. The development of productive forces moves within the narrow limits of state boundaries while it has already outgrown those limits. Under such conditions there inevitably arises a conflict, which, given the existence of capitalism, is settled through extending the state frontiers in bloody struggles, a settlement which holds the prospect of new and more grandiose conflicts*" (Bukharin, 1915).

Capitalism tends to create a single world economy, but development does not take place uniformly. Instead, it is characterized by combined and uneven development. Economic, military, and political power are concentrated in a handful of countries. Kautsky called this anticipated phase of capitalist development "ultra-imperialism," and he interpreted the formation of the League of Nations at the end of the war as part of the shift to ultra-imperialism (in "Ultra-imperialism," Die Neue Zeit, 1914). WTO, World Bank, and IMF are the modern equivalent of the League of Nations.

Lenin in his book, Imperialism the Latest Stage of Capitalism (1917), wrote that capitalists had found a new way to prosper, through exporting and earning finances for their business in their colonies in Africa, Latin America, and Asia exploiting the workers in those countries and their natural resources. When in the mature capitalist countries, rate of profit started to decline, capitalists found ways to restore and enhance it through globalization.

Capitalism has so far failed to maximize social welfare through the maximization of individual's profit. The resultant discontent will grow substantially due to the 'Globalization' process, which will intensify deprivation in the pursuit of efficiency across the globe. However, under global capitalism, this modernization dynamic confronts severe constraints associated with the dynamic of overproduction, magnified by trade liberalization. The theory of 'overproduction' is based on the trend that fewer workers are needed to produce, in both agriculture and manufacturing, for larger and larger markets. Consequently, wages as a conduit to support buying power are choked off, leading to under-consumption, which is the corollary of overproduction.

If the economic system imposed from outside does not correspond to the national culture or the philosophy of life, it will collapse sooner or late due to its own inherent contradictions. According to the Hindu philosophy of life, we are in the era of the merchants or the capitalistic system. This system cannot last forever due to the tyranny, oppression, and degenerations it creates just like other systems those came before it.

Relationship between culture or the philosophy of life of a country and its economic and social system is important for all nations. Humanistic aspects of Indian national culture, i.e., renunciations, selfless work, sacrifice, work without any attachments to the results, do not correspond to the acquisitive consumerism glorified by the capitalism which is the philosophy of the 'Globalization' process. The essential characteristics of national cultures can be traced on these basic human values signified by the ancient philosophy of life, which suggests that the present acquisitive consumerism or the capitalist system controlled by the merchant class cannot last, but would be replaced by an alternative system.

While the market economy is based on materialism and selfishness, the ideals of Hinduism are exactly opposite to these. Sri Krishna has described utilitarian men very clearly, "*They say: 'this world has no truth, no moral foundation, no God. There is no law of creation" (Bhagwat Gita, Ch16, verse 8). Their highest goal is sensual enjoyment and they firmly think that is all" (Bhagwat Gita, Ch 16, verse 11). "In their chain of selfishness and arrogance, of violence and anger and lust, these malignant men hate me" (Bhagwat Gita, Ch 16, verse 18).*

Market system is based on profit; every work must be justified by the results. Hindu ideals are based on selfless work without expecting any rewards. "When work is done as sacred work, unselfishly, with a peaceful mind, without lust or hate, with no desire for reward, then the work is pure" (Bhagwat Gita, Ch 18, verse 23). Sri Krishna also said, *when a man dwells on the pleasures of sense, the lust of possession arises, which leads to anger, ruin of reason and ultimate destruction* (Bhagwat Gita, Ch 2, verse 62). Thus, market economy is against the Hindu ideals.

As capitalism dehumanizes human beings by turning them into mere factors of production, which can be discarded if market demands that, humanism is not associated with capitalism at all. Maximization of profit irrespective of its social consequences is the rational behavior under capitalism. In this system, workers are deprived from the fruits of their toil thus making them alien to the production system in which they are the essential part. This alienation creates discontent among the workers and that leads to the social and economic contradictions, leading to revolutionary changes in the society (in Economic and Political Manuscripts of 1844, Karl Marx).

Sri Aurobindo has explained it further in 'Life Devine' (1947). Principal contradiction of human life is that between the individual and society or aggregate, the essence of ideal law of human development demands that the individual should harmonize his life with the life of the social aggregate.

Individualism, the ideal of Western culture, propagated by capitalism and the 'globalization' process, does not correspond to the ideal view of life according to this universal law of nature. Thus, according to both Swami Vivekananda and Sri Aurobindo, fundamental ideas of Hinduism are the same as those of 'Integral Humanism,' a system of non-capitalistic nature based upon religion.

Greed, possessiveness, and desires to create wealth are the virtues of capitalism but for Sri Krishna these are the gates of hell and enemies of the soul. Those who are attached to these are described by Sri Krishna as those "*who hate me*" (Bhagwat Gita, verse 18, chap 16).

Thus, Hinduism considers both social and economic inequality and the resultant arrogance as unacceptable. Swami Vivekananda wrote in 'On India and Her Problems' that, "*I consider that the great national sin is the neglect of the masses, and that is one of the causes of her (India) downfall.*" Down the centuries he wrote, "*…the rulers and the dominant castes neglected the interests and the lot of the simple people, and that was one of the greatest social evils.*"

Rabindranath Tagore (1941) also wrote, in his essay 'Crisis of Civilization' that capitalism, as a civilization, is incapable of ensuring humanity's progress. After visiting the efforts of construction of that socialist state the Soviet Union in 1930 Tagore (1960) wrote, in Letters From Russia, "*This (Soviet) civilization spreads the power of humanity.*"

Swami Vivekananda has analyzed the history of the world and came to the conclusion down the centuries, the rulers, and the dominant castes neglected the interests and the lot of the simple people and that was one of the greatest social evils (Vivekananda, On India and Her Problems). The rulers and the oppressors increased their material wealth forgetting that wealth was created for men and by men. In this system, "fight between labour and capital is constant" (Vivekananda, *The Complete Works*, Vol. IV, p 307). Thus, highly developed production and material well-being cannot by themselves make men happy if their spiritual civilization is low. "The great national sin is the neglect of the masses and that is one of the causes of her (India) downfall" (Vivekananda, *On India and Her Problems*, p. 23).

According to him, this age is dominated by the Vaisya or the merchant class, "whose battle fields are the market places of the world" (Vivekananda, *Complete Works*, Vol. IV, pp. 384–385). However, the supremacy of the Vaisyas (*merchant class*) is now coming to an end. In future, the supremacy of the Sudras (*workers*) must emerge according to the laws of nature. Under it, just distribution of material values will be achieved, equality of the rights of all members of society to ownership of property established, and caste differences obliterated. "If it is possible to form a state in which the knowledge of the priest period, the culture of the military period, the distributive spirit of the commerce and the ideal of equality of the Sudra period can all be kept intact minus their evils, it will be an ideal state" (Vivekananda, *The Complete Works*, Vol. VI, p. 343). The first three periods have already occurred in India, and now, the time has come for the fourth, during which "New India" will be built. 'Integral Humanism' is the foundation of that new India.

The economic ideology of Swami Vivekananda and Sri Aurobindo, who have expressed in modern language the wisdom of Bhagwat Gita, Upanishad, and the Vedas, calls for a harmonious, caring social model where the state will take care of every aspects of the welfare of the people and will not reject anyone who may fail. Swami Vivekananda asked every Indian to say with pride: "*Wretched Indians, poorest Indians, illiterate Indians are my brothers*," not to reject them as 'underclass.'

In the 'Rama-Rajya,' the king is even responsible for the snakebite on a boy. That idealistic Hindu state demands a totalitarian government where ordinary people would be taken care of from 'cradle to the cremation ground' as it was the case in the former Soviet Union or in some countries in the Western Europe today. Anglo-American ideas like competition, profit-motivated efficiency, small government with total freedom for the business community to exploit the people, cannot uphold that Hindu idealism.

After the Second World War, the structure of global politics changed dramatically with the emergence of two dominant countries, the US and the USSR. Wars continued on the peripherals countries resulting in millions of deaths, but there was no war between the US and the USSR. With the Eastern European revolutions of 1989 and the subsequent disintegration of the Soviet Union itself, the structure of the global system has witnessed revolutionary changes with repercussions felt everywhere.

Britain provides the first example of industrial capitalism, as opposed to exchange between individuals. British Industrial Revolution created large industrial enterprises, and their supporting small and medium-scale industrial manufacturing units. All these were financed through the profit from the trans-Atlantic slave trade and exploitation of Bengal in India where in 1757 East India Company got the contract to collect taxes, which eventually became Britain's Indian Empire.

The conquest of the Americas by the Spaniards and Portuguese in the sixteenth century, then by the French and the British, was the first modern form of imperialism and colonization: An extremely brutal form, which resulted in the genocide of the Indians of North and South America. Indian societies, those who had survived that 'Holocaust' in both the Americas, were thrown into slavery and black slaves were imported from Africa to work throughout the continents, North and South Americas. During all the stages of capitalism, the plunder of the resources of the peripheries, the oppression of colonized peoples, and their direct or indirect exploitation by capital remain the common characteristics of the phenomenon of colonialism. Hobson (1902) wrote, "*The economic root of Imperialism is the desire of strong organized industrial and financial interests to secure and develop at the public expense and by the public force private markets for their surplus goods and their surplus capital. War, militarism, and a 'spirited foreign policy' are the necessary means to this end.*" Lenin remarked, "*Finance capital does not want liberty, it wants domination*" (Lenin, 1917).

Kautsky's assessment was that there is an alternative to war between the rival capitalist countries, "*the joint exploitation of the world by internationally united finance capital in place of the mutual rivalries of national finance capitals. Such a new phase of capitalism is at any rate conceivable*" (Kautsky, 1914). WTO was created for that purpose. However, a global system with peaceful "re-divisions" can be excluded, because the various sectors of the capitalist world economy developed at different stages. China is a growing capitalist imperial country; today, the US is a mature capitalist country. Thus, conflicts between these two powers are inevitable, according to Thucydides trap, what explained the war between an old power Athens and a new power Sparta in the year 411 BC.

References

Basu, D., & Miroshnik, V. (2016). *Structural revolution in international business architecture*. Basingstoke: Palgrave Macmillan.
Bentham, J. (1780). *An introduction to the principles of morals and legislation*. London: Payne and Sons.
Bhagwat Gita. (1962). Translated by Juan Mascaro. London: Penguin.
Brown, M. B. (1974). *The economics of imperialism*. Baltimore: Penguin.
Bukharin, N. (1915/2013). *Imperialism and world economy*. California: Createspace Independent Publisher.
Cohen, B. J. (1973). *The question of imperialism*. New York: Basic Books.
Davis, M. (2000). *Late Victorian holocausts: El Nino famines and the making of the third world*. London: Verso.
Einstein, A. (1948). *Reply to soviet scientists*. New York: Monthly Review Press.
Fieldhouse. (1967). *The theory of capitalist imperialism*. London: Longmans.
Gilpin, R. (1981). *War and changes in world politics*. Cambridge: Cambridge University Press.
Hobson, J. A. (1902). *Imperialism: A study*. London: George Allen & Unwin.
Kautilya. (1992). Artha Shashtra (Translated by Rangarajan). London: Penguin.
Kautsky. (1914, September). Ultra-imperialism. Die Neue Zeit.
Lenin, V. I. (1917/1963). *Imperialism, the highest stage of capitalism*. Moscow: Progress Publisher.
Marx, K. (1957). *India's first war of independence*. Moscow: Progress Publisher.
Marx, K. (1959). *Economic and political manuscripts of 1844*. Moscow: Progress Publishers.
Mill, J. (1817). *The history of British India*. Edinburgh: Baldwin, Cradock and Joy.
Mill, J. S. (1863). *Utilitarianism*. London: Parker, Son and Boum.
Rolland, R. (1930). *L'Evangile Universal*. Paris: Stock Vichy Wallon.
Schumpeter, J. (1919). *Sociology of imperialism*. Tubingen: JCB Mohr.
Smith, A. (1776). *Inquiry into the nature and causes of the wealth of nations*. London: Strahan and Cadell.
Sri Aurobindo. (1947). *Life devine*. Calcutta: Arya Publishing House.
Tagore, R. (1941). *Crisis of civilization*. Shanti Neketan: Vishwa Bharati Press.

Tagore, R. (1960). *Letters from Russia*. Shanti Neketan: Vishwa Bharati Press.
Vivekananda. (1946a). *The complete works* (Vol. VI). Calcutta: Adaitya Asram Press.
Vivekananda. (1946b). *On India and her problems*. Calcutta: Adaitya Asram Press.
Weber, M. (1946/2002). *The protestant ethics and the spirit of capitalism*. London: Penguin.
Younkins, E. W. (2002). *Capitalism and commerce*. New York: Lexington Books.

Conclusion

Free trade was the instrument of Britain's industrial supremacy holding back development elsewhere. However, British capital investment in Europe and North America, and in other lands of European settlement, created the necessary expanding markets for manufactured exports. Between 1870 and 1914, Britain profited from capital exports. Income received in various forms from foreign investments was substantially larger than the net export of British capital: some £4,000 million against £2,400 million. The same is true, on an even larger scale, of US investments since 1945.

Under colonialism, explicit policy decisions were taken by the colonizers to prevent economic development in the colonies; to make their economies subordinate to the needs of the colonial power. The smashing of Indian handlooms by the British was an example as Marx (1957) illustrated. The import substitution model was always opposed by the rich countries but was finally put away during the 1980s under structural adjustment.

With the debt trap, created by the Reagan Administration with increased US interest rate for the developing countries, came structural adjustment policy packages imposed by the IMF (as the lender of last resort) in order to increase export earnings of the developing countries to pay off their debts. The reforms required under structural adjustment,

© The Editor(s) (if applicable) and The Author(s), under exclusive license to Springer Nature Switzerland AG 2021

D. Basu and V. Miroshnik, *The Economic and Political Dangers of Globalization*, https://doi.org/10.1007/978-3-030-79895-6

repackaged as the Washington Consensus in the late 1980s, obliterated any trace of import substitution and replaced in the 'conventional wisdom' by the 'export-oriented' development paradigm.

The Clinton Administration pushed through policies of economic globalization designed to bind the other major powers into relations of dependency on the US in the World Trade Organization. Simultaneously, it also followed a policy to expand NATO eastward in order to weaken Russia. This culminated with military interventions in the former Yugoslavia, then Iraq, Libya, and Syria intended to maintain dominance of the US armed power. However, at the same time, the economic foundation of the US is being demolished by China.

The 51st World Economic Forum (WEF) starting on January 25, 2021, has as its theme "A crucial year to rebuild trust." This is the continuation of the theme on the "Great Reset" that WEF founder Klaus Schwab and Prince Charles launched in 2021, when the word faces global challenges that require global solutions and action (Schwab, 2021). One of those global leaders was Chinese President Xi Jinping, whose country either by accident or by deliberate action spread a deadly virus all over the world causing death, unemployment, and destruction of lives of millions of people all over the world. He last spoke at Davos in January 2017 promoting globalization and against protectionism. WEF wants to exploit the coronavirus crisis to remake the world economy, put it under the control of an unaccountable technocratic elite, and impose a new world order under which the people will be monitored and measured, controlled and commanded, and oppressed.

The ideas are not new. These are a revised version of the UN's decades-old sustainable development agenda. Before COVID-19 was discovered, the UN and the WEF had agreed to work together to advance the sustainable development agenda, now known as the Great Reset.

The 'Great Reset' is in essence an advocacy of "stakeholder capitalism," the increasingly fashionable idea that a firm's managers should be responsible not just to shareholders, but also to vaguely defined "stakeholders." The way to that end is for the state to "steer the market towards fairer outcomes," using such tools as wealth taxes and new rules over intellectual property, trade, and competition; to ensure that investments advance "shared goals," such as equality and sustainability; and to "harness the innovations of the fourth industrial revolution to support the public good," which means essentially applying new digital technologies to redesign the society. These are lofty goals but without any realistic tools. Thus, like all other such ideas emerged from the UN, these ideas are just words.

In the 'First Globalization,' Russian Empire was destroyed by a new power Britain through continuous military attacks by itself and through Turkey and Japan. In the new 'Globalization' of today, are we going to witness the old power the US, to be destroyed and defeated by the new power China through continuous economic attacks, when China is perhaps the only country that has gained from the World Trade Organization?

References

Schwab, K. (2021). *Stakeholder capitalism*. New York: John Wiley.

Schwab, K., & Thierry, M. (2021). *Covid -19: The great reset*. Geneva: Forum Publishing.

Index

© The Editor(s) (if applicable) and The Author(s), under exclusive license to Springer Nature Switzerland AG 2021
D. Basu and V. Miroshnik, *The Economic and Political Dangers of Globalization*, https://doi.org/10.1007/978-3-030-79895-6